Bobby Sands

Writings from Prison

Foreword by Gerry Adams
Introduction by Seán MacBride

ROBERTS RINEHART PUBLISHERS

Published in the United States by Roberts Rinehart Publishers,
5455 Spine Road, Boulder, Colorado 80301

Distributed in the U.S. and Canada to the trade by Publishers Group West

ISBN 1-57098-113-2

Library of Congress Catalog Card Number 96-70064

First published in Ireland in two volumes, *One Day in My Life*
and *Skylark Sing Your Lonely Song,* by The Mercier Press,
5 Frenchchurch St., Cork and 16 Hume St., Dublin 2

Foreword © Gerry Adams, 1997

Introduction © The estate of Seán MacBride, S.C.

© The Bobby Sands Trust, 1983, 1997

Design:
Ann W. Douden, Boulder, Colorado
Typesetting:
Red Barn Publishing, Skeagh, Skibbereen, Co. Cork, Ireland
Printed in the United States of America

Contents

Foreword by
Gerry Adams

Bobby Sands was twenty-seven years old and sixty-six days on hunger strike when he died in the H Blocks of Long Kesh, on 5 May 1981. The young IRA Volunteer, who had spent almost the last nine years of his short life in prison, was world-famous by the time of his death, having been elected to the British parliament and having withstood pressures, political and moral, for him to abandon his fast which was aimed at rebutting the British government's attempts to criminalise the struggle for Irish freedom by criminalising Irish political prisoners.

Apart from all of the very obvious historical and political contradictions for the British in pursuing such a strategy, they had one other immediate problem: hundreds of prisoners were held in Long Kesh under a regime of political or special category status. This status had been introduced by the British government in June 1972 after a successful hunger strike by republican prisoners in Belfast jail. But now as part of its ridiculous new strategy, the London government dealt with this anomaly by introducing legislation which classified all prisoners arrested and sentenced after 1 March 1976 as criminals. Those arrested after midnight, 1 March, were deemed to be criminals, but before midnight they were political!

I first met Bobby in the cages of Long Kesh where we were held with special category status as political prisoners. From our cage, Cage 11, we could see the building site where the H Blocks were being constructed to house prisoners sentenced under London's new criminalisation legislation.

In those days Bobby was a slightly-built young man with a mane of long hair, an intense manner whether engaged in a game of football, a political discussion or a guitar lesson. He read extensively, and wrote quite a few arrangements and songs for his guitar.

But who was Bobby Sands? He was an ordinary young Irish man who lived and died in the extraordinary conditions which exist in the occupied part of Ireland. In the course of his short life he came to challenge these unjust conditions in an extraordinarily heroic and unselfishly courageous way.

He was born in 1954 in Rathcoole, a predominantly loyalist district of north Belfast. He always had an interest in Irish history and when the

Civil Rights Movement burst on to the streets in 1968 the reaction of the RUC to peaceful protest evoked a nationalist response in the hearts of most Catholic youths.

Bobby left school in June 1969 and worked as an apprentice coach-builder for the next three years. He never expressed any sectarian attitudes. In fact, Bobby ran for a well-known Protestant club—the Willowfield Temperance Harriers. But at work he came under increasing intimidation and by 1972 the Sands family were forced out of their home by threats and attacks.

They moved to Twinbrook—a new housing estate in nationalist west Belfast. Eighteen-year old Bobby was the eldest in a family of four children, the others being Marcella, Bernadette and John.

Bobby joined the Irish Republican Army in his late teens and in 1973 at the age of eighteen he was arrested and sentenced to five years' imprisonment on an arms charge. That was when I met him. I had been caught attempting to escape from Long Kesh internment camp, was charged and was now a sentenced prisoner. We shared Cage 11 with a large number of other men including some who would go on to play pivotal roles in the H Block struggle: Brendan Hughes, Brendan (Bik) McFarlane, Larry Marley and Pat Beag McGeown among others.

Bobby was released from Cage 11 in April 1976 and rejoined the struggle. As well as engaging in IRA activity he worked within his local community in Twinbrook. He helped to form a tenants association and a youth club. He was also married with a three-year-old son, Gerard.

However, six months after his release, Bobby was arrested on active-service following a bomb attack on a furniture warehouse. There was a gun battle between the IRA unit and the RUC and two of Bobby's comrades were wounded. One shortarm was caught in the car and the four occupants were all charged with possession of this one gun. Bobby was taken to Castlereagh where he was interrogated for seven days. He refused to talk to the Special Branch detectives and refused to recognise the court when charged. One of those also arrested with him was Joe McDonnell who replaced Bobby on the hunger strike after his death and who himself eventually died after sixty-one days on 8 July 1981.

Bobby was sentenced to fourteen years' imprisonment in September 1977. This time, in keeping with Britain's attempts to project militant Irish republicanism as a criminal conspiracy, he was denied special category or political status and was imprisoned as an "ordinary prisoner" in the H Blocks of Long Kesh.

Writings from Prison

For over a year the British government had been attempting to force the political prisoners in the H Blocks and in Armagh prison to conform to regulations, to wear a British criminal uniform and carry out compulsory menial, often degrading, prison work.

The Irish republican prisoners who had been arrested under special laws, interrogated in special interrogation centres and sentenced in special non-jury courts refused to be criminalised, to wear the prison uniform or to carry out prison work. In order to keep themselves warm the prisoners wrapped themselves in a blanket—and so the blanket protest began.

For years the prisoners were held in solitary confinement and subjected to beatings, although eventually, due to overcrowding, many came to share a cell with another blanket man. In Armagh prison republican women also resisted the criminalisation programme and they too were persecuted by warders.

In March 1978 the prison authorities in a further attempt to break their will refused the H Block prisoners access to toilets and washing facilities and forced the prisoners to live in filthy conditions. This no wash/no slop-out protest continued until March 1981.

Shortly after he arrived in the H Blocks, Bobby Sands was selected as PRO of the blanket men. His statements from the Blocks traced developments within the prison: the build-up of the blanket protest, the beginning of the no wash protest, the beatings, cell shifts, and mirror searches, and throughout it all the determination and dignity of the blanket men, who, despite the violence and the propaganda of the British government, continued with the longest prison protest ever by Irish republicans.

The policy of attacking and demoralising a struggle by attacking prisoners had been employed before by the British against past generations of republican prisoners—against the Fenians in English prisons and against IRA Volunteers following the 1916 Rising. (Indeed, Britain, which first invented the concentration camp in South Africa, had also attempted to criminalise nationalist movements in its restless colonies.) In resisting criminalisation IRA volunteers had resorted to the hunger strike protest, the most famous case being that of Terence MacSwiney MP, Lord Mayor of Cork, who died on the seventy-fifth day of hunger strike in Brixton prison in 1920. (MacSwiney's protest directly inspired Mahatma Gandhi.)

In 1980 despite the best efforts of a broad based campaign of support and after years of prison protest the British government persisted with its criminalisation strategy. In Autumn of that year a number of H Block men and Armagh women began a hunger strike which lasted for fifty-three days and which ended without fatalities when the British government promised to introduce a more liberal prison regime. Bobby, who was not on this hunger strike, had succeeded Brendan Hughes as the Officer Commanding of the prisoners.

It was the failure of the British government to live up to the settlement of the first hunger strike and to implement a promised enlightened prison regime which directly forced Bobby and his comrades on to a second hunger strike. He led the hunger strike on 1 March 1981, two weeks ahead of Francis Hughes, hoping that the sacrifice of his life and the political repercussions which it would unleash would perhaps force the British government into a settlement before any more of his comrades would have to die.

Shortly after Bobby went on hunger strike, the independent MP for Fermanagh and South Tyrone, Frank Maguire, who was a champion of the prisoners' cause, died of a heart attack. In the ensuing by-election Bobby stood on a "political prisoner" ticket and was elected as MP for Fermanagh/South Tyrone in a blaze of international publicity.

The result of this historic action showed the extent of support for the prisoners among the nationalist people—British propaganda had described the prisoners as having no support—and should have been the occasion for the British Prime Minister, Margaret Thatcher, to settle the hunger strike crisis. Instead, the British not only refused to negotiate but enacted legislation to change the electoral law and prevent another republican prisoner candidate from standing for election. So much for British democracy! The election, held against a background of harassment and intimidation of his election workers by British crown forces, was unique, not least because of pressure put upon the nationalist electorate by the SDLP leadership, the Catholic hierarchy, and British politicians. Despite these pressures, Bobby Sands received 30,492 votes, a clear sign—for those who doubted it—that the nationalist people recognised republican prisoners as political prisoners and supported their prison struggle.

But despite the election result, the British government remained intransigent.

On 5 May, IRA Volunteer Bobby Sands MP died on the sixty-sixth day of hunger strike. His name became a household word in Ireland, and his sacrifice, like that of those who followed him, overturned British propaganda on Ireland and had a real effect in advancing the cause of Irish freedom.

Writings from Prison

By August 1981, nine other blanket men—Francis Hughes, Raymond McCreesh, Patsy O Hara, Joe McDonnell, Martin Hurson, Kevin Lynch, Kieran Doherty, Thomas McElwee and Micky Devine—also died on hunger strike.

On Saturday 3 October 1981 the prisoners reluctantly abandoned their hunger strike after a series of incidents in which families, encouraged by a campaign waged by the Catholic Church, sanctioned medical intervention when their sons or husbands lapsed into unconsciousness. The prisoners were effectively robbed of the weapon of the hunger strike and so decided to end the historic fast which had lasted a marathon of two hundred and seventeen days.

As well as being the leader of the blanket men and of the second hunger strike, Bobby Sands was also the most prolific writer among the H Block prisoners. He not only wrote press statements, but he also wrote short stories and poems under the pen name "Marcella", his sister's name, which were published in *Republican News* and then in the newly merged *An Phoblacht/Republican News* after February 1979.

Bobby's writings span the last four years of his life in H Blocks 3, 4, 5, or 6. They were written on pieces of government issue toilet roll or on the rice paper of contraband cigarette roll-ups with the refill of a biro pen which he kept hidden inside his body. He also wrote as "a young West Belfast republican" and as PRO of the blanket men in the H Blocks 3, 4, and 6.

This collection contains creative pieces—writing of an extremely high standard—as Bobby describes penal life in a compelling and graphic manner. When one recalls that all of his writing was accomplished in almost impossible conditions, one cannot but admire his achievement, an example of the ingenuity and determination of the republican prisoners about whom he writes.

There is a premonition of personal tragedy running through his writings: that his H Block cell will, literally, become a tomb. His admiration for his comrades and his feelings for supporters and for oppressed people outside of prison emerge in the words which he expertly uses as a weapon against a regime which tries vainly to break and dehumanise him. Bobby's diary is a unique piece of literature, his last written words.

During his formative years Bobby, as he says himself, was "a budding ornithologist." As one well-known H Block ballad goes, ". . . A happy boy through green fields ran/And kept God's and man's laws." He also read and was influenced by the nationalist poet Ethna Carberry (Anna McManus) who coincidentally also grew up in Belfast.

So Bobby put many of his own thoughts into verse. My favourite is "The Rhythm of Time," but his H Block Trilogy must surely rank with Wilde's *The Ballad of Reading Gaol* and has recently and very brilliantly been staged as a drama by H Block prisoners. Two of Bobby's songs, "Back Home in Derry" and "McIlhattan" were also recorded by Christy Moore.

In his own poetry Bobby asserts that the spirit of freedom and injustice has been innate to humankind from the beginning. In tracing this spirit he demonstrates an exceptional grasp of history and memory recall. (He was denied books, newspapers, radio or TV, and mental stimulation for the last four years of his life.) Wat the Tyler, for example, was an English peasant who in 1381 challenged and led an uprising against the English monarchy. The persecuted early Christians, slaves, peasants, native American Indians and Irish republican freedom fighters share the stage of history against tyranny. And the driving force against oppression, as Bobby concludes, is the moral superiority of the oppressed.

As Danny Morrison wrote in an introduction to an earlier collection of Bobby's poetry:

It has been said that were Bobby alive to see these poems today he would have rewritten or changed some of the simpler rhyming words. But that is to miss the point. These poems were written by a young man under the most depressing of conditions. More importantly his poetry is the raw literature of the H Block prison protest which hundreds of naked men stood up against their cell doors (in the late of night when the Screws left the wings) to listen to and to applaud.

It was their only entertainment, it was a beautifully rendered articulation of their own plight. Out of cruelty and suffering Bobby Sands harnessed real poetry, the poetry of a feeling people struggling to be free. . . .

I could not have put it better myself. Bobby Sands lives in these pages.

Gerry Adams, Belfast, Ireland, January 1997

Introduction by
Seán MacBride, s.c.

O Wise Men, riddle me this:

What if the dream come true?

What if the dream come true?

And if millions unborn shall dwell

In the house that I shaped in my heart,

The noble house of my thought?. . .

Was it folly or grace?

No men shall judge me, but God.

Pádraig Mac Piarais

The pages that follow are a human tale of suffering, determination, anguish, courage and faith. They also portray frightening examples of man's inhumanity to man. They make sincere, but harsh, reading.

Why then publish them? Is it really necessary to read them? It is to the answer to these two questions that I propose to address myself in this introduction.

The reaction to the hunger strike and the death of Bobby Sands and his comrades‡ [see over] has been varied and contradictory. To the British establishment which rules that portion of our country known as Northern Ireland it appeared a victory in a contest of wills between "Irish terrorists" and a strong-willed British prime minister: "By God, we have taught them a lesson! They will now know that we mean what we say. We have broken their morale!" To the IRA and their supporters it was a triumph of endurance and courage. If proof were needed, it was evidence of their determination to pursue unflinchingly their campaign of violence until British forces and administration were withdrawn from Northern Ireland. It was a morale booster for their cause, a cause that depended more on integrity and courage than on what politicians and lawyers term "reason and common sense."

To the bulk of the Irish people it was a tragedy that tore asunder the strings of their heart and their conscience. Many of them disagreed with the methods used even though they had sympathy for the objectives that the men of violence were seeking to achieve.

There were also some Irish people who through some perverted form of intellectual snobbism had become hostile to the concept of a united and free Ireland; there were others too who, for reasons of personal advancement, still hankered after the trappings of British influence in Ireland. These were comparatively few and indeed did not include the majority of those who had given allegiance to the former pro-Treaty party. Be it said in fairness to the Fine Gael rank and file that probably the majority of them are by now supportive of a united Ireland and were sympathetic to Bobby Sands. Fianna Fáil was clearly sympathetic; so were the Labour supporters with the exception of two or three anti-national mavericks.

Centuries of oppression, bribery and duplicity have led to a certain ambivalence in a section of our people: this is best described as "the slave mentality," or the "gombeen" psychosis. This makes it difficult to assess the real sentiment of some of our people on certain issues.

The majority of the ordinary decent people of England are not really interested in what happens in Ireland. Their knowledge of Anglo-Irish relations is minimal. They have been taught to regard the Irish people as impossible and irrational, even if somewhat amusing and gifted. They could not care less as to what is happening in Ireland. They are oblivious to the fact that the partition of Ireland has been created, imposed and fostered by the British establishment. They have been led to believe that the British presence in Northern Ireland is essential in order to prevent "those

---

‡ Francis Hughes died 12 May 1981; Raymond McCreesh and Patsy O'Hara died 21 May 1981; Joe McDonnell died 8 July 1981; Martin Hurson died 13 July 1981; Kevin Lynch died 1 August 1981; Kieran Doherty TD died 3 August 1981; Thomas McElwee died 8 August 1981; Michael Devine died 20 August 1981.

impossible Irish from killing each other." They conceive their role as that of an honest broker who is keeping the peace in this turbulent island. They ignore, and do not particularly wish to know of, the grievous sufferings which have been inflicted on the Irish people in the course of the British conquest and occupation of Ireland. Whenever this is mentioned, they just complain that our memories are too long and that we should forget the past.

They are not aware, or do not admit to being aware, of the brutal repression and injustices from which Ireland suffered right up to the Treaty of 1921. They are not aware that the settlement which they imposed on the Irish people under threat of "immediate and terrible war" in 1921 caused a Civil War in Ireland which lasted for several years and which prevented any normal political development. They are not aware that the enforced partition of Ireland has resulted in a virtual state of continuous civil war, both in Northern Ireland and in the Republic, since 1922.

The reality, however, is that the partition of Ireland by Britain in defiance of the will of the overwhelming majority of the Irish people has disrupted the life of Ireland—North and South—for over sixty years. It has cost thousands of Irish—and indeed British—lives. Irish jails have been continually filled to bursting point. Several hundred thousand Irish men and women have passed through Irish and English jails over the last sixty years because of partition. The normal application of the rule of law has been disrupted since 1922 in both parts of the country. The Statute Books contain every conceivable form of coercive and repressive legislation. The normal protection of human rights under the law is subject to so many exceptions and qualifications that we cannot adhere to the international standard without constant derogation.

Worse still, successive Irish governments have been placed in the absolutely false position of attempting to justify and defend partition. It is upon the Irish governments that the task of manning and sealing an impossible border which is unacceptable to the majority of the Irish people falls. The army and the police have to be constantly augmented in order to maintain this unwanted border. This puts Irish governments, opposed as they are to partition, in an increasingly difficult position *vis-à-vis* their own constituencies as they have to jail and oppress their own young people in order to protect British rule in the north-east corner of our island. The subversive organisations naturally trade on this situation and are able to obtain the support of the younger generation. Thus the cycles of violence and repression continue to escalate; this weakens the authority of the government, the courts and the police. The financial implications resulting from this situation are incalculable; it has been said, probably correctly, that the cost of partition to the Irish government in terms of increased security measures, prisons, special courts, compensation, extra police and military, amounts to twenty percent of the total state expenditure.

There are a number of responsible persons in England who do appreciate Britain's responsibility in trying to correct the workings of history. One such person is a leading Anglican theologian Dr John Austin Baker [‡], who was the chaplain to the Speaker of the British House of Commons. During the hunger strike, in a sermon in Westminster Abbey on 1 December 1980, he pointed out:

> *No British government ought ever to forget that this perilous moment, like many before it, is the outworking of a history for which our country is primarily responsible. England seized Ireland for its own military benefit; it planted Protestant settlers there to make it strategically secure; it humiliated and penalised the native Irish and their Catholic religion. And then, when it could no longer hold on to the whole island, kept back part to be a home for the settlers' descendants, a non-viable solution from which Protestants have suffered as much as anyone.*

Our injustice created the situation; and by constantly repeating that we will maintain it so long as the majority wish it, we actively inhibit Protestant and Catholic from working out a new future together. This is the root of violence, and the reason why the protesters think of themselves as political offenders.

In Northern Ireland itself, the ordinary laws were abrogated and a police-state regime was installed. Because the British authorities and those who supported British rule in Northern Ireland feared that the nationalist minority would increase more rapidly than the pro-British population, which was generally Protestant, a regime of wholesale discrimination was installed. The reason for installing a draconian system of discrimination, based on religious beliefs, was that by preventing Catholics from obtaining

---

[‡] The Right Reverend Dr John Austin Baker, who was a distinguished lecturer in theology at Oxford and was rector of St Margaret's, Westminster, became Bishop of Salisbury in 1982 until his retirement in 1993.

employment or housing, their numbers could be kept down. They would not be able to get married and they would not be able to obtain employment. This would force them to leave the area, thus ensuring that the Catholic population would decrease.

A new generation of young people, however, resented the discrimination that was being implemented to their detriment. They could get neither employment nor housing. All employment and promotion within all services was strictly reserved to non-Catholics. Notices were displayed outside factories proclaiming: "No Catholics employed here."

Gradually, as was inevitable, the rising generation of young people resented a situation in which they were treated as third class citizens and were precluded from obtaining employment or housing. They became dissatisfied and disillusioned with existing political parties in the North as well as in the South and they started a perfectly legal and constitutional civil rights campaign demanding an end to the discrimination which prevailed and insisting on their civil and political rights. They obtained the support of the majority of the nationalist population in the North and indeed the active support and sympathy of the population in the rest of the country. Bernadette Devlin McAliskey became one of their leaders and swept aside the existing more moderate politicians. The rise of this new Civil Rights Movement was met with violent repression by the British forces and the police. Their members were arrested, interned and subjected to systematic police harassment. Their meetings were broken up by the police. This culminated in the killing of thirteen civilians by British soldiers at a perfectly legal public demonstration on 30 January 1972, now known as Bloody Sunday, in Derry city.

These acts of oppression by the British forces had two results. In the first place they solidified and increased the support for the Civil Rights Movement, and on the other hand they influenced the young people to turn more and more towards the IRA and physical force. The IRA availed of this situation to become the defenders of the Catholic population against the attacks of the police and the British military forces. The methods used by the British forces became more and more indefensible. Prisoners were systematically tortured by means of sophisticated methods imported from England. This was fully exposed and condemned in the course of legal proceedings brought by the Irish government before the European Commission of Human Rights in Strasbourg, and assurances were given by the British government that these methods would be discontinued. It is claimed by the

IRA that these methods have not been discontinued, but are now being applied more secretly.

As the extent and nature of the oppression grew, so did the IRA reaction to it, and we have had a constant escalation in what is now a full-blown guerrilla war, in the course of which some 628 members of the British forces have been killed and 7,496 wounded in the period 1969–June 1981. In the same period, 1,496 civilians were killed and 16,402 wounded. The total number of persons killed in this small area over the last ten years is 2,124, and the number wounded is 23,898. There are at present in Northern Ireland 1,244 Republican prisoners. These are variously described by the British authorities as terrorists or criminals; by the nationalist population they are regarded as political or Republican prisoners.

As a result of this situation there were, on 11 June 1981, 1,244 male prisoners serving sentences in British prisons in Northern Ireland for what the British describe as terrorist-type offences. In addition, there were on the same date approximately fifty women prisoners also serving sentences. It must be borne in mind that none of these prisoners were convicted after trial in due process of law. They were tried by single-judge courts without any juries. These courts are known as "Diplock" courts. These are courts which follow procedures that do not conform with those applicable to normal trials under the rule of law. Of some 1,300 prisoners serving sentences in British jails in Northern Ireland, 328 have been receiving what the prison authorities describe as "special status treatment." The balance of some 966 have been denied this "special status treatment" because they were convicted on a date subsequent to the withdrawal by the British authorities of the "special status treatment." In effect, what the hunger strikers in the H Blocks at Long Kesh were demanding was that they should receive special status treatment. This had been spelled out by the hunger strikers and the other prisoners in five specific demands concerning:

1. The right to wear their own clothes at all times.

2. The prisoners requested that they should not be required to do menial prison work; they were prepared to do all the work required for the maintenance and cleaning of the portions of the prison occupied by them. They also asked that study time should be taken into account in determining the amount of work which they were required to do.

3. They requested the right to associate freely at recreation time with other political prisoners.

4. They requested the right to a weekly visit, letter, or parcel, as well as the right to organise their own educational and recreational pursuits in the prison.

5. The right to remission of sentences as is normally provided for all other prisoners.

The prisoners believed that the refusal of the British authorities to grant them the "special category status" which obtained in regard to other prisoners was a political decision taken in order to criminalise their status. Several hundred of them went on what is called "the blanket protest," from September 1976. This protest consisted of refusing to wear prison clothes and wearing a blanket instead. As from March 1978, they escalated their protest to a "no-wash protest." A number of them went on hunger strike in October 1980 and the hunger strike ended on 18 December 1980 on the basis of an agreement put forward by Cardinal Tomás O Fiaich and Bishop Daly. In the course of the negotiations between Cardinal O Fiaich and Bishop Daly, the British government had agreed substantially to the demands made by the prisoners provided that they were not described as "an acceptance of political status." This proviso was accepted by the prisoners. However, the British government failed to implement the recommendations that had been made by Cardinal O Fiaich and substantially accepted by them. This caused considerable bitterness and distrust among the prisoners. They considered that they had been tricked into giving up the hunger strike by subterfuge in which the British government availed of the good offices of Cardinal O Fiaich, but then reneged on the agreement they had made with him.

Cardinal O Fiaich and Bishop Daly also considered that they had been misled by the British government. It is in this atmosphere that the later hunger strike was started on 1 March 1981. However, on this occasion, the prisoners started the hunger strike with the preconceived determination that they were not going to allow the British government to trick them again, or to use intermediaries; they insisted that they would continue the hunger strike, until death, in relays until such time as the British government gave categorical assurance to them concerning the future treatment of prisoners, and the granting of the five requirements which they had specified.

In the meanwhile, a succession of well-intentioned intermediaries, including a number of members of the Irish parliament, representatives of the European Commission on Human Rights, representatives of the Irish Commission on Justice and Peace and representatives of the International Committee of the Red Cross sought to mediate, but the attitude of the British government throughout had been:

> *We cannot accept that mediation between the government and convicted prisoners, even by international bodies of the highest standards, is the right course.*

They also refused to negotiate directly with the prisoners. In reality, the attitude of the British government had been to avail of all the intermediaries in an effort to break the determination of the prisoners and to avoid negotiating with the prisoners, thus not binding themselves to alterations in the prison rules. The prisoners accused them of playing a cynical game of brinkmanship, waiting for one prisoner after the other to reach the dying point, hoping that this would break the morale of the other prisoners. Indeed, in the course of a press interview given by Mr Michael Alison, British minister of state for Northern Ireland in the British embassy in Washington, he made the startling but candid admission that negotiations about the hunger strikers was like:

> *the efforts of authorities to keep plane hijackers occupied while plans are developed to subdue them.* (Irish Times, 13 July 1981)

The death of Bobby Sands and his writings are but a fallout resulting from the cruel interference by Britain in the affairs of the Irish nation. I wish it were possible to ensure that those in charge of formulating British policy in Ireland would read these pages. They might begin to understand the deep injuries which British policy has inflicted upon this nation and now seek to heal these deep wounds.

As was pointed out by the Taoiseach, Charles Haughey, "For over sixty years partition has not worked, and it is not likely to work now." Why not face up to this situation now without any further strains on Anglo-Irish relations?

No one in Ireland would wish to impose any discrimination or injustice upon any minority, religious or political, that may exist in any portion of Ireland. In a united federal Ireland I am sure that special guarantees could be ensured that would protect any religious minority that felt threatened. I am sure that, within the context of the European Convention for the Protection of Human Rights and Fundamental Freedoms, special mechanisms could be instituted to ensure the administrative and judicial protection of any minority within the Federated Republic of Ireland.

However, such a solution will only become possible when Britain finally relinquishes any claim of sovereignty over any portion of this island. The withdrawal of British forces can, if necessary, be phased over a period of years. More important, and more urgent, would be the immediate cessation of overt and covert British secret service operations in any part of Ireland; these are now commonplace, and are a grave source of danger. Such secret service operations can only aggravate the situation and cause an added complication in the already difficult relations which exist between our two islands.

Lest this introduction by me to these harrowing pages be construed as a tacit endorsement of violence I should explain my attitude. I do not agree with violence. Throughout the hunger strikes I did not participate in any of the H Block Committee activities lest this might be construed as an approval of violence. This was a difficult decision for me to make as I was only too conscious of the provocation and intolerance which was a feature of the policy of the British authorities *vis-à-vis* the hunger strike. I did make my views known to the British authorities in no uncertain terms but did not do so publicly. Because of persistent misrepresentation of the facts involved in the hunger strike by the British authorities in the United States I did make one speech in New York under the auspices of the American Irish Unity Committee on 22 July 1981 in order to set the record right.

In their own country and in countries which they do not seek to dominate, the British are reasonable, fair-minded and even lovable. It is otherwise in areas which they regard as their preserve. In regard to Ireland, the British government and establishment are just incapable of being objective, fair-minded or just. A typical illustration of this was provided recently.

The British forces in Northern Ireland have been using rubber or plastic bullets indiscriminately for a number of years. They have argued that they were harmless. Over fifty people—mostly children—have been killed or permanently maimed in Northern Ireland by these plastic or rubber bullets. This was denied by the British who maintained that they were harmless. When extensive riots broke out recently in Britain the possibility arose of using rubber or plastic bullets for crowd control. An alarmed Conservative British Home Secretary said immediately that he would oppose their use "in mainland Britain because they are lethal!" (*Irish Times*, 11 July 1981) It is all right to use them in Ireland and to kill women and children there—but not "in mainland Britain"!

In the early stages of the last decade, Paul Johnson, one of Great Britain's most distinguished journalists, editor of the *Spectator*, and one of Prime Minister Margaret Thatcher's most ardent supporters, wrote in the *New Statesman*:

> *In Ireland over the centuries, we have tried every possible formula: direct rule, indirect rule, genocide, apartheid, puppet parliaments, real parliaments, martial law, civil law, colonisation, land reform, partition. Nothing has worked. The only solution we have not tried is absolute and unconditional withdrawal.*

Why not try it now? It will happen in any event!

> Some had no thought of victory
> But had gone out to die
> That Ireland's mind be greater
> Her heart mount up on high;
> And yet who knows what's yet to come.
>
> William Butler Yeats

SEÁN MacBRIDE, 1982

Seán MacBride (1904–88)

President International Peace Bureau (Geneva); President NGO Committee (Geneva); Member International Commission of Jurists; Hon. President World Federation United Nations Associations; President Irish United Nations Association; President Irish Section Amnesty International.

Mr MacBride, who was one of the founder members of Amnesty International, was Chairman of its International Executive for thirteen years, was Secretary-General of the International Commission of Jurists for seven years, and was President of the International Commission for the Study of Communications Problems (1977–80); he was Assistant Secretary-General of the United Nations and Commissioner for Namibia (1973–6); Mr MacBride acted as a member of several International Commissions of Enquiry.

He was the holder of the Irish Military Medal (1920–21); Nobel Prize for Peace (1974); the International Lenin Prize for Peace (1977); the American Medal of Justice (1978); Medal of the International Institute for Human Rights (1978); UNESCO Medal of Merit (1980); Dag Hammerskjoeld Award (1981).

The following honorary degrees were awarded to Mr MacBride: Doctor of Letters (D. Litt.), Bradford University (1977); Doctor of Laws (LL.D.), Saint Thomas, Minnesota (1975); Doctor of Laws, Guelph University, Canada (1977); Doctor of Laws, University of Dublin (1978); Doctor of Laws, University of Cape Coast, Ghana (1978); Doctor of Laws, Florida Southern College (1979); Doctor of Laws, Suffolk University, Boston (1980).

One Day
In My Life

It was still dark and snowing lightly when I woke. I don't think I got more than an hour's sleep during the long, restless, torturous night. The cold was intense, biting at my naked body. For at least the thousandth time I rolled over on to my side, hugging the blankets close to my body. The sleep that the bitter cold had denied me hung above me, leaving me tired and drowsy. I was somewhat exhausted, and every bone in my body seemed to be protesting at the ordeal of having spent yet another night on a damp foam mattress on the floor. No sleep again worth mentioning! I was frustrated, cross and curled up in a little ball to get warm. If I had had something to boot, I would have booted it, that's just how I felt. I had tried lying in every sort of position to get warm, but the cold still penetrated. My three flimsy blankets were no match for the bitter, biting cold that came creeping through the bars of my window, situated above my head.

Dear God, another day, I thought, and it was a far from pleasant thought. Naked, I rose and crossed the cell floor through the shadows to the corner to urinate. It was deadly cold. The stench rose to remind me of my situation and the floor was damp and gooey in places. Piles of rubbish lay scattered about the cell, and in the dimness dark, eerie figures screamed at me from the surrounding dirty, mutilated walls. The stench of excreta and urine was heavy and lingering. I lifted the small water container from amongst the rubbish and challenged an early morning drink in a vain effort to remove the foul taste in my throat. God, it was cold.

It was beginning to grey outside as dawn approached, and the crows began to assemble themselves in long black lines upon the snow-covered barbed wire fencing. One morning I am going to wake up out of this night-mare, I thought, as I huddled in under the blankets again. Apart from the caws of the crows it was sinisterly quiet. I was sure many of the lads lay awake, probably just lying huddled up trying to get warm. The prospect of cold, tasteless porridge along with two slices of bread and half a mug of lukewarm tea for breakfast was depressing. It was simply demoralising just thinking of it.

The dawn broke and out of the shadows of the dead night materi-alised the daily nightmare. The dirt and filth, the scarred walls—the inner confines of my stinking, smelly tomb greeted me once again. I lay listening to my own gentle breathing and to the caws of the crows.

The snow lay deep upon the outside yard. Didn't I know it only too well, having spent half the night huddled up in the corner while it fell in through the bars of my window to its earthly destination upon my bed. In the first light of morning boredom began to set in. The day ahead would seem like eternity and depression would soon be my companion again. I lay there, freezing cold and uncomfortable, feeling a bit sorry for myself with the thought of yet another day churning around in my head.

A key clinked against the steel. Footsteps came charging along the outside corridor breaking the silence. The crows fled in an explosion of chattering caws; my mind fought to register the meaning of the disturbing confusion. Panic gripped me as the heavy steel door rattled and flew open. A wave of black uniforms swept into my cell, blotting out the door space. A gruff, intimidating voice yelled, "Right you, get up!"

I was already halfway to my feet before the last syllable left his rowdy mouth, wrapping my threadbare old blue towel around my shivering waist.

"Bears in the air" echoed throughout the wing as those awake and alerted by the invasion warned the rest of the lads that there were screws in the wing.

"Wing shift," someone shouted, leaving me in no doubt as to what was to come.

"Right you, out and up to the top of the wing and be quick," rowdy mouth snapped. I moved out of the cell, the corridor was black with uniforms, batons dangling by their sides.

"Not quick enough," rowdy mouth snapped again.

Two strong pairs of arms gripped me from behind. My arms were wrenched up my back and my feet left the floor. A mass of black thronged around me and moved in a sudden burst of speed dragging me along with it. I came back to earth and a well-polished pair of leather official issue boots ground into my feet. A screw on the perimeter of the now excited gang kneed me in the thigh. I felt like vomiting and screaming surrender but I remained mute. A table loomed up before me where half a dozen or so screws converged, gaping and inspecting me— their first intentional prey. I was left standing in the midst of the black horde who awaited their cue from the mouthpiece.

"Right," screamed the self-appointed tyrant. "Drop that towel, turn round. Bend down and touch your toes."

I dropped my towel, turned a full circle and stood there embarrassed and naked, all eyes scrutinising my body.

"You forgot something," the mouthpiece grunted.

"No I didn't," I stammered in a fit of bravado.

"Bend down tramp," he hissed right into my face in a voice that hinted of a strained patience. Here it comes, I thought.

"I'm not bending," I said.

Roars of forced laughter reinforced by a barrage of jibes and abuse erupted. "Not bending!" the confident bastard jibed.

"Not bending! Ha! Ha! He's not bending, lads," he said to the impatient audience.

Jesus, here it comes. He stepped beside me, still laughing, and hit me. Within a few seconds, in the midst of the white flashes, I fell to the floor as blows rained upon me from every conceivable angle. I was dragged back up again to my feet and thrown like a side of bacon, face downwards on the table. Searching hands pulled at my arms and legs, spreading me like a pelt of leather. Someone had my head pulled back by the hair while some pervert began probing and poking my anus.

It was great fun; everybody was killing themselves laughing, except me, while all the time a barrage of punches rained down on my naked body. I was writhing in pain. They gripped me tighter as each blow found its destination. My face was smashed against the table and blood smeared the table under my face. I was dazed and hurt. Then they dragged me off the table and let me drop to the floor. My first reaction was to wrap the towel which lay beside me around my reddened waist. Again I was gripped by the arms from behind and dragged towards the other wing. I just caught a glimpse of one of my comrades being beaten and dragged to the table, while in the background someone else was being kicked out of his cell. A cell door opened and I was flung inside. The door slammed shut and I lay on the concrete floor, chest pounding and every nerve in my body strained. Could have been worse, I tried to tell myself as a consolation. But this didn't convince me or my aching body one bit.

The cold drove me off the floor. Every part of my body protested as I made the slow ascent to my feet. A trickle of blood ran from my mouth on to my long shaggy beard and dripped on to the floor. My skin was finely emblazoned with a host of bruises and marks. I was trembling. I hadn't really had very much time to be frightened; everything had moved too fast. Thank God I had not been asleep when they came.

We'll get those bastards someday, I told myself. We'll see how big they are then, I thought, as I spat out a mouthful of blood into the corner.

We'll see how great they are then.

I began pacing the floor. The cold streamed in through the open window and, still clad in only a towel, I really felt it. God, I was sore.

More bodies were dragged down the wing.

The bastards were shouting their sadistic heads off, revelling in the blood and pain, all of it ours, of course. God only knows how long it will be before they decide to throw us in a blanket. An empty freezing cold cell, an aching black-and-blue frozen body, a bunch of psychopaths beating men to pulp outside the door and it isn't even bloody-well breakfast time yet!

Suffering Jesus, can it get any worse? I asked myself, and then answered, you know bloody well that it will. That's what was worrying me.

Regardless of my aching body, I continued to pace the floor trying to get some sort of warmth into my body. My feet were now blue with the cold and I thought my entire body was going to give up to the freezing cold. The shock had worn off and the pain and cold were attacking me relentlessly. The snow had begun falling again. On the outside wire there wasn't a crow to be seen.

A few of my comrades shared their experiences and injuries out the windows of a few cells down the wing. I heard the rattle of the trolley and I knew breakfast was coming, and still no blankets or mattress. Don't forget to see which screws are on the wing today, when the door opens, I reminded myself. We could do with a few quiet screws after this morning's episode, I thought, as the cell door opened and two orderlies with sneers on their freshly washed faces planted the morning offering right into my hands—mug of tea in one hand and a bowl of porridge with two slices of bread lying on top of it in my other hand. A little rat-faced figure with a black hat poked his head round the open door he was leaning against and wearing a smirk said, "Good morning! Would you care to put on the prison clothing and go to work, clean your cell, wash yourself or polish my boots?". . .

"You wouldn't! Ah well, we'll see after!" The door slammed shut.

"Bastard," I said, retreating to the corner to inspect the second catastrophe of the day—the breakfast. I salvaged whatever dry bit of bread I could, and having fished the two slices from the soggy porridge I threw the remainder, porridge and all, against the far wall. Disgusted, I literally forced the meagre bit of bread and lukewarm tea into me. It was bitter cold, so cold that in between sips of tea I had to keep pacing the floor. I thought of the three screws who had stood outside the door while I received my breakfast. Warders A—, B— and C—. That was all I needed. Three out-and-out torture-mongers and they'd be here all day. Bloody marvellous, I thought.

The screw who had just spoken to me was A—. He was heartless, sly and intelligent when it came to torturing naked men. There was no physical stuff from him. All purely psychological attacks and cunning tricks. He was a right-out-of-Belsen type, and like the majority of the screws he took great pleasure in attacking the dignity of the naked prisoners-of-war. He was on a constant ego trip, but then weren't they all once they donned their little black suits with the shining buttons, and were handed their baton and pistol?

The second screw that I had seen was B—, a sectarian bigot. He was of medium build, black hair, good looking and all go. He was also an alcoholic and handy with his baton, especially on the younger lads, and that was a regular practice of his.

The remaining screw, and perhaps the worst of the three, was C—. He hated us more than B—, the bigot, and he constantly went out of his way to prove it. He never smiled, never spoke unless to make a derogatory remark or hurl abuse. He carried an extra large chip on his shoulder, which we had to bear.

Three perfect bastards, I thought, and I cursed the cold, my aching body and the pangs of hunger that never left me. I continued on my journey to nowhere as I circled the cell floor like a guinea pig, stopping here and there for a moment or two to identify the scratched names on the door and walls; the simple testimony and reminder that others had been and still were in my position. A certain quality of pride seemed to attach itself to the scrawled names of the tortured writers. They were entitled to be proud, I thought, as I moved off to read the scribbled Gaelic phrases and words, noting the progress of the other wings in the Gaelic classes.

"Gaelic classes," I said it again. I sounded rather odd. But then it was odd, considering that it meant standing at the cell door listening to your mate, the teacher, shouting the lesson for the day at the top of his voice from the other end of the wing when the screws happened to be away for their dinner or tea.

I walked on. The biting cold refused to yield. If I didn't get a blanket or two soon I'd be in trouble. You don't ask for them either. I learned that a long time ago. Show one sign of weakness and you've dug your own grave. Besides, there were forty-three of my comrades in the wing in exactly the same predicament as myself. So forget the moaning and get some heat into your body, I thought, rebuking myself for dangerously playing with thoughts of self-pity and thinking too long and too much of the hardships. It breeds depression and depression is worse than the cold and my aching body put together. My thoughts turned to food. Friday, fish for dinner. Cold potatoes and hard peas. But there was always that vague hope that it might be served hot and with salt on it. I don't know why, because it never was. Maybe it was just something to look forward to, like winning the pools or the Irish Sweepstakes. More chance of winning the pools, I admitted to myself. Wasn't it all just living from one stinking cold meal to the next, creating false hope for oneself, clinging to every rumour that came your way? *Scéal, Scéal, Scéal!* The Irish word for news or story that was now so worn out that even the screws used it.

"Have you any *scéal*?"

"Did you hear any *scéal*?"

"The *scéal* is bad, or heavy or fantastic."

It was perfectly understandable. You had to have something to hope for, to look forward to, to speculate on or to cling to. The way a good bit of *scéal* could liven up the wing was unbelievable. Like after the Coalisland to Dungannon march when one of the lads brought back an estimate of the turn-out, plus a smuggled photograph. I nearly cried myself and I'm sure more than a few of the lads did. I'll never forget it, sitting in the midst of a living nightmare without even a friendly face in sight, and when it came to my turn to see the picture I looked at it and I never felt so happy in all my life. I just stared at it and stared at it, never wanting to let go of it. Aren't they grand people, I thought. I felt proud to be fighting for them. It brings a lump to my throat even thinking of it now. Ah, dear God, if it wasn't so cold and if I wasn't so sore I could maybe sing a wee song or two to pass the time. But I'm in no mood or form at all for it.

Nobody at the windows talking. Too busy pacing the floor and licking their wounds.

"Bear in the air," someone shouted, warning that there was a screw in the wing outside the cells. That was the call we used when someone detected the jingle of a key, the squeak of a boot or a passing shadow. All warned of a hovering screw. I squeezed up close to the door and put my eye to a little chip in the concrete where the door met the wall. I'd noticed it earlier and, as I hoped, it afforded me a restricted but welcome view of a few yards of space on the outside corridor. I caught a glimpse of the shadow first, then the familiar form of A—. He had a few letters and a few packets of tissues in his hand.

"Screw giving out letters," I yelled in Gaelic at the top of my voice out the door to ease the strained, alerted nerves. A— jumped a little, my voice startling him as it broke the sinister silence. But he carried on with what he was doing. It was normal to shout if anyone knew what was going on. It let everyone else know. There was nothing as nerve-wracking or as frightening as sitting naked behind a closed door not knowing what was going on when danger was lurking, and in our predicament danger was constantly lurking.

The screws didn't like Gaelic being shouted about the wing or its use in conversations. It alienated them, made them feel foreign and even embarrassed them. They didn't know what was being said. They suspected that every word was about them and they weren't too far wrong!

I began my journey to nowhere again. As I turned by the window a key hit metal. A shiver swept through me as the lock shuddered and my door opened. A— stood there clutching a couple of packets of tissues and some letters.

"I've a parcel for you," he drawled in his hateful accent, staring at me, wearing his dominant "I'm better than you" look.

Some parcel, I thought. A couple of packets of Kleenex tissues.

"You're lucky; you are the only one who got a parcel today," he said.

Jesus! I felt like vomiting. This was A—, the psychologist at work. Reading me like a book, he said, "Why don't you put on the prison clothes, then you can have some privileges."

I felt like telling him what to do with his stinking privileges and his parcel for that matter, but the tissues would come in handy for standing on the cold floor.

Keep your head, Bobby, I told myself as he handed me a Parker pen to sign the large book for the parcel. He was loving it all: making it seem as if I was signing a million pound contract for three lousy packets of tissues. He had a letter for me as well. I'd spotted that long ago but he was waiting for me to ask him for it. I didn't. I ignored it. He replaced his expensive pen in his top pocket, grinned and made some comment about the smell of my unwashed body and the stinking, evil stench of my cell. He turned to close the heavy steel cell door. "Oh," he said, "I've a letter for you." He handed it to me. I took it from him and cradled it like a new-born child. The door slammed. I pressed my eye against the small hole to see if he was going up to his office at the top of the wing. He was. I yelled in Gaelic again, "Bear off the air," to let the boys know and retreated to the corner feeling like a new man with my prized possessions—a letter and three packets of tissues! I spread the tissues about the floor and stood on them. They felt like luxurious carpeting compared with the naked concrete. I slid the priceless, several times read and censored pages of my letter out of the already opened envelope. The letter was scarred with black censored lines here and there, but not as bad as last month's, I thought. I immediately identified the familiar handwriting as my mother's. Old faithful, never lets me down! I began reading.

My dear son,

I hope you received my last letter all right. I've been very worried about you and your comrades. Is it cold there, son? I know that you have only three blankets and I read in the Irish News *that many of you have severe flu. Keep yourself well wrapped up as best you can, son. I'll say a wee prayer for you all.*

Your sister Marcella had a birthday party for Kevin some time ago. He was one year old. He is a lovely child. You haven't seen him yet son, have you? Your father and brother were asking for you, and so was Bernadette and Mr and Mrs Rooney. I was down at the march on Sunday and there was ▆▆▆▆▆▆▆▆▆▆

▆▆▆▆▆▆▆▆▆▆▆▆▆▆▆▆▆▆▆▆▆▆▆▆▆▆▆

▆▆▆▆▆▆▆▆▆▆▆▆(Censored! The Bastards! I cursed them.) *Everything is going well, son. Maybe it won't be long now.*

The Brits raided the house twice last week and smashed my new Celtic harp that the boys in the Cages sent to me at Christmas. I don't think the Brits are very pleased at the minute son, with all the ▆▆▆▆▆▆▆▆▆▆▆▆▆▆▆▆▆▆▆

▆▆▆▆▆▆▆▆▆▆▆▆▆▆▆▆▆▆▆▆▆▆▆▆▆▆▆

▆▆▆▆▆▆▆▆▆▆▆▆▆▆▆▆▆▆▆▆▆▆▆▆▆▆▆

their heads must be turned son.

Your brother Seán was down in Killarney and there's slogans painted on all the roads and walls about ▆▆▆▆▆▆▆▆▆

▆▆▆▆▆▆▆▆▆▆▆▆▆▆▆▆▆▆▆▆▆▆▆▆▆▆▆

(H Block!! you Bastards, I said to myself.)

Well son, I must finish off. It's started snowing. I hope you are all right. We are all behind you, son. I had the child up in the house on Sunday. He says he is going to be a Volunteer when he grows up and get you out of that terrible place. God help him. I'll be up with your father and Marcella on your next visit on the 12th. Well son, God bless you all. I'll see you soon. We all miss you.

Your loving Mother

God bless her, I said.
Visit today!
"Yahoo!"
"You all right in there, Bobby?"
"All right, Seán. Just remembered I have a visit today. Forgot all

about it after that bloody massacre this morning," I said to my next-door neighbour.

"How did you get on yourself, Seán?" I shouted back.

"I think my nose is broken, Bobby. What about yourself?"

"Not too bad, Seán. The usual—plenty of bruises and a few cuts. Here, I got a letter. I think there were plenty of bombs and a big turnout at the parade. It was all censored as usual, but I'll find out today on my visit. I'm away to walk, Seán; have to get warm. It's really cold, comrade. Keep your heart up. I'll give you a shout later."

Yahoo! Visit today. Where are those bloody blankets? I'm freezing to death.

I might see the wee lad today. I haven't seen him in almost nine months. It's the health risk. I'm taking a chance seeing him anytime, I thought, but I just have to see him again. The thought of the stringent body searches I would have to face just to receive a solitary monthly half-hour visit was demoralising.

"Bears in the air! Bears in the air!"

I was at the door like a flash, eye to the small hole. Nothing! I couldn't see a thing. I heard them but I couldn't see them.

"Turnover! Turnover!"

Jesus, cell searches! There's nothing in the bloody cells to search. We'd got a right turning over this morning.

A lock on someone's door shot. I caught a glimpse of B— and C— entering a cell facing me. It was Pee Wee's cell. I heard C— yelling, but I couldn't make out what he was saying. The words were barely audible, but I heard B— screaming, "Bend over, you little cunt!"

Jesus, they were doing a body search on Pee Wee. Barely turned eighteen and they were forcibly bending him to probe his anal passage. I heard the all-too-common dull thud of blows striking Pee Wee's naked body.

B— and C— came swaggering out of the cell like two gunslingers, smiling.

"Stinking bastards!" Seán screamed out of his cell door at them.

"Mr A—, a van for the Punishment Block, please. Pee Wee O'Donnell just assaulted Mr C—," said B—, giggling.

Must be bad, I thought. He must be bloody bad when they are sending him to the boards to charge him. All part of the cover up. Accuse them and you have another charge of false allegations. War criminals! I said to myself. They're a stinking, dirty shower of war criminals, every last one of them.

They took Pee Wee out of his cell. I caught a glimpse of his small harmless figure. His face was red with blood. His right eye was swollen and his nose gushing blood.

They'll forcibly bathe him and cut his hair on the boards. In other words they'll batter him to pulp for the third time today!

The wing was deadly quiet. It was very tense, but the evil atmosphere never left and the tension never lifted.

We'll get you C—, I said to myself. We'll get you. And I never meant anything so much in my life.

I was shivering, but I stood at my post at the little accidental spyhole in case they decided to come back and try the same on someone else. I heard them laughing and boasting in their office of how they had beaten Pee Wee up. Word of what had occurred was filtering down the line to the wing O/C. B— was rattling a bucket and shouting to C— about carrying out a slop-out. He made sure we all heard it. They'd come around with the bucket and enter the cells kicking the contents of the filthy chamber pots about the floor. We couldn't empty them out the windows or doors until late at night. But I knew B— was playing on the already strained nerves of the lads. A— was in charge. He might not risk it. The boys were really angry after what happened to Pee Wee. There would be more trouble. Besides the bedding wasn't in the cells to soak yet. As I was thinking of the bedding and the torturing cold the orderlies came down the wing pushing a trolley carrying our mattresses and blankets.

"Blankets on the air!" I yelled in Gaelic to let the boys know. The cells erupted in a mêlée of shouts, yells and cheers. The doors began opening and after what seemed like an eternity with the cold apparently growing more intense, my cell door finally opened and the orderlies threw my three flimsy blankets and filthy mutilated mattress upon the floor.

C— gave me his dirty I hate-your-guts look and slammed the door. And I hate your stinking guts too, C—, I said to myself and dived at the blankets. I wrapped one around my waist and drooped one over my shoulders poncho-fashion, putting the towel around my head and neck like a scarf. I pushed the filthy, damp foam rubber mattress in along the wall and sat down on it, wrapping the third and last blanket around my feet. I was like something last seen in Stalag 18 or Dachau. And to tell the truth I felt like it too. My beard became irritated by the towel and the horse hair blankets irked my aching body. It was cold and one of the boys commented out his window that it was snowing again. It could snow in on top of me like last night and the night before. I wasn't moving. I wonder how Pee Wee is? Probably near dead in those Punishment Blocks. Jesus, it's been a bad day, I thought, and I felt very tired. The exhaustion of the last two nights without sleep suddenly hit me. My feet warmed a little and I thought of the afternoon visit. The wing was silent except for the occasional roars of laughter from B— and C—. B— would be back after dinner, drunk and dangerous, I thought. I closed my eyes hoping to escape for a while through sleep till dinnertime. God, it's hard. It's very hard.

I rose slowly from the mattress testing every movement. I made it to my feet and placed the mattress against the wall. I spread a blanket on the floor and with another blanket wrapped around my waist and a towel around my head and shoulders I set off once again like a nomad on my journey to nowhere. It was still cold but the morning bite had gone from the air. The snow still lay heavy on the ground outside and the light was unusually dim for midday.

The dinner will be here shortly, I thought, and then it's only a few hours to my visit. The thought of seeing my family was comforting. It was the highlight and only highlight of each long torturous month. Twelve highlights per year! Half an hour of comparative happiness each visit. That's six hours of comparative happiness a year. I did a quick bit of mental arithmetic: that's six hours out of 8,760 per year. Six lousy hours and they harass you and your family for every minute of it, every single minute of it!

I walked on, anger beginning to surge up inside me.

"Bastards," I said and stopped to gaze out of the open but concrete barred window. I won't have this much longer either, I reminded myself, thinking of how they'd started to block up the windows in the other wings with corrugated iron and timber, blocking out all sunlight and the sky. There wasn't much to see anyway except the birds, the night sky and the clouds. The rest was just a downright depressing eyesore, although at present the snow was unusual and it hung on the miles of ugly, gruesome barbed wire and clung to the impersonal, usually depressing, corrugated iron. Everything was either a dreary grey or a brilliant white. At night there would be a bit of colour while the snow lasted, with the thousands of assorted bright lights and beaming spotlights reflecting on the white carpet.

Wouldn't it be a relief and delight to stroll through a lush green field and touch the blades of shining grass and feel the fresh texture of a leaf on a tree or sit on a hill and gaze upon a valley filled with the buzzing life of spring, smelling the fresh, clean, healthy scent with nothing but miles of space around me.

Freedom: that was it. Freedom to live again. I turned from the window to continue my relentless pacing, disheartened a little by the thoughts of freedom. I looked at the stinking, dirt-covered walls, the piles of disease-ridden rubbish and decaying waste food that lay scattered in the corners on the damp floor. The mutilated, filthy mattress, torn to shreds by a thousand searches. The tea-stained ceiling, to cut the glare reflecting off the bright light, the scraped and scarred door, and the disease-ridden chamber pot that lay beside the door. It was getting harder and harder to conjure up the picture of that beautiful lush green field. Every minute my nightmarish surroundings screamed at me. There was no escaping this nightmare unless I gave up! A few—a very few—had already given up. They had put on prison clothes and conformed. Not that they had wished to do this. They just couldn't bear the unrelenting burden of torture, the continued boredom, tension and fear, the deprivation of basic necessities like exercise and fresh air, no association with other human beings except through a shout from behind a closed heavy steel door.

The depression, the beatings, the cold—what is there? I said to myself. Look out the window and concentration camp screams at you. Look around you in the tomb that you survive in and you are engulfed in hell, with little black devils in the forms of A—, B— and C— ready to pounce on you each minute of each stinking nightmare-ridden day.

I pulled my mattress back to its former position on the floor and sat down. The first clouds of depression fell upon me. I tried to think of my coming visit to cheer myself up. I thought of Pee Wee and I was about to kill B— and C— in another fantasy, when a cheer arose announcing the arrival of the long awaited dinner. The "Happy Wagon," as they called the lorry that brought the food from the cook house to the H Blocks, had arrived. And thank God for that, I thought, forgetting the threatening depression. There was a bit of a buzz in the wing as signs of life suddenly appeared from within the tombs around me. A few of the lads went to the windows and a bit of chatter ensued. The arrival of the dinner did not only mean food. It also meant that the screws would be departing shortly for their two-hour dinner break. It meant comparative safety for two short hours and it also meant that you would only have half a day left to battle with. A slight drizzle of rain fell outside. I hoped to God it wouldn't rain heavily for if the snow melted they'd be out with the hoses, hosing the outside of the cells and the yards. That meant we'd get hosed down with the high-powered apparatus. In this weather we'd freeze to death if we or our bedding were saturated. It's murder trying to hide in the corner to escape the powerful jet of freezing water. With no panes of glass in the windows there's nothing to stop it.

A lock shuddered and a door opened.

"Dinner up!" one of the lads shouted in Gaelic.

I abruptly forgot about the high-powered hose and headed towards my little peephole. They were moving down the far side of the wing. I'd get my dinner last, I thought. The plastic plates were piled on top of each other on the trolley. The orderlies were handing them into each cell. B— stood breaking off pieces of fish from the plates and was in the process of eating them. I was raging.

"Fenian steaks for dinner," B— was shouting. He was laughing at his own sick wit.

"I hope they choke on them," said C—, putting his little dig in as usual. The food procession moved on with A— bringing up the rear. They reached the bottom of the wing and turned. I heard the doors on my side of the wing opening and slamming as they drew nearer.

B— shouted, "Mr A—, there seems to be a fish short."

A sickening feeling hit me right in the chest, almost crippling me. I was the last man. That stinking bastard B— ate it. I felt like screaming it out the door, but that was what they wanted me to do.

"Ah! Mr A—," said B—. "I seem to have made a mistake. There's not a fish missing at all." My heart lifted.

"There's two missing, Mr A—!"

I thought Seán was going to go through the door. I knocked on the wall quickly to remind him that he wasn't on his own. I could hear him cursing them up and down. I felt as sick as the fish must have felt when it was hooked. The most eatable part of the dinner would be missing. It was a catastrophe and Seán knew it as well as I did.

Seán's door opened and closed. Then mine opened. I stood there as if nothing had occurred. I took the sparse-looking meal from the orderly as A— drawled, "We seem to be a few fish short. I shall inform the cook house to send them to us as soon as possible."

That really meant, "Too bad you are not getting any."

I caught a glimpse of B— ceremoniously licking his fingers while wearing that hateful smile of his for the occasion. I turned away from the door not having uttered a single word or given them any hint of my utter disgust and dejection. The door slammed like a cannon-shot behind me. They all had a jolly good laugh on their way back to their little office, orderlies and all.

I sat down and inspected my meagre dinner of one unpeeled cold potato and about thirty or forty equally cold and hard peas. The orderlies began their daily session of drumming out and whistling *The Sash My Father Wore*. B— would see them right with a few cigarettes, crack a few sectarian jokes with them and encourage them to keep up their incessant racket. The orderlies, for their stinking part, crawled right up his sectarian ass and grovelled as only informers and rabble can grovel. They'd sell their own mothers for a cigarette. What they did to us for the same price and an easy time of it would make their poor mothers sick.

I began to salvage some of the cold dinner, eating as much as I could, which was an effort, and throwing the leftovers into the corner with the rest of the filth and rubbish.

The Sash My Father Wore ceased and a few seconds later the cell doors began opening to the shouts of "Collecting the dishes" which echoed along the wing. I began walking, not bothering to have a sly look out of the peephole. They continued on their way, collecting the dishes and moving from one cell to the next. I heard Seán telling his neighbour to tell the O/C that he was going to ask the screw for bog roll (toilet paper).

The thoughts of my afternoon visit were getting the better of my nervous system, the excitement in just the thought was getting the better of my constipated bowels of five days as they began to churn.

The party had reached Seán's door.

"Any chance of a bit of toilet paper, mister?" asked Seán.

"Wipe it with your hand," snapped C— and slammed the door.

One and all went into hysterics over C—'s sick wit! My cell door opened, the orderly removed the plate in the midst of the hilarious uproar. No mention of my missing fish, just B—'s chirping "That was a good one Mr C—," and then more convulsions of laughter.

"Ah, no doubt, Mr C—, a cracker. Ha, ha, ha, ha!" The door slammed. C— delighted in humiliating us. There was an excuse for B—: he had the mentality of an idiot. A— revelled in it, and the four orderlies competed with each other to win their stinking favour. I rapped on the wall.

"Seán," I called, "I'll rig up a line with a bit of towel thread and swing a few tissues into you, *mo chara*."

"Hold on till the screws go for their dinner," I added.

"*Maith thú*, Bobby," he said. I sat down again to engineer the line, tearing long bits of thread from the towel and twining them together. Just about made C—'s day that, I thought, working away at my line.

"Mr B—, are you on the night guard tonight?" enquired a screw from the top of the wing.

"Yes, that's right," B— shouted back from the office.

Ho! Ho! Good or bad? I asked myself. He'll be going home now but he'll be back at 8.30 tonight for the night guard. He'll be drunk—and I knew right away what that meant.

"You hear that, Bobby?" shouted Seán.

"I heard it, comrade," I answered, thinking Seán had reached the same conclusion as myself.

"Trouble tonight!"

I stood up and lifted a small half-rotten potato from the rubbish and tied it on to the end of the completed line to weight it. The office door slammed, and the hated keys jingled. They were going and good riddance to them, I said, going to the window and tying several tissues on to the end of my line. I knocked on the wall.

"You there, Seán?"

"I'm here, Bobby," he said.

"Well, put your hand out and I'll swing these tissues to you," I said.

I put my arm out the open window and began swinging the weighted line across the five foot gap. It hit Seán's hand a few times before he caught hold of it.

"I've got it, Bobby," he said.

"*Maith thú, Seán*. Take it to you," I said.

He pulled the line in and secured the badly needed tissues and then rapped on the wall in acknowledgement. I answered with a knock on the wall, and retreated into my thoughts again. What else could I think of but my visit—seeing my family again. And I'd get a smoke too. That was something to look forward to. It had been a long while since I'd seen a cigarette and with a bit of luck I'd have some tonight for myself and the boys. That would be an achievement and a morale booster!

My bowels began to churn again. That's it, I thought (and in a way it was a welcome thought after five days of severe constipation), I'm going to have to go to the toilet, which sounded a bit ridiculous, as I lifted some tissues and retreated to the corner of my cell which did not afford a view from the spy hatch in the cell door. Despite the relief from constipation I felt like an animal squatting in the corner of the cell among the rubbish and dirt. But there was nothing else for it. It had to be done, however humiliating and degrading. More so to the lads who were two to a cell. At least I had some privacy!

Who among those so-called humanitarians who had kept their silence on the H Blocks, who among them could put a name on this type of humiliation and torture, when men are forced by extreme torture into the position that they had to embark upon a dirt strike to highlight the inhumanity poured upon them! How much must we suffer, I thought. An unwashed body, naked and wrecked with muscular pain, squatting in a corner, in a den of disease, amid piles of putrefying rubbish, forced to defecate upon the ground where the excreta would lie and the smell would mingle with the already sickening evil stench of urine and decaying waste food. Let them find a name for that sort of torture, I thought, rising and moving towards the window to seek fresh air, the beatings, the hosing downs, starvation and deprivation, just let them bloody well put a name on this nightmare of nightmares.

The drizzle had ceased and the snow remained intact. I was not so cold now but a chill remained. There were several sparrows trudging about on the snow searching for food, which brought to mind again the fish that I never got, nor would ever get! I gathered a few crusts of bread from the floor and flung them out the window to the smaller citizens, the sparrows, and stood watching them pecking their little hearts out. Many an hour I passed at this window just watching the birds, I thought. The sparrows and starlings, crows and seagulls were my constant companions, and the little wagtails who stayed to entertain me, fluttering about the yard until the last shadows of day departed. They were my only form of entertainment during the long boring days and they came every day now since I began throwing the crusts of bread out to them. They liked the maggots, I thought, thinking of the sweltering summer months when the cells were like ovens and the stench from the putrefying piles of rubbish and decaying waste food was almost overwhelming. That was when the white, wriggling, crawling maggots made their way out of the rubbish piles in their thousands.

I'll never forget that, I said to myself, reflecting on the morning I woke up and my blankets and mattress were a living mass of white maggots. They were in my hair and beard and crawling upon my naked body. They were repulsive and, dare I say it, frightening at first. But like everything else I had come to terms with them sharing my cell with me. At night I could hear them actually moving about the floor, disturbing little bits of paper, now and again causing a rustling noise as they headed in the direction of my mattress, where they would finally embed themselves and in the warmth harden into an egglike cocoon before hatching into flies. They would give off a sharp crack whenever I stood on them in my bare feet in the darkness, squashing them. Needless to say their end product was a pest, and very annoying, hundreds of fat, bloated flies that clung to the ceiling and walls, continually pestering my naked body day and night, hovering around my face as I tried to sleep or awakening me in the mornings when I would catch a glimpse of a black cloud ascending in panic as I stirred. But the maggots had another use, as I quickly discovered. I soon became so used to them that I would gather them up in my hands off the floor and from the rubbish piles in the corners. There would be thousands of them wriggling and sliding about. Having gathered them together between my palms, I would throw the white wriggling mass out of the window, scattering them over the jet-black tarmacadam yard, and against the black background their white wriggling little forms were easily spotted. The wagtails came fluttering about in a frenzy, their quick little legs darting them from one maggot to the next, feasting upon what to them must have been a delicacy. Within two or three minutes the yard would be cleared of every single maggot. I suppose it was something to do, to pass the time. Who would believe it if you told them you spent your summer gathering maggots to feed the birds?

I lifted a few crusts of bread from the corner and flung them out the window remembering my little friends again. Winter was a hard time for the birds, with the snow coating the ground and hiding the land.

I went back to my pacing once again as one of the boys shouted *Rang anois*, summoning the lads to their doors for an Irish language class.

The teacher was at the far end of the wing. He began to shout out the lessons at the top of his voice from behind his heavy steel door, asking questions, spelling out words and phrases, while the willing pupils scratched and scribbled them upon the dirty, mutilated walls. It was a rough and rugged way of teaching but it worked, and everyone endeavoured to speak what they learned all the time until the words and phrases became so common that they were used instinctively. The Irish class continued in the background as I returned to my thoughts. Thinking of how they would be getting ready in the house now to come up on the afternoon visit, if they weren't on their way already. They were probably as excited as I was, wishing the time away.

It would be a long hard day for them, waiting and queuing, being herded about like cattle from one gate to the next. From one degrading search to another. Enduring the insults and despising, dirty glances from the screws before they finally reached the visit-box. Then they would have to go though it all again to get out.

A screw began jeering and shouting from the top of the wing trying to disrupt the ongoing Gaelic class but the lads continued, disregarding him. It happened all the time. The screws, achieving nothing, soon got fed up and departed. I sat down upon the mattress again, my body still sore, the bruises colouring more as each hour passed by. I was very tired, becoming easily exhausted, not having had exercise or fresh air for so long, and I was bored stiff. The thought of my afternoon visit left me barely able to think. But there is always someone worse off than yourself, I told myself, remembering only too well my dead comrades and their families.

"At least I can see you once a month," my mother would say. "Better where you are than Milltown Cemetery."‡

But then there were times when Milltown would have been the preferable alternative when things became so unbearable that you just couldn't care less whether you lived or died just as long as you could escape the hellish nightmare. Aren't we dying anyway, I thought. Aren't our bodies degenerating to a standstill? I am a living corpse now. What will I be like in six months' time? Will I even be alive after another year? I used to worry about that, churning it around in my mind for hours on end. But no more! Because that is the only thing left that they can do to me: kill me. I have known this for some time and God knows that it isn't for the want of trying that they haven't achieved that on some one of us yet! But I am determined that I shall never give up. They can do what they will with me but I will never bow to them or allow them to criminalise me.

I find it startling to hear myself say that I am prepared to die first rather than succumb to their oppressive torture and I know that I am not on my own, that many of my comrades hold the same. And I thought of my dead comrades again. My friends who had stood beside me one day and were dead the next. Boys and girls just like myself, born and raised in the nationalist ghettos of Belfast to be murdered by foreign soldiers and lackey

---

‡ Bobby was eventually buried in Milltown Cemetery.

sectarian thugs. How many have been murdered at their hands throughout the occupied Six Counties. Too many! One boy or girl was one too many! How many more Irish people would die? How many more lives would be lost before the British had decided they had murdered enough and were forced to get out of Ireland forever? Inside and outside of gaol it was all the same—oppression bearing down upon you from every direction. Every street corner displaying an armed British soldier, every street having endured its share of suffering and grief at their hands.

I was proud to be resisting, to be fighting back. They couldn't defeat us outside; they are torturing us unmercifully inside their hellholes and have failed to defeat us again. I was frightened but I knew I would never give up. I would face the imperial might of their entire torturous arsenal rather then succumb. I tugged at my blankets to wrap them round me and rolled over hoping to doze for a while. The screws would not be back until after two o'clock. B— would be back at 8.30 p.m. tonight and I wondered who would be his replacement meantime. I'll find out soon enough, I thought, closing my eyes and my mind to my surroundings.

"Slop out on the air! Slop out on the air!" I awoke with a jump.

"Slop out on the air!"

The tin bucket clammered and rattled and a cold chill swept through my body leaving an empty hollow sensation in the pit of my stomach. I rose quickly but wearily, dreading the thought of a cramp. I was okay, although for several seconds my eyes fought to clear the blackness of a light head and threatening blackout.

I defeated it and sprang to my peephole at the door. The door next to Pee Wee's cell opened. A—, B—, and C—'s replacement, D—, stood in a semicircle around the entrance, the four grovelling orderlies flanking them, one clutching a squeegee (a pole with a rubber fitting used to push pools of water down drains). John O'Brien stepped into the doorway, his blanket hanging around him, and emptied his chamber pot of urine onto the ground in the wing, then stepped back into the cell. The orderly with the squeegee needed no signal. He stepped forward and brushed the pool of urine back into the cell again, all around John O'Brien's mattress. Most of the lads were lashing the contents of their po's under the doors using the empty po to push the urine that remained out into the wing. The bottom of my door was too tight. There was a large gap at the top and side, but too awkward for this type of operation. I would have to take the hard way out and heave it into the wing as John O'Brien had done when the door opened. It had to be done. If they got a po of urine in your cell it would end up over you and your bedding. There is more than one way to skin a cat or, in our case, more than one way to try to break a prisoner-of-war, and this was a well-worn one. They were switching cells, going from one side of the wing to the other. It didn't matter whose door they opened, it was just another harassment exercise, a build-up to more torture. I grabbed the po and stood poised for action! Better if I had had a cell mate, I thought, wishing for moral support. But Seán was on his own as well, and so was poor Pee Wee this morning. They were going to get someone else, I could sense that this was the whole object of the slop-out, and we all knew that only too well.

My lock rattled, alerting me. I stood poised and ready, po in hand, hoping for the best. The door opened. I didn't even glance at them. I lowered the po towards the ground, jettisoning the contents in the middle of the manoeuvre, hoping none would splash around their stinking, shining boots. I stepped back, lifting my head, expecting a blow that never came. I glanced at their faces. C— and D— were steaming drunk. A— was grinning as usual. The orderly appeared and began to brush the reeking mess back into my cell, saturating the sides and bottom of my mattress, before he decided to retreat. The door slammed. I lifted my mattress and began squeezing the urine out of the filthy foam onto the floor. I then started to scrape and push the pool towards the bottom of the door. It was a long, slow process. The door was tight and narrow. The urine trickled out slowly. In the wing the slop-out continued. The bucket rattled, spelling out danger. The occasional splash announced another emptied po. The tension was almost sickening.

Then it happened. A sudden eruption of noise, shouts, yells and venom-filled screams. The bucket clammered on to the ground and a barrage of dull thuds carried along the wing. What sounded like someone's head colliding with the steel pipes came ringing through the cells. I dropped my po and put my eye to the peephole, hearing a voice scream, "Give them more!" The ruckus continued until I heard A— shout, "That's enough!" Several screws came tearing down the wing from the opposite direction, their heavy boots squelching and splashing in the pools of reeking urine that lay on the corridor floor.

"Get a van for the punishment cells," screamed D— in his hateful, ignorant voice. There were more thuds and banging, then footsteps and evil laughter, followed by the gradual build-up of running feet, bumping, and what sounded like the swish of water. Four black uniforms darted past my area of vision dragging a naked body by the feet, his back scraping and scratching the ground and his head bumping off the concrete. It passed so quickly that I was unable to recognise who it was. But there had been blood on his face and body whoever he was.

For several seconds nothing stirred. A sinister, expectant silence resumed. The pools of urine rippled and waved, then settled into a calm pool just as the same noises built up again; the speedy build-up of feet gaining speed, the thuds, bangs and swish, as another mass of black figures soared past my line of vision dragging another blood-stained body by the feet. The swish died away and the squeaks of the naked body, burning as it reached and contacted the dry, shiny surface at the end of the wing, faded. The sinister silence resumed its ugly role. Tension hung like a guillotine. No one dared to breathe aloud, fearing it would fall upon them. It was soul-destroying and seemingly endless. A scream came shrieking and hurtling down the wing.

"*Tiocfaidh ár la!*" bounced and rebounded in frightening echoes off the walls, shattering the silence like the impact of a brick crashing through a window, raising hearts, bitterness and hate rivetted to every single syllable. "Our day will come!" That's what it meant and our day would come, I told myself, and God help you, A—, C— and D—, and you, too, B—, and every stinking last one of you, because you are all the same—torture-mongers.

"*Tiocfaidh ár la!*" I screamed out the door. One of the boys down the wing began to sing. *A Nation Once Again* resounded and echoed from behind every door and everyone joined in to break that ungodly silence, lifting our spirits and bolstering our shaken morale. The stench from the reeking urine streamed in through the door, flooding my eyes with tears and catching the back of my throat. The orderlies attempted a rendering of *The Sash*, but were drowned out with an explosion of noise as the now empty po's rattled and battered the scarred doors in defiance and anger.

"*Tiocfaidh ár lá!* All right!" I said, "and the sooner the better."

I went back to my task of getting rid of the small remaining pool of urine at my feet, pushing it out under the door. The noise began to die away as the last drops of urine disappeared in a trickle out the door. I threw the po into the corner upon the rubbish and sat down on my mattress, my feet avoiding the damp area, my mind in a turmoil, exhausted and strained, begging relief and comfort that was never granted.

The noise died completely. Seán rapped on the wall, concerned as ever.

"All right, Bobby?" he called.

"I'm all right, Seán. What about yourself?"

"They didn't even come to my cell," he replied.

"Who was dragged out?" I asked.

"I don't know," he said, adding that he had sent down the line to find out. "But I think that C— and D— did all the beating," he said.

"They probably did," I offered in agreement.

"Hey, Seán!" one of the lads shouted up the line, "it was Liam Clarke and Seán Hughes. C— and D— did most of the beating. The orderly with the squeegee beat the two lads stupid with the pole. No reason, Seán. Same as usual. They pounced on them when they were turning back into the cell."

I left Seán to discuss with the lads at the windows what had happened and began walking the floor once again, keeping in mind that I could be called for my visit at any minute. The beating up of the two lads—and Pee Wee O'Donnell earlier—had temporarily dampened my enthusiasm. I couldn't help but think of them lying there now on the boards, in the punishment block, where they probably got another brutal beating at the hands of the sadistic screws who appropriately managed that torture centre within a torture centre.

I knew only too well what it was like in there. It was dreaded by one and all. The punishment block stood for torture, brutality and inhumanity. Even the screws knew it but would not say. I spent three days there a few months ago—three of the longest and most unbearable days of my entire life. The screws removed me from my cell naked and I was conveyed to the punishment block in a blacked-out van. As I stepped out of the van on arrival there they grabbed me from all sides and began punching and kicking me to the ground. Not one single word had been spoken, not even so much as a threat. I was a Republican blanketman and that was all the go-ahead that was needed. I barely realised what had occurred or what was happening as they dragged me by the hair across a stretch of hardcore rubble to the gate of the punishment block. One of them rang the bell to summon the screw inside to come out and open the gate to admit them. I lay at their feet, dazed, shocked and panting for breath. My heart was pounding and my body felt like it was on fire, torn to ribbons by the rough concrete that had cut and hacked at my naked skin. My face was warm and wet from the blood spurting from a gash on my head. I lay stock still, playing possum, hoping they'd be content thinking that I was unconscious. My cheek rested upon the cold, hard, black surface but my body was unaware of the biting cold. I mumbled a "Hail Mary" to myself and a hurried "Act of Contrition" as I heard the approaching jingle of keys. Several gloved hands gripped and tightened around my arms and feet, raising my body off the ground and swinging me backwards in the one movement. The full weight of my body recoiled forward again, smashing my head against the corrugated iron covering around the gate. The sky seemed to fall upon me as they dropped me to the ground. The second impact sent a mass of tiny white stars exploding in front of my eyes like a fireworks display that suddenly became extinguished by a cloud of inky blackness. I regained consciousness lying on the floor of one of the cells in the punishment block.

I opened my eyes. My head was reeling. The bright light in the ceiling spiralled downwards and blinded me. The pain in my head was enormous and sickening. My whole body was seized by crippling pains and aches. I lay transfixed to the ground, afraid to move, the taste of blood on my swollen lips, fighting to work out where I was and what had happened. The concrete floor was intensely cold and I knew I would have to get off it or pay the consequences of perhaps pneumonia later. I rose slowly to my knees first. The walls came hurtling towards me. I fell. After an eternity I tried again though spasms of pain almost rendered my body useless. I made it to my knees. My skin was burning as the raw flesh from the mass of cuts and scrapes clung to the cold floor. I got up. I made it to my feet. I almost fell again but with the aid of the wall I staggered to the concrete block that served as a stool and slumped upon it. I felt as if I were dying. I was so distracted by pain and shock that I didn't know what to do. I simply couldn't think. The slightest movement of my body sent me shivering and gasping in agony. I was on the point of screaming out when the cell door opened revealing a white-coated figure of an orderly who stepped into the cell. The glorified screw with the white coat began to examine me, fiddling about my body, poking and probing, imitating the antics of a doctor, trying to impress the audience of screws who stood around the entrance of the cell.

Having made his observations, or whatever he had done, he arrogantly informed me that to see the doctor and receive treatment I would firstly have to bathe. I glared at him in disbelief. He repeated what he had said only in a sterner threatening voice. He knew what he was doing. He knew I was hurt and in need of immediate attention, but he was putting me under duress, holding me to ransom. No bath—no treatment. Besides, I was so sore I could barely move, let alone bathe, and I hadn't any intention of breaking my protest. Hurt or dying I was not going to concede to him or anyone else. I knew what was coming. His ultimatum changed to a command.

"Drop dead!" I said angrily. The hovering pressgang without so much as "Where are you hurt?" and without any ceremony lifted me as a man would lift a bundle of rags and carried me to the already-full bath, dropping me into the water like a bar of soap. The shock of the ice-cold water engulfing my tattered body almost stopped my breath.

Every part of me stung unmercifully as the heavily disinfected water attacked my naked, raw flesh. I made an immediate and brave attempt to rise out of the freezing, stinging water but the screws held me down while one of them began to scrub my already tattered back with a heavy scrubbing brush. I shrivelled with the pain and struggled for release but the more I fought the more they strengthened their iron grip. The tears came, flooding to my eyes. I would have screamed, had I been able to catch my breath. They continued to scrub every part of my tortured body, pouring buckets of ice-cold water and soapy liquid over me. I vaguely remember being lifted out of the cold water—the sadistic screw had grabbed my testicles and scrubbed my private parts. That was the last thing I remembered. I collapsed.

I was taken to the prison hospital wrapped in a large fawn blanket where the doctor examined me. I remained there for two hours, and patched up like a mummy, sporting a black eye and seven stitches in my head I was returned to my punishment cell. I sat there wrapped in a solitary filthy blanket that reeked of urine and stale smoke. I had regained my composure although I was a little disorientated and still trying to piece together my awful ordeal. But that soon became overshadowed by the thoughts of what was to come. No one could do anything for me. I could not tell a soul as I was isolated, alone and vulnerable. I was simply at their mercy and I had already discovered and learned that they did not know the meaning of the word. Perhaps worst of all I was freezing cold, unable to walk and exercise to warm myself, and I was feeling sorry for myself. The screws came back later in the day and once again dragged me out of the cell to appear naked before a Prison Governor to be tried in the normal farcical court. I stood naked before them, humiliated and embarrassed, my head bursting with the pain from my earlier beating. I was charged with "disobeying an order"—that is, refusing to cooperate with the screw who was endeavouring to probe and search my anal passage. In other words, I refused point-blank to allow this. But I was charged because it took three or four of them to hold me down to do it. The screw in question had been the whitecoated one. It would have made little difference to me had he been a brain surgeon, as the motive was purely to degrade and humiliate me, which was all part of the general torture to break our resistance. I was found guilty—not that I expected anything else—and sentenced to three days to be spent in the punishment cells, to be fed on what was politely termed a "number one diet," a starvation diet. I also lost one month's remission, the equivalent of a two month prison sentence! To wrap things up nicely, I was charged with assaulting the four screws who had almost murdered me that morning and, to rub it in, I was also charged with causing self-inflicted wounds to myself and informed in a roundabout way that if I dared to make a formal complaint I would also be charged with making false allegations against prison officers. How can you win, I thought, and felt like vomiting as they dragged me back to my cell again, being remanded to appear before the Board of Visitors. I would be here three days, then back again at the end of the month for another fifteen days. The B.O.V. would ensure that.

The cell was freezing cold, bare and lonely. I'd been here once before, therefore I knew just how lonely and unbearable it would get. A board on the concrete floor served as my bed, a concrete slab as a table, and a concrete block as a stool. A Bible, po and water container were the only other visible items. I remained there for the three days, being beaten up twice more but not as severely as the initial hiding I received. When the filth in the po needed to be emptied they attempted to hold me to ransom.

Put on prison clothes to empty it, they said.

I refused. So it spilled over on to the cell floor and lay there. I plodded through it regardless. I had to get warm. My body was continuously numb. For the first two days I was barely able to walk at all and I was growing weaker as the starvation diet took its toll. My daily food consisted of two slices of bread, dry and stale, and a mug of black lukewarm tea for breakfast. Then for dinner I had a small bowl of watery soup. My evening tea was the same as breakfast. On the third day I collapsed once again and lay upon the cold concrete floor regaining consciousness sometime later of my own accord.

When I returned to H Block even the screws stared in shock at my deathlike appearance. I was physically wrecked and mentally exhausted.

The starvation, beatings, forcible bathing, the boredom and cold remained in my mind, scarring me deeply with hatred, bitterness and thoughts of revenge. Two weeks later I endured another fifteen days there. It was the same nightmare only multiplied by five. I lived like an insane animal, eating with my hands. Every other three days they starved me and once again I plodded through the dirt and filth, exercising to keep warm, taking the beatings, praying to myself, crying in my sleep, always fighting the urge to give in to them, to surrender.

But I survived. I beat them again. The torturous dungeons and the sadists who manned them had destroyed my body but had failed to break my spirit. It was three weeks later before I recovered from my torturous ordeal. My mind will never recover from it. God only knows how many of us have been subjected to that nightmare. Poor Pee Wee and the other two lads will be going through it all now. How many more will be subjected to it and how long can it go on before someone is beaten to death, I wondered. Where is it all going to end? I asked myself, sitting down upon my mattress again.

The afternoon was growing older and the first tinges of worry began to cross my mind. Where was my visit? I sat listening and willing the phone at the top of the wing to ring to inform A— that my visitors had arrived. I began stripping pieces of thread from one of my flimsy blankets and started to plait them together to pass the time, making a long line that hopefully would come in handy later. A skiff of snow fell in through the open window as another heavy fall threatened to follow once more. The afternoon light was beginning to fade, growing dimmer with each passing minute. The cawing of the crows making their way home from the nearby fields came plainly on the slight evening breeze. I rose and stood at the window, watching the crows fade into the distance and the thousands of different-coloured lights illuminating their designated vicinity one by one, as they were switched on. The entire area before my eyes was soon a mass of brilliant lights, causing the snow-coated wire to sparkle and glitter. The winter light of day died and darkness took over. It was getting very late, I thought, hiding the plaited line in a hole in my mattress and feeling the ever-increasing panic setting in more and more. I was wondering and speculating as to what could have happened to my visit. It must be at least 4.30 p.m., I thought. What has happened? The telephone rang. I stiffened my muscles, hoping to hear the long-awaited words. A— was summoned by the screw at the top of the wing. That's it, I thought excitedly and sat down impatiently awaiting developments. The minutes dragged by and still no indication to confirm that my visit had arrived. Five minutes! Now ten minutes! Then the rattle of keys and approaching footsteps. The warning rattle of the lock and the door opened. C— and D— stood there.

"Visit, tramp," C— rasped at me, hatred hanging to every syllable. If C— had his way I would be put up against the nearest wall to be shot. I rose from the mattress pulling the blankets off me, letting them drop to the ground and wrapping a towel around me. I stepped out of the cell door into the urine-covered corridor of the wing.

It was warmer in the corridor than it was in the cells. I noticed that immediately. I trod on through the river of urine until I reached the end cell where the prison garb was stored. Going on a visit was the only time that we donned the prison uniform. I glanced around me and grabbed the nearest set of clothing. I was just about to put on the shirt when D— said, "Right! Drop your towel and stand over by that mirror," pointing to a large mirror which lay on the floor. I did as he said. He then told me to bend over and touch my toes. I refused. A— was called and he entered the cell. All three of them proceeded to grab me and forcibly bend me over. A— and D— held me while C— inspected my anus. After several seconds they released their grip and I straightened myself up and began to dress.

"Bastards," I said to myself. They didn't even ask me to open my mouth. They were not interested in searching me but in humiliating me!

I left the cell, dressed and disgusted, storing in the back of my mind the fact that they didn't search my mouth and reminding myself that the worst had yet to come! They locked me between the steel grills at the top of the wing. I was a sorrowful-looking sight: dirty face, shaggy hair and beard, with the prison uniform that was several sizes too large hanging on me. I didn't give a damn. But the sooner I got it off me the better and to hell with my appearance! I was being tortured, not manicured. A screw came and opened the gate of the grill whereupon another screw awaited to escort me to my visit. He led me out and into a blacked-out transit van that sat outside the door of the yard, engine running and the exhaust smoke belching out underneath the back of it into the darkness. I shivered as I sat down upon the hard benchlike seat. I had been hoping that some of the lads from the other wings or Blocks might have been in the van going on a visit also but it was empty and dark. My escorting screw climbed into the back of the van and closed the door over, throwing the confines into total darkness.

"Right!" he shouted to the van driver who immediately drove off. We passed out through the front gate of the H Blocks—the front gate of Hades, I thought to myself. The screw cursed the loose rattling door and held it to stop it flying open. He tried to make conversation with me.

"How long have you been on the blanket now?" he enquired and added immediately, "Don't you think you'd be as well packing it in?"

"No, I don't," I answered him dryly.

"Yous aren't getting nowhere," he said matter-of-factly.

"No one ever does until they reach what they set out for," I said sharply.

"You must be mad," he said. "I wouldn't do what you are doing if I were in your position."

"I'm quite sure you wouldn't," I said. "Maybe that's because you're a screw and I'm a political prisoner." He didn't like that last remark, I thought, as he became very quiet in the darkness. I'm sure his face is red, I said to myself.

"Besides," I said, putting the boot right in, "at the end of the day you will be entitled to feel more let down than anyone."

"How's that?" he muttered.

"Well," I added, "when the British government, through the stroke of a political pen, grant political status to us again or, better still, declare their intention to withdraw, which they will do all right when necessity forces them to, it's going to make a proper ass out of you. What are you going to do then?"

"That won't ever happen," he said nervously.

"It will happen all right," I said. "And better still they've done it before in places like Cyprus, Aden and Palestine. Yes, they will most certainly do it again," I added just for good measure as the van came to an abrupt halt. He opened the door and stepped out, beckoning me to follow him. He wasn't so chirpy now, I noticed. It frightened the best of them. None of them relished the thought of being left high and dry, especially with the atrocities that they had committed, and still were committing, to be answered for. I passed by the search boxes that were doing a brisk trade on those returning from their visits. They were all remand prisoners and ordinary prisoners. The special search hut for blanketmen was set apart from all the other huts, looking sinister and evil. Patches of snow were clinging to the sides of its wooden structure, giving it a lonely, desolate appearance but it was in operation all right. A heavy, dull thud and a shout coming from its interior soon testified to that.

I entered the visiting building and stood there in the bright light while the screw went to find out what visiting box I was to be brought to. Dozens of screws eyed me up and down as they passed me by, making the occasional snide remark and jibe at me. I ignored them. The bustle around me seemed unreal. I was unused to such a change in atmosphere. It was not the murderous tension-filled atmosphere that surrounded and hung over me every day in the H Block. There were plenty of nasty screws here all right, but they were concerned with other business which, thank God, wasn't me for a change!

The screw came back and led me to a large visiting room.

"Box 7," he said.

Jesus, I thought, Box 7 is one of the end boxes where most of the prowling screws congregated. The screw opened the visiting room door and I walked into a large room. It was like walking into a play. The buzz of whispered conversation struck me first, then the clouds of smoke, the colourful clothing worn by the huddled little groups of visitors who hung over the tables in the open boxes whispering and muttering, the black mass of screws pacing up and down the floor, hanging over their shoulders, cracking jokes amongst themselves and filling the air with their loud-mouthed laughter. I glanced at the numbering of the boxes—12, 11, 10, 9—and made my way towards Box 7. Friendly, sympathetic faces smiled encouragement at me from the open boxes. Old women, wives, daughters, sisters and brothers, the children and fathers of my comrades. I smiled back as best I could, feeling more than sorrow and sympathy towards them.

"God bless you, son," some old woman shouted at me. "Keep your chin up," she added.

I felt like crying.

"Move along," one of the screws snarled at me. In a daze I scanned the boxes as I passed them by. My comrades and their families were smiling and calling to me. I turned into Box 7 and, not thinking, sat down on the wrong side of the box. The prowling screws nearby nearly ate me.

"Get off that chair and get around to this side of the table," they snapped, seemingly competing with each other to see who could be the most dominant and nastiest.

I changed sides.

"Bastards," I said to myself.

"How are you, son?" called some old fella with a Derry accent as he passed by my box.

"I'm surviving," I said, which was just about right and no more!

"Good for you, son, and God take care of every one of you," called another passerby, a middle-aged woman with what sounded like a Tyrone accent. Some distance to travel, I thought, for a half-hour visit.

The screws continued to prowl up and down, ever vigilant and listening to every word that was being spoken. Three more plus my escort stood by the side of my box talking. Three or four people came around the partition directly beside my box. Then my mother appeared, my father and sister following directly behind her. I stood up to greet them as they approached the visiting box. I saw my mother taking a quick glance around her a split second before she started to hug me, then I felt her hand touch the side of the baggy coat that I was wearing. The congregation of screws were partially covered by the approach of my father and sister. Those prowling past the boxes had their backs turned. It was a quick move. I knew what it was and I knew that it was now in my left-hand pocket. My sister had reached me and threw her arms around me while my father shook my hand at the same time. My eyes were scanning the faces of the screws for a telltale sign of discovery. There were none but my heart stopped as they moved towards the box. My mother sat down and I sat down beside her. My father and sister went around to the other side of the plain wooden table, which served as the division between prisoner and visitor.

"Right!" shouted a screw.

I nearly fell off the chair, discovery screaming at me from every side.

"You'll have to move away from the prisoner to the other side of the table," the screw said to my mother.

My heart was pounding and a sickish feeling gripped my chest. I thought for several terrible seconds that I had been caught. That just about would have made my day.

"Prisoner?" my mother said, exasperated. "That's my son. Surely I can sit beside my son?"

"No, I'm afraid you can't," he said.

"That's right you can't. Prison Rules," another one chipped in.

I was too busy regaining my composure from the awful fright to argue. My mother, fearing the loss of the visit, somewhat hesitantly moved her chair around to the other side of the table beside my sister and father.

The screws, having adamantly stood there to see their word decreed, now moved off, retreating a bare three feet from my visiting box, where they stood in a group talking in hushed voices and staring at us all the while. I turned around in my chair, turning my back to them, and began talking to my family.

"How are you, son?" my mother asked.

"I'm not too bad, Ma," I answered, seeing the anguish in her face as she examined my terrible appearance.

"Your beard has got a lot longer since I last saw you," my father said jokingly, and my sister began asking me was it cold in the cells. My father took out a packet of cigarettes and gave me one. I took a light from the solitary match that they were allowed to bring with them. My mother held my other hand in hers. I heard the shuffle of feet behind me. I was in no doubt that the warders were watching my every move and weighing every word that was spoken.

"How are you all?" I asked, adding that I thought the three of them looked grand. The cigarette was making my head light but I had dreamed of this cigarette too bloody often to discard it.

"How is everyone else keeping?" I asked, and listened eagerly to the answers. All three competed with each other to get talking. There was so much to be told and so many questions I had to have answered. It was one excited babble of conversation. We ignored our unwanted listeners and reduced our voices to barely audible whispers when something arose that we did not want them to hear. I would have preferred them to hear nothing but what could be done? My father and mother continually glanced towards them but I knew that that would not move them a single inch. My sister was telling me bits and pieces of news. I was trying to lodge them in my mind to tell the lads later while at the same time struggling to remember other things I wished to ask them. My mother whispered to me to be careful with the small parcel in my pocket. She said that there was a little bit of tobacco squashed as small as possible, cigarette papers and a wee note from my sister, Bernadette. My mind was in turmoil, collecting news, asking this and asking that. Such and such was dead or dying, everyone seemed to be getting married, soldiers wrecked the house again and such and such's young son was charged. There were a lot of strikes brewing here and England was plagued with them. It was in the papers about the flu epidemic, the forcible baths and haircutting in the H Blocks. There had been a Christmas tree on the Falls Road beside Dunville Park, with all the blanketmen's names on it.

I was storing every scrap of information in my mind and all the while thinking of the powder keg in my lefthand pocket. I gave them a quick run-down on things in the Blocks, telling them to drop into the H Block Information Bureau on the Falls Road and tell them there what I had told them about Pee Wee O'Donnell, Liam Clarke and Sean Hughes and what had occurred during this morning's wing shift. My beard was hiding the marks on my face which I had received that morning, but my mother and sister were searching my hands and face for the telltale traces of a beating and continually asking me was I sure that I was all right. I lit another cigarette from the one I was about to extinguish, feeling a lot more up to it now. The other visiting boxes were emptying rapidly. I could hear the people moving towards the exit door behind me. I did not look around. I'd seen it all before and didn't wish to see those sorrowful, pitiful faces again. My sister was telling me how her young son was doing. My mother followed that up with what was in last week's *Republican News* and my father added to it.

I gave them a few messages that I had for some of the lads' families that they could pass on to them. I sat listening intently to how the parade went. My father interjected again to tell me of the growing interest and concern that was gathering in America, France and other European countries over what was going on in the H Block. Our conversation continued and I lit another cigarette. Twelve minutes left, I noted, keeping an eye on my father's watch.

"Good luck to you boys and God bless every one of you," a departing visitor shouted aloud to one and all. I became conscious of the fact that my unwashed body must be smelling but I ignored it. As ever no comment was forthcoming from my people. My sister was now telling me how things were in the district and who had been around in my mother's house enquiring about me and how her husband was keeping. My mother began to tell me about a recent riot in the district when the screw interrupted her.

"Right, that's it. Time up," he barked over my shoulder, handing the visiting permit to my mother, emphasising that he wished her, my father and sister to depart.

"There is still eight minutes of my half hour left," I said coldly to him.

"Too bad. See the Governor," was his aggravating reply.

My mother and sister looked towards me anxiously.

"It doesn't matter, son. Sure it's only a couple of minutes," my mother said, worried that I would reap the repercussions of an argument when they got me outside the visiting area. I rose from the chair knowing that the visit would be over no matter what I said. I was disgusted and angry but I didn't wish to leave my family worrying. There was more than enough to worry over as it was. My mother and sister began hugging and kissing me goodbye, tears rolling down their cheeks having suddenly appeared from nowhere.

I was shattered.

The screws were harassing me from behind.

"Come along, come along. Right. That's enough! Come along!"

"I'll see you next month," I said to my mother and sister, my father stealing a quick handshake just before the screws literally bundled me towards the exit door for prisoners. I caught a glimpse of the remaining little huddled groups whispering amongst each other around the little tables. In some boxes a screw sat right beside the visitor. These were the notorious "appeal visits." One word out of place not pertaining to the appeal case and the watchdog screws sprang upon you and terminated the visit. I caught a final glimpse of my family as they waved goodbye before the screw almost slammed the door in my face.

"Right you!" he roared. "Wait there!"

He was not my original escort, who had apparently disappeared, but it looked like I was stuck with this bastard who had now gone off to check me out of the visit. I stood there shaking a little, feeling disorientated and somewhat sick, being unused to being out of my small, stinking, concrete tomblike cell. The sight of other people with smiles to offer, friendly, sympathetic faces, colourful expressions and clothes, the comfort of simply seeing my family again was just too much for my physically wrecked body and tortured mind to cope with or adapt to.

There was a bustle of activity going on around me. Screws all over the place.

Jesus, Mary and Holy Saint Joseph! The wee parcel! I worked my hand in panic to the other side of my coat. It was still there. I could feel it. I glanced around and when it looked good put my hand into my pocket and took it out. A screw passed me, eyeing me up and down. I held the wee parcel like a bomb. It was concealed in my fist. I was praying that the screw who was escorting me wouldn't come back now.

All clear. I made my move. Like a flash it was up and out of my hand into my mouth. It was fairly small and wrapped in "stretch and seal" plastic. I gazed at the window in front of me looking at my reflection. My beard hid any telltale bulge. I would just have to sweat it out now. Other screws came walking past me, their searching, probing eyes glaring at me as if I were something out of the ordinary. But then I was, I thought, staring at my reflection in the window again: my uncombed hair ruffled and shaggy and my long beard untamed and wild like a bramble bush, and from somewhere in between, ghostly white and, dare I say it, somewhat frighteningly, appeared my own face, rugged and aged before its time. My cheeks and eyes were sunken and withdrawn into my face, creating a hollow from where my glassy, piercing eyes peered back at me, and unseen and covered by the prison garb stood my dilapidated, physically wrecked body.

"Right you, move along," came that growling bark again, interrupting my thoughts and self-scrutiny, setting me in motion towards the search huts that stood outside. I passed by the first hut where the ordinary prisoners were frisked, searched, and then the second hut where the remand prisoners were dealt with in a similar fashion. The third hut, which I knew only too well, sitting apart from everything else and looking drab, desolate and sinister, was the "special hut" where only we were taken—the blanketmen, the Republican prisoners-of-war. My escorting screw, as ever behind, barked another command, "Right you, in there!"

I could hardly swallow my spittle with the parcel in my mouth. I detected the eagerness in his voice. He could hardly wait to get me inside. He almost threw me in through the door. The inside of the search hut was as drab as the outside. Several screws stood warming their hands over an oil-fuelled fire. It was cold outside. A coating of snow still lay upon the ground. Panic was rising in me as each of them glared at me and—as was only to be expected—at my face. I was waiting on the fatal words—What's that in your mouth? But they never came. I stood there for an eternity, my eyes scanning the room. The inside was a lot warmer than the stinking, freezing tomb I was returning to. A few chairs were scattered about the room, a plastic basin filled with a blue-coloured disinfectant sat upon the oil fire where a stack of paper towels lay adjacent to it, and upon the floor and looking out-of-place was a large mirror secured to a wooden handle. The screws began to mill around me, batons dangling at their hips. For some stupid reason I thought of a dental surgery! I don't know why, as any dentist that I have ever encountered was considerate.

"Right, tramp," snapped a harsh voice. "Strip!"

I stripped, standing naked before them. They stood around, glaring at my naked body. I was embarrassed and humiliated, but I couldn't grasp the full significance of it. The humiliation was secondary to my parched throat, the potential bomb in my mouth and the thoughts churning around in my mind of what lay ahead of me. More so if I had to spit out contraband.

Jesus! I thought, what they had to do to us to discover and catch the odd love letter from one of the lads' sweethearts, the worrying note from a distracted mother or the lousy, meagre little parcel of tobacco! It is just pure torture and harassment.

"Turn around," growled another bully-boy screw. I turned, making a full circle. Panic gripped me as they scrutinised my body. (I was waiting on the fatal command every second: "Open your mouth.")

"Turn around again," snapped the screw who had escorted me.

That's it, I thought, they are really rubbing this humiliation bit in! If I had been able to speak I would have told them that they had humiliated me enough and any more humiliating to be done *they* could do it. They had forced me to degrade myself enough already. I stood there silent and still. He threatened me and yelled his command once more. I ignored it. I thought the roof had fallen upon them. They were momentarily dumbstruck, so startled that they just stood staring at me in utter disbelief that I had disobeyed their word. Their faces were flushed and perplexed, anger was building up inside them. Here it comes, I told myself, here it bloody well comes!

"Get up against that wall and spread-eagle," one of them finally mumbled, breaking the seemingly eternal silence. I remained unintimidated but not unperturbed. I was shaking and it wasn't from the cold! I was scared stiff, frightened to the verge of panic. I thought I was about to vomit out the parcel on the floor.

They grabbed my arms and threw me up against the wooden wall. The impact made a dull thud. They held me in spread-eagle fashion. Someone punched me in the ribs and my feet were kicked to part my legs. A terrible pain tore through my outstretched arms and my already aching, bruised body hurt all the more. They continued to hack at my ankles with their heavy issue boots, constantly screaming and shouting, cursing and threatening me.

I felt the cold chamfered edges of the large mirror being pushed between my legs. They were scrutinising my anus, using the mirror to afford them a view from every angle. A foreign hand probed and poked at my anus and, unsatisfied, they kicked the back of my knees, forcing me down into a squatting position where they again used the mirror and, to finish off, they rained more kicks and blows on my naked, burning body for good measure. I fell to the floor, which was wet and dirty from the melted snow carried into the hut on their boots. I rose immediately, half conscious of the pains as they streaked through my body. I made a desperate attempt to swallow my spittle and not only did I almost choke on the parcel but I almost spat it out on the floor. My face was contorted and red as I fought to hold back a cough. I grabbed the clothing I had been wearing and dressed as quickly as I could, racing to get finished before they finished washing their sadistic hands in the basin of disinfectant.

"Maybe that will help you find your tongue!" rasped one of them, drying his hands with a paper towel. Jesus! I thought, the very mention of anywhere in that vicinity made me panic! I raced to dress. A hand from behind me lifted my hair to see if I had anything hidden behind my ears. I panicked and almost made a move to switch the wee parcel from my mouth to a pocket which they wouldn't search again. But the searching hand withdrew to a vacant space that had just appeared around the disinfectant basin.

Clothes half hanging off me, and realising just how sore I was, I struggled towards the door, my growling companion of a screw falling in behind me. I stepped through the door waiting on—Where are you going to? We're not finished— but again nothing happened.

My throat was burning. The fresh air hit me, refreshing me and reviving me a little. A few of the lads from the other Blocks stood there, their faces as white as ghosts, as white as the snow they stood on, awaiting their turn, no doubt having heard the yells and thuds of my fate and knowing only too well that it was to be their fate next.

"Okay, Bobby?" one of the lads asked.

I couldn't answer. I nodded in recognition and sympathy, thinking of where they were going and took consolation from the relieving fact that at least I had the torturous ordeal behind me. I trudged onwards towards the H Block. There was no van about and I was only too glad of the short walk, gorging myself in the luxury of a few minutes of fresh, clean air. That's the worst and first hurdle over, I thought.

The road ahead of me was wide and white with snow. It hung on the dull grey timbers and clung to the miles of tangled, gruesome barbed wire. There was fencing and barbed wire everywhere. A jungle of it flanked at intervals by looming, sinister, camouflaged gun posts where armed British soldiers scanned the camp from perimeter to perimeter. It reminded me of a clip of film I once saw, when I was young, of a Nazi concentration camp in winter, and I remember, although young, feeling shocked but also secure in my chair by the fire, thinking that that type of place was a horror of the past and could not nor ever would be allowed or tolerated again, least of all in Ireland and never upon me.

I thought of families whispering together around the tables of the visiting room, the faces of mothers lined with sorrow, speechless fathers and crying, whimpering children watching their daddies being bundled away by the monsters in black uniforms, the same heartless monsters who hung over your shoulder listening to every word and syllable spoken, who kept your people queuing for hours on end for a half-hour visit, herding them about like cattle through one gate to the next, through one degrading, humiliating search to another, treating them like animals.

They despised our people as much as they despised and hated us. They insulted them, harassed them and broke their hearts by torturing their sons and daughters. I was naïve when I was young. Here I was now going back to a filthy concrete tomb to fight for my survival, to fight for my right to be recognised as a political prisoner-of-war, a right for which I would never stop fighting.

The H Block loomed up ahead of me on my right. I stood waiting for the gate to open—the gate to hell. A sinister silence reigned: not so much as a sigh from the wind stirred, not one bird sang, but there was nothing in Belsen to sing about either, I thought, going through the gate to hell.

I walked across the yard to the front door of the H Block. On my left the boys in the other wing were standing at their windows. The lights were on in a few cells. The rest of the cells were in darkness. Those cells with the lights on looked like little caves, the inhabitants wrapped up in their shabby blankets. They were scary looking, their long beards and pale faces peering out at me from behind the concrete bars. I could see the slight movements of shadowy figures in the cells that were in darkness.

"All right, Bobby?" one of the boys shouted. I couldn't answer so I waved back, feeling a little stupid.

"Won't be long now!" someone else shouted and the boys began joking and staring out the windows. I looked to my right at the other leg of the H, which was my wing. There were no windows, not even a shadow of light to be seen. The entire outside length of the wing was shrouded with the corrugated iron and timber structure which blocked out all light and view of the outside. Thank God they haven't got around to my side of the wing yet, I thought. But they would soon!

I entered the Block and stood waiting at the iron grill gates, my unwanted barking escort disappearing. I was passed from one grill to the next until A— appeared and admitted me back into my wing again. The high-pitched whining, droning noise of the machine which was sucking up the pools of urine still lying upon the corridor was echoing around the wing. The tea trolley was parked outside the search cell. I passed by it, noticing the coat of slimy skin that had formed upon the freezing cold tea. The slices of bread were piled high and were curled up and stale. The food lay on the plates. A piece of meat that represented a beef burger was almost surrounded, but not quite, by twenty or so beans.

I walked on into the search cell, all thoughts of food disappearing in a flash as I saw C— and D— standing there. Walking ahead of my escort from the visit, I had been able to move the parcel about in my mouth and swallow my spittle, but my throat was now parched again. I began to strip the clothes off me— two minutes and I would be safe. Just two more minutes! I took the trousers off and wrapped the towel around me again. I no sooner had it around me when D— said, "Drop your towel and turn round!" I was waiting for the bending-over bit. I dropped my towel and turned around but to my surprise nothing came. I grabbed my towel and rewrapped it around me, making for the cell entrance. That was it. I've made it or I haven't! I walked on out the door still waiting for the words that would hail discovery, but they never came. I could barely believe my luck. A— sniggered at me and said, "You'd be as well to take your tea back to your cell with you in case it gets cold." C— and D— found that very amusing. The hovering orderlies went into hysterics. I ignored them and took the plate and cup, noticing the meagre contents.

I walked on down the wing which by now was dry at the end where I was walking. The screw with the machine was still working away at the far end and was almost finished. The drone was mind-wrecking. I was as happy as a lark. I couldn't wait to get back into my cell. I dreaded the thought but it was purely to be able to spit out my well-travelled contraband. A— opened the door and I stepped back into the darkness of my filthy cold tomb. The door slammed behind me and I stood in the darkness. Victory!

I wished I could have told them that I had outdone them, that I had put one over on them, especially that bastard C—. I could hardly believe that I had made it back safely.

Yahoo!

I set my cold tea on the floor and took the parcel out of my mouth. It was a relief. The wee parcel was wet and I dried it on the end of my towel.

I couldn't examine it in the darkness. I would do that later. I wrapped the three blankets around me and put my wee parcel in the fold of the blanket that was wrapped around my waist. The doors were opening and slamming shut as the cold tea was being handed into the cells. The drone of the cleaning machine continued unabated and they'd probably leave it on for a few hours to try and drive us insane. I wondered had anything else occurred while I was away. I threw the cold tea out the window and took a quick look into the corners where the rubbish lay, just in case an adventurous rat had decided to have a look around while I was out. It wouldn't have been the first time that that had happened to me; it even happened during the night on one occasion. I sat down on the mattress and began to eat my cold food, reflecting on the highlight of my month, my visit. I finished off my cold, meagre tea and set the plastic dishes at the door. Back to my fight for survival, I thought, feeling the cold and rising to resume where I had left off on my endless walk to nowhere in the darkness. I checked that my little parcel was secure and revelled in the self-esteem of success. I couldn't figure out why C— and D— didn't try to forcibly bend me over when I arrived back to carry out another humiliating body search. They had seemed somewhat eager to get me back to my cell again.

The floor was very cold so I stopped to spread a blanket on it to enable me to continue my endless pacing. The snow still lay on the ground outside and began to fall again slowly, little flakes floating in through the open window. The cleaning machine, deliberately left on, droned in the background. I tried to overcome the harassing sound with thought. I would have liked to tell Seán the good news of the victory, but he wouldn't hear me with the continuous noise. I began to think about the wee bits of *scéal* that I had heard on my visit to tell the boys later on. It wouldn't be long until suppertime, for the tea had been served very late, but that wouldn't be anything to look forward to either, probably a mug of lukewarm tea and a round of bread and margarine. All it really meant was that it wouldn't be long until lockup when the screws would go home for the night and no more cell doors would open until tomorrow morning.

I gazed out the window thinking that I could always watch the rats running up and down the yard when it got really quiet later on. I wouldn't be able to get into my bed on the ground too early. The cold wouldn't allow me to sleep. I was tired; in fact I was exhausted but the day was not over yet by any means. I wondered how the boys on the boards were. Perhaps someone in another Block or wing may have come back from the boards today and could tell if anything else had occurred. The shouting to the other wings and Blocks would start when things settled down later, when the screws went home.

I heard the slam of the cell door facing me. It had been barely audible. They were probably collecting the dishes. No use shouting out the door with the drone, as no one would hear it.

My cell door opened and the light was turned on. The orderly lifted the dishes and the door slammed shut again. I didn't see the screws as the illumination of the cell left me temporarily blinded. The sudden change from darkness to light cut at my eyes. My stinking surroundings came screaming up at me once again. The white squares of discarded stale bread added a new feature to the rubbish piles in the corners. I noticed the marks in the sides of the slices of bread and lifted one from the rubbish. It was blue moulded. Thank God I hadn't eaten the bread, I thought, examining the rest of the slices to find that they were the same. I knew immediately what had happened, why C— and D— didn't forcibly bend me over and why they were so eager to get me back to my cell to eat my tea in the dark. I had been too busy thinking of my mouth full of contraband to scrutinise the bread on my plate on my way back to the cell.

The cleaning machine droned and whined in the background. The cell light was very bright and already my eyes were hurting. I felt the dreaded, early warning tinges of a migraine headache building up inside the back of my head. I kept pacing the floor, taking deep breaths of air at the window to try and clear the stuffy, wheezy sickliness that was also beginning to bother me. The machine became more annoying. The temperature was falling outside and the coating of frost on the wire grew thicker. I took out my little parcel and had a peek at it. It was intact. I could see the contents through the "stretch and seal" plastic wrapping, the wee note, the cigarette papers and the brown tobacco. I couldn't open it up now so I put it back again in the fold of my blanket for later. Being the possessor of a wee note from my sister, cigarette papers and a quarter ounce of tobacco made me feel like a king.

What would it be like if they were to open the door now and throw me out to freedom? I wouldn't be able to cope with it. Dear God! I could hardly bear up to a visit. I just couldn't imagine what state I would be in if I were to be released from this torture. I knew how to appreciate small, seemingly unimportant things now that one time or another I would have taken for granted or probably not even noticed. When was the last time I received a decent warm meal? Funny how one can adapt to things—especially when you are starving, I thought, remembering the times during the summer when the orderlies and screws had dropped maggots into our dinners and all we could do was search for them and remove them, then eat our dinners as if nothing had happened. It was either that or starve!

The drone from the cleaning machine suddenly stopped and a terrible unnatural silence fell once again. I heard the footsteps of the screw who had turned off the machine returning back along the wing. I put my eye to the little spyhole. It was A—. He walked on past towards the little office. I heard the sound of the television going but was unable to make out any words. The orderlies were shouting and carrying on between themselves. I heard C— shouting, "Right," and the carry on of the shouting orderlies died immediately to be replaced by the rattle of the tea trolley.

"Tea on the air," some of the lads shouted in Gaelic. The cell doors began to open and close. They passed by my cell going down the other side of the wing. One of the lads a few cells down was singing to himself and a bit of life came back into the wing. The tea trolley finally arrived at my door. The usual hated faces were standing there when the cell door opened. The orderly handed me a mug of tea and a slice of bread doubled in two. I caught D— sniggering as he saw me glancing at the bread for any signs of blue mould. It was all right.

The door slammed and I retreated to the mattress detecting an unnatural warmth and seeing the steam rising from the plastic mug. It was hot! I could hardly believe it. I sat down and somewhat sheepishly tasted it. It was as weak as water. In fact it was simply coloured hot water, but I decided to brave it. Anything hot was a Godsend on a night like this, I thought, even hot water. I ate the slice of bread and sipped the warm weak tea. It won't be long until lockup, I thought, relishing the thought of the parcel and the smoke.

My mother and father and sister would be at home now and most likely they wouldn't be feeling the best. They would have had a terrible hard day and having seen my appearance they would do nothing else but worry. I thought of the families who had two or three sons inside and those with sons on the blanket protest, or those with daughters on protest in Armagh. It must be really hard on those families. There was heartbreak everywhere. That's all that ever came out of the stinking hellholes—heartbreak and grief.

I couldn't drink any more of the weak tea. It was growing cooler and becoming a bit sickening. I rose and threw it out the window upon the snow and watched the puff of steam rise as it buried itself into the snow. Setting the cup at the door I returned to my pacing as the doors began to open and close.

"Cups off the air," came the cry.

My feet were getting colder. I stamped them on the blanket on the floor. The cold was going to be very intense tonight all right. The singer down the wing began to sing a new song to himself. There was nothing to sing about but one had to overcome the terrible monotony some way or other. I was getting bored myself but it was more impatience than anything else as my wee parcel was burning a hole in my blanket so to speak.

My cell door opened and the cup was removed. I didn't even bother to look round. The door slammed and the procession of screws and orderlies proceeded towards the end of the wing. I sat down on the mattress once again to rest. There were eight of the boys on the other side of the wing who smoked, plus nine on this side, but three were away to the boards, so that left fourteen smokers, including myself. I would be able to manage a cigarette for everyone tonight with perhaps a bit to spare. It would mean shooting a line under the bottom of the best door across the wing to the cells opposite to get the cigarettes over to the other lads. The boys on the other side of the wing couldn't swing or pass things out of their windows because they were blocked up. But they had engineered little holes in the walls where the pipes ran through which would enable them to pass the cigarettes up and down the line, as well as a light. A light for the cigarettes would be engineered by one of the lads using a piece of glass, a small flint and a wee bit of fluffy wool. A wick would be made and lit, allowing the glowing material to be passed carefully from one cell to the next, until everyone got a light. Getting a line across would be tricky and dangerous. It always was. The screws knew we did it and they were always on the prowl, lurking and tiptoeing around the wing at night. B— would be on tonight, on night guard, which meant that we would have to be extra careful. I checked to see if the long line that I had plaited earlier was still there. It was all right.

Seán knocked on the wall.

"Down to the pipe," I said, getting down to the corner on top of my mattress with my head right to the wall where the pipes ran through. There wasn't a great deal of heat coming through the pipes. What there was went streaming out the open window into the dark cold night.

"Well, Bobby," came Seán's enquiring voice through the small hole in the wall.

"*Go h-an mhaith*, Seán," I said in delight. "I made it back with the other." He knew what I meant.

"*Maith thú*," he said, and I began to tell him about my visit and related the happenings with the searches and all the rest. I sensed the excitement building up in Seán's voice as I told about all the happenings, the great turn out for the parade and the massive offensive in the war effort. In general things were going better than ever before. The British government's attempts to criminalise the Republican Movement had failed miserably and now everyone realised just exactly what the motives behind the tortures in the H Blocks were aimed at. I continued my conversation with Seán for some time until I began to feel cramped lying in my unnatural position at the pipes and wall. So I decided to go back to pacing the floor once again. My feet were numb with the cold. Seán understood. He was in much the same condition. I told him that I'd call him later and we both left our corners to resume where we had left off in our endless pacing.

The screws began to lock grills and doors in preparation for the nearing lockup. The orderlies had left the wing for their dormitories which were two large rooms adjoining the wings especially opened and equipped with such luxuries as television, radio and record player and a host of other things: the payment for their dirty work that they did exceedingly well. Some orderlies didn't bother us but they were very few and hard to find.

A—, C— and D— were hovering at the top of the wing talking and joking and waiting on the call to lock up. It couldn't be too far away, I thought, perhaps fifteen minutes. There were two head counts to be done yet—one by the leaving screws, A— and company, and the other by the night guard who would be arriving shortly. The night guard would only consist of four screws. Sometimes they watched television, played cards or drank themselves into a stupor and wouldn't bother us. But most times there was trouble and more so if there was someone like B— on. And B— was on tonight!

I was bored pacing up and down so I decided to sit down and risk opening my wee parcel. The chances of a cell search now were slender but the danger was always there so one had to be very careful. It would be a terrible thing to get caught after what I had gone through today but I was impatient to get reading my wee note, so I took out my little treasured parcel and began peeling the glossy "stretch and seal" off it until I had the note. Before I began to read my sister's letter, I wrapped the loose "stretch and seal" back around the rest of the contents, just in case. I sat quietly for two or three minutes taking in every word of her neat handwriting. When I had finished, I re-read it. It was good to hear from her again. It seemed an eternity since I had seen her but she seemed to be doing all right, more worried about me than anything else and enquiring about the other lads that she knew. I would have to try and get a wee note to her as soon as I could. We had one miserly pencil and a pen refill that were constantly in use around the wing, going from one cell to the next, back and forth from one side of the wing to the other, eating up sheets of "bog roll" (toilet paper) for the wee smuggled notes to worried wives, mothers and girl-friends; for the letters to the newspapers and the quickly scribbled notes to the H Block Information Bureau telling of the beatings and horrors that took place every single day. I would have to wait my turn for the pen or pencil.

I tore my sister's wee note up into shreds and threw it out the open window watching it blow across the snow-covered yard until it disappeared along with the falling snow. A— and company were still at the top of the wing at the grills. I could hear the jingling of the keys and the occasional murmuring voice. I decided to take another chance and open the parcel once again to roll the cigarettes and have them ready for the lads and the line to be shot across the wing later. I unwrapped the covering again and took out the small lump of tobacco that was very fresh and squashed for convenience sake. I began to shred it and loosen it up to enable me to roll the cigarettes. The small lump grew into a small stringy pile. The aroma of the tobacco was a pleasant change from the evil stench that usually hung in the air of my cell. I stripped the cigarette papers that clung to each other into a pile until I had enough for my requirements and a few left over. When I had everything ready I commenced my task of rolling them, my ears alert for the slightest telltale sound of a footstep or key, while telling myself all the time that it wouldn't be long until I was lying on the mattress smoking one of the cigarettes that I was making now.

Five completed! I began the sixth, thinking how much one lousy ciga-rette meant and how it could lift morale, even of the lads who didn't smoke. Somehow or other everybody realised and took satisfaction from the fact that somebody or other had gotten one over on the bastards like A— and C— and that meant a great deal. I lifted another cigarette paper to begin the seventh cigarette . . .

"Bears in the air."

I heard the jingle of a key and whipped the blanket over the contraband as the lock on my door rattled and the door flew open. I tried to act normally in my panic, shock flooding my entire body. A— looked into the cell.

"One," he said as C— slammed the door shut again.

"Head count on the air," I yelled, terror clinging to my voice.

"Two," I heard A— say as Seán's door slammed.

"Four, six, eight," as they continued down the wing.

A cold wave swept my body. That was close, I thought, as I looked at the blanket that covered the tobacco and cigarettes. One cigarette was half visible, but they never saw it. I sat glued to my mattress as the head count continued.

"Twenty, twenty-two, twenty-four, twenty-six." A— counted.

"Bears off the air," one of the lads shouted, signalling the all-clear as the final number tallied and A—, C— and D— left the wing slamming the office door shut as they departed. I recovered my composure and contraband and went back to my rolling. I should have everything finished before the next and last head count I thought. Besides we'd hear B— long before he'd even reach the wing, as he would most certainly be drunk. I worked on until I had completed all the cigarettes whereupon I divided them into two parcels. One contained the cigarettes for the lads on the other side, and the other one contained a cigarette each for the boys down this side.

I got the long, thin line that I had plaited earlier and tied both parcels to it and attached a bit of stale blue moulded bread to the end of it to weight it before rapping on the wall for Seán.

"Hello," he shouted.

"Put your hand out," I said and began swinging the line to him. When he caught hold of it I explained the contents of the parcels, telling him to send the line and the parcel down the wing to the man who would be doing the shot to the other side so that he could get things ready. Seán knocked on the cell wall next to him and began to get things boxed off with the lads. I put my own cigarette, plus an extra one for myself and Seán, under the pillow.

The rattle of grills and keys sounded, then footsteps followed by a mouthful of obscenities as B—announced his arrival. The footsteps came tramping down the wing and the final head count began on the other side of the wing to another barrage of slamming doors. They worked their way around the doors and then my door opened. B— peered in. He was barely able to stand, let alone count. He half stumbled away and the door shut again.

"Bears off the air." The all-clear came. No one had even bothered to announce their arrival. It was obvious enough. A hush fell upon the wing and one of the men down the wing called out, "Right lads, we'll say the Rosary now. Who is going to say the first mystery?"

"I will," someone shouted.

"And the second?"

"I will," said Seán, and three other lads volunteered to say the three remaining decades.

"It's the sorrowful mysteries tonight," the same voice said, blessing himself and saying the opening prayers himself. The Rosary continued being answered by the boys out the doors. Midway through the third mystery a screw decided to bang the grills with his baton. The Rosary carried on and as usual the screw got fed up and departed. When the Rosary ended the wing was a flurry of activity and buzzing with conversation.

The boys down the wing decided to do the line across the wing before B— came prowling, or some other screw.

"Hey, Bobby. Will you keep watch?" one of the boys shouted.

"Okay. Go ahead," I shouted back, going to my little spyhole at the door.

Shooting the line across would be a tricky operation.

"Hey, Seán, can you see out your door?" the same voice asked.

"No way," Seán answered.

"I can," one of the lads at the bottom said.

"Can you see Gerard's door?"

"No problem," came the reply.

"*Maith thú*," said the man who was about to do the shot. "You can guide us."

"You there, Bobby?" someone asked, double checking. If the line was caught it would be a catastrophe.

"I'm here," I said, not daring to move my eye from the little hole. The long line would be secured to a button and flicked along the ground under the door and across the corridor. The man on the other side would search for it outside his door, using a strip of paper. When he detected it he would slide the paper underneath it and pull it in under his door. Then the ferrying of notes, cigarettes or whatever, to and fro began! The cigarettes would be tied on to the line and like a long train dragged across.

"You ready, Gerard?" the shooter asked.

"Go ahead, Pat," came the reply. There was a sharp crack and the scrape of the button sliding across the floor.

"Can you see it, Brian?" the shooter asked the man, guiding him down the wing a bit.

"Too far to the left," he said. "Shoot it again."

The line was drawn in and the sharp crack sounded again as the button slid across the corridor. The wing was deadly silent, every ear listening for the slightest telltale sound.

"What's that like, Brian?"

"Too short," came the tense reply.

The line was drawn in once again. The third shot was too hard and bounced off the door and had to be tried again. The fourth sharp crack sounded.

"How's that?" came the nervous voice of the shooter. The whole wing listened in anticipation.

"Leave it where it is," came the excited reply.

"Put your piece of paper out, Gerard," the spotter directed.

The paper rustled as it slid out underneath.

"Move it to the left," he directed again. "Another few inches. That's it. Leave it there. Now, push it out as far as you can. No good. Try it again."

My eye was beginning to hurt being pressed against the little hole. The silence remained. No one dared to speak except the team at work. The paper rustled again.

"Push it on out, Gerard, nice and gently. That's it! Easy, easy! *Maith thú*, Gerard. The button's sitting on top of the paper. Pull it back in to you slowly! Go ahead, go ahead! Take it easy."

"I've got it," came the successful disclosure.

"All right up there, Bobby?"

"Okay. I think so anyway, Pat."

"Pull the line on over in to you, Gerard," Pat said, "but don't tug too hard."

The cigarettes slid out underneath the shooter's door and across the corridor.

"Take it easy," the spotter said, "or they will stick underneath the door."

All the cigarettes got under Gerard's door except the last one which got entangled in the line.

"Don't pull it," Brian said. "Flick the line a little. That's it. It's sorting itself out. Try it now," he said. I caught a glimpse of a moving shadow and the squeak of a boot.

"Bear in the air!" I yelled as he shot past my line of vision.

"Pull it on in, Gerard!" Brian yelled. There was a scuffling noise as the screw tried to grab the line. Then silence followed by the retreating footsteps of the screw. I caught a glimpse of his face as he passed by. He was a stranger.

"All right, Gerard?" Pat asked.

"Okay, Pat. I got all the 'blows' in but the screw got the button." At least the cigarettes were okay. The loss of the button wasn't a catastrophe but a loss all the same in these conditions.

"Okay, lads. Slop out now," the O/C said. We began to filter the reeking urine out the doors. If we didn't do it then the screws would do it for us first thing in the morning. It's not a pleasant thing to be awakened by the splashing contents of a filthy po of urine! There wasn't too much left in the po's due to the slop-out earlier on. I worked at the foot of the door trying to get it out. When I'd finished, I retreated to the mattress to rest. I was completely out of breath and panting, a good indication of just how bad a state my physical health is in, I thought, when I became exhausted that easily. I sat back awaiting the arrival of the glowing wick which would provide me with a light. Lucky enough with the "blows," I thought. If the screw had arrived a few minutes earlier he would have caught the whole lot. Seán knocked on the wall.

"Right, Bobby, here's the effort."

I knew what he meant and I put my hand out the window to catch the swinging line with the glowing, improvised wick dangling at the end of it. I took it in and lit my cigarette.

"Here you are, Seán," I called.

"Go ahead," he answered, as I swung the line back into him. He knocked on the other wall to pass it down the line again as I lay down to smoke the cigarette. It was soothing and a relief to lie and enjoy something without the worry of the door bursting open. The keys for the doors were not kept in the H Blocks but elsewhere. The boys in the other wing would see the arrival of any strange screws bearing keys and raise the alarm.

"Bears in the yard," came the warning, but there was no real need for concern unless you were in the process of swinging something to another cell. The screws were down at the bottom of the yard hurling abuse at the lads further down. I finished off my cigarette then I got up to the window to see who they were. They came swaggering up the yard. B— was shouting and slobbering his head off. There were two others along with him who were endeavouring to add their fourpence worth of abuse. They passed on by in the direction of the other wing. The O/C called for everyone's attention and silence fell immediately as he asked did anyone see or make out what happened during the earlier incidents concerning the slop-out and Pee Wee O'Donnell. I told him what I had heard and seen out the door. Several others were able to put more to it. He then asked what were the injuries received during the early morning wing shift. The bloody accounts of damage were given out the doors.

"Okay," he said when everyone had finished. "Nothing else?" That was all the business concluded and noted for the Information Centre outside.

"Any *scéal*, Bobby?" some of the lads asked, and for about five minutes I related all that I had heard.

"I think that's the heap, lads," I said, when I was certain I had yelled it all out.

Yahoos and yahoos and cheers followed. Then the conversations at the windows, pipes and doors resumed, discussing, debating and speculating upon every little piece of news. The *scéal* was good and that meant a terrible lot. Reports were coming across the far yard to the lads whose windows were blocked up from the other wing about what had taken place that day in the other two wings of the Block. One man from each wing was away to the boards. One man was beaten up very badly, six cells hosed down and the daily horror reports kept coming in. The stench from the outside corridor was sickening. I rose and moved to the window to try and get some air. The snow glistened in the brilliance of the mass of lights and the noise of shouting and singing came on the breeze from the other blanket blocks. Hundreds of naked, physically wrecked men had come alive. It was bitter cold now. I wrapped all the blankets around me and put the towel around my head like a scarf once more. The boys in the other blocks were shouting to each other, passing messages back and forth and the horror reports began to be shouted from the other blocks. Several men severely beaten during a wing shift. Two men taken to the boards. Three men scalded in another wing and two men sent to the boards having been caught with tobacco coming back from visits. One man returned from the boards and had been beaten up and forcibly bathed while he was there. Several men beaten up and forcibly bathed on the boards. Pee Wee O'Donnell taken to the hospital, and the others badly bruised.

"You hear that, Seán?" I said.

"I heard it, Bobby," he answered. The horror reports continued: forty-four men beaten, bathed and had their heads shaved in another wing; two men in hospital and two more missing, probably on the boards. The reports in Gaelic continued. H5 began to tell H3 that several men were hurt during a slop-out done by the screws and one man was taken to the boards. H3 received six new blanketmen sentenced the day before. The shouting continued. The distance to each block was quite a bit but the sound echoed and carried in the night across the snow over the grey timbers and barbed wire. Several messages had to be repeated before they were understood and several times words had to be spelled out a letter at a time. But with a bit of perseverance and patience the communications system worked. But with the blocking up of the windows, that would finish also!

"Lights out," one of the boys shouted on the other side of the wing. The screws were extinguishing the lights. They'd most likely be around in the middle of the night to put them on again; not that we'd get much sleep with the cold anyway, I thought, as the screw put my light out. I knocked on the wall for Seán.

"Hello," he said.

"Get the effort up the line," I said.

"*Maith thú*," he replied and called up the line for the improvised wick.

"Are you listening, Seán?" I asked and added, "I'll swing you in a 'blow' when I'm sending the line back again. Okay?"

"*Maith thú*," he replied once again.

The line reached Seán's cell and he swung it in to me, whereupon I lit the second cigarette, tied on the one for him and swung it back to him again.

"Okay, comrade?"

"Sound," he replied.

I sat down once again. I kept thinking that the chances I had taken had been worth it. The smoke streamed upwards in the dim light and out the windows and for another few minutes the stench was blotted out by the aroma of tobacco. It was very cold. I decided to go back to my pacing when

I had finished my cigarette. Poor Pee Wee, I thought, lying in the prison hospital or maybe even in Musgrave! The rest of the lads on the boards would be lying battered and sore. I wasn't feeling the best myself. My earlier wounds grew more and more painful but I knew that I was a lot better off than the boys on the boards. I watched the reddened ash of the cigarette die on the blackened floor and I rose once more to walk the floor for another while, carpeting the floor with one of the blankets.

"Bears in the yard!" came drifting across from one of the other Blocks. It was really cold now and the snow lay deeper in the yard and continued to fall steadily. I wondered what the torture-mongers would be doing now. A—would most likely be sitting drinking in the screws' club in the camp with the rest of his mercenary friends and Brit soldiers; C— and D— would be in their houses with their families and I wondered what they'd say if their children asked them, "What did you do today, Daddy?" Or better still, what would their wives and children say if they knew what they did and just how much suffering, grief and torture they were causing and perpetrating upon hundreds of naked men?

I paced onwards in my endless circles to nowhere. The lads were still talking and joking, one or two singing and humming to themselves. I was about to sit down once more upon my mattress when the warning shout rang out.

"Bears in the air! Heavy gear!"

I knew just what that meant. I dived at the mattress and put it standing lengthways, in the farthest corner from the door, against the wall and put all the blankets behind it, wrapping the towel around my waist, forgetting the cold and securing the remains of my little tobacco parcel in the waist band of the towel. I heard the first splash of lashing liquid at the cell facing me.

Heavy gear, all right! I could smell it already: ammonia-based detergent, a very strong and extremely dangerous disinfectant. The screws were lashing it in under and through the splits in the sides of the doors. I braved a quick glance through my little spyhole as the lights in the corridor were turned on. It was a very foolish and dangerous thing to do because if the disinfectant hit me in the eyes it would burn my eyes out, blind me in a matter of seconds. B—was lashing a full bucket of the sickening liquid in under the door facing me and shouting to the other screws to hurry up and fetch more. I heard the chokes and coughs of the man across from me. The boys on the other side of the wing were in trouble. Their windows were blocked up. The fumes from the disinfectant were similar to tear gas, they cut at the eyes and throat, bringing on fits of vomiting and temporary blindness. I heard the hose being unravelled at the top of the wing.

"Hose on the air," I yelled and stepped back from the door. B— was lashing the disinfectant in through the doors like a mad man, laughing all the while. He had been wearing a small face-mask that protected him from the fumes and no doubt he and his companions were clad in their blue nylon overalls. The hose burst into life and the thundering jets crashed against the bottom of the doors. I heard a swish and saw the greenish coloured liquid flooding in under the door. Immediately the terrible fumes struck me and I began coughing and spluttering, my eyes watering as I made my way to the window. My stomach was turning and I thought I was going to be sick as I fought for gasps of air at the window, my head pressed tightly against the concrete bars. Every single man must have been at his window coughing. That's all I could hear with the swish of the high-powered hose in the background. The tears were tripping me. I couldn't see a thing. Then the water came pouring in the sides of the door and came flooding across the blackened floor. I couldn't have cared less. I was shattered and coughing, my throat burning and dry. The water would dilute the disinfectant. I knew that. But it would be several minutes before the fumes cleared. The water from the hose was still streaming in under the door then it ceased as the screw moved on to another cell. I was still coughing and spluttering but the fumes were clearing. I could hear Seán vomiting violently. The whole wing was filled with moans and groans and coughing. B— was literally screaming, "See how yous like that. See how yous like that." Then he began singing the only song he knew—*The Sash.*

The screws turned the hose off. I braved it to the spyhole to see B— plodding through the river of water, disinfectant and urine with his face-mask in one hand and an empty bucket in the other. He was laughing like a madman. The other screw came behind him, dragging the deflated hose, whilst the third screw hurled obscenities and abuse from the end of the wing. My eyes were burning but I wasn't too bad. The coughing still went on in the other cells. There was at least an inch of water on the floor, the end of my mattress was submerged in it, but the blankets were safely tucked in behind the mattress on the pipes. I began the long exhausting job of scraping and pushing the ocean of liquid out under the door as best I could.

"All right, Seán?" I yelled.

"No! I'm shattered!" he answered. The coughing in the other cells died out to be replaced by the noise of scraping po's as the drying-up operation began. The stinking, putrefying rubbish was floating about around my feet and clogging whatever little gap there was at the bottom of my door. I had to keep clearing it with my hand, lifting handfuls of soggy bread, dirt and filth and flinging them back into the corner. The water level began to subside. The fumes of the disinfectant still hung in the air but they were mild. I glanced at the window. The snow was falling really heavy now and a soft breeze was directing it in through the window.

Dear God, I thought, what next? My feet were numb and soaking but my exhausted body was sweating as I continued to scrape and push the water out. When I had most of it out, I took the mattress and tried to squeeze the water out of the saturated part at the bottom of it. Then I tore a lump off it and began to soak up the remaining damp patches on the floor, leaving the soaking end of the mattress against the pipes in the hope that it would dry out. I took another peek out of my little spyhole and gazed at the river of urine and filth and everything else that lay like a lake outside in the wing. They'd be around in the middle of the night with the cleaning machine to clean and dry it all up. I threw the damp piece of foam into the corner and stood at the window to catch my breath. I was exhausted but I couldn't stand too long on the freezing cold floor. The snow flakes were still coming in through the window. I had still only the towel wrapped around me so I lifted the blankets and wrapped myself up again. The floor was still slimy and damp. I would have no alternative but to put the mattress down on it later knowing that the dampness would seep up through the foam and attack my body. But it was either that or walk all night which I wouldn't be able to do. It was going to be a long, freezing cold, restless night. I listened to the boys describing their predicament out the windows. Several of the lads' mattresses were completely saturated. The blankets of others were in the same state. I wasn't too bad. At least it was only the lower end of my bed that was wet.

All the noise had died and mattresses and blankets were being dried as best they could. Does anyone fancy a sing-song? came the familiar question. After what had just occurred we had to do something to bolster our morale, and besides everyone would be pacing the floor. A bit of a cheer went up and the first singer was called to a roar of applause. I paced back and forth listening to the first singer singing *The Old Alarm Clock*. The next singer was one of the Derry lads. He sang *My Old Home Town on the*

Foyle, and after that the singers kept stepping up to their doors as they were called. Then came my call and I braved it to the door to give my rendering of *The Curragh of Kildare* and all the while, as I sang, I was waiting for B— to return and slip up unnoticed to lash a bucket of disinfectant into my face through the side of the door. I finished my song, being somewhat breathless, to a round of applause and went back to my pacing as the next singer was called. My feet were numb. The floor had dried very little and was still slimy. I couldn't walk any more, so I threw my mattress back onto the ground and crouched up in the corner on the dry half of it. The bruises I had received in the wing shift and search outside the visits were hurting.

I was tempted to roll another cigarette for myself and Seán but I decided against it as I knew I might well be able to manage one "blow" between two down the line tomorrow night and the way things were going it most likely would be more than welcome then. The singing continued. It broke the monotony and the tension-filled air and for a few minutes helped to take your mind off your surroundings and situation. There was no sign of B— returning. Most likely he was lying on his back around in the screws' mess or else filling himself with more booze. Someone was singing a self-composed song about the blanketmen which was very good indeed. Then one of the lads began to sing *Ashtown Road.* The wing went deadly silent and I sat, slightly shivering, listening to every note and word of the beautiful rendering as the singer sang on in his very sad voice. I felt my morale rising and once again I was glad I was resisting. Better suffering while resisting than being tortured without fighting back at all. The singer finished and the lads nearly tore the place down. The Master of Ceremonies called on the same singer to sing the last song and away he went again with *The Wind that Shakes the Barley.*

The snow was still coming in the paneless window which reminded me of the night when we had to smash them with our bare hands when the screws, lashed gallons of the heavy disinfectant in through the doors. The lads on the other side must have got it really bad tonight. I had heard them cursing the blocked up windows when B— had lashed the disinfectant through their doors.

The singer finished the last song of the night, and everyone gave him a grand round of applause. A bit of chatter followed and someone on the other side was getting a message shouted over in Gaelic from the other wing, which was passed on to the O/C. Some lad was very sick in the other wing. They rang the bell and the screws turned the emergency bell off and ignored the sick man. Another lad's mother had died yesterday and he had been refused parole like all the rest who had been in the same sorrowful position before him.

I got to my feet and stood on the mattress gazing out the window once more. The frost was thick on the wire which sort of reminded me of the inside of a fridge. Some of the boys down below were saying goodnight to each other; others were saying that they were going to try and walk as long as possible as their mattresses were soaking. Only a few remained talking at the windows. Seán knocked on the wall.

"*Oíche mhaith*, Bobby," he shouted.

"*Oíche mhaith*, Seán," I replied and added, "is your mattress wet?"

"No, it's not too bad," he replied. "I'm going to try and get warm under the blankets."

"*Maith thú. Oíche mhaith, a chara*," I said.

"*Oíche mhaith*," he shouted again.

The snow had stopped falling and only a soft breeze blew. The once smooth untarnished surface of the snow was marred by the footprints of the screws. The white puffy snow clouds had forsaken the sky and the inky-black sky returned, bearing a few stars that twinkled here and there. Most people would be in bed now, I thought. I wonder how they would feel if they had to wake up to what lies in front of us tomorrow? Is it any wonder, I ask myself, that I've had several nightmares this past few weeks and everyone of them connected with this hellhole. Dear God, where is it all going to end? It's bad when you can't even escape it through sleep, I thought.

The noise had died completely in the other blocks and those who had remained at the windows drifted away to either sleep or stay up because of the state of their mattresses. It was very quiet. The snow glinted and glistened as the multi-coloured brilliant lights reflected on it. The silence was ugly and sinister. A curlew cried out in the darkness as it passed overhead. The spotlight of a hovering helicopter danced about in the black ocean of sky far in the distance and I wondered if my family were all right. They would be worried sick until another month's visit came around. It had been a hard day but wasn't every day the same and God only knew what tomorrow would bring. Who would be the unlucky unfortunates tomorrow, supplying the battered bloody bodies for the punishment block? Who would be hosed down, beaten up or torn apart during a wing shift? Tomorrow would only bring more pain and torture and suffering, boredom and fear and God knows how many humiliations, inhumanities and horrors. Darkness and intense cold, an empty stomach and the four screaming walls of a filthy nightmare-filled tomb to remind me of my plight, that's what lay ahead tomorrow for hundreds of naked Republican political prisoners-of-war, but just as sure as the morrow would be filled with torture so would we carry on and remain unbroken. It was hard, it was very, very hard, I thought, lying down upon my damp mattress and pulling the blankets around me. But some day victory would be ours and never again would another Irish man or woman rot in an English hellhole.

It was cold, so very, very cold. I rolled on to my side and placed my little treasured piece of tobacco under the mattress and felt the dampness clinging to my feet.

That's another day nearer to victory, I thought, feeling very hungry.

I was a skeleton compared to what I used to be but it didn't matter. Nothing really mattered except remaining unbroken. I rolled over once again, the cold biting at me. They have nothing in their entire imperial arsenal to break the spirit of one single Republican political prisoner-of-war who refuses to be broken, I thought, and that was very true. They can not or never will break our spirit. I rolled over again freezing and the snow came in the window on top of my blankets.

"*Tiocfaidh ár lá,*"‡ I said to myself. "*Tiocfaidh ár lá.*"

---

‡ Our day will come.

you do not lie like pigs in sty
   upon a concrete bed
or watch them come before the sun
   to count the living dead
and ask of Christ this Sacrifice
   Maybe you penance paid.

you do not pray through each long day
   or pray into the night,
take our worships with prayer on lips
   to sleep May Steal your fright.
and Cross yourself in silent dread
   as darkness turns to light.

From wall to door he walked that floor
like a Man trapped in a time
and looked at the Quite desperately
behind a Mask of grime.
for with each step he sunk a depth
   From which he had to climb.

and time is but an endless rut
and each Man in his own
and some climb out and some do not
and some lie dead and prone
while time goes by like cloudy sky
its destiny unknown.

Now keeping time to a squelch of slime
he Marched a Quickened pace
those blazened eyes like angry stars
rolled Round his ashened face
and on he went like a Regiment
   that fled the battle Place.

he ran that floor from wall to door
and glared at me Quite dumb
and I at him like Mortal sin
for words just would not come
for this was hell and in this cell
   a soul was on the run.

each wretched soul in that vile hole
had one thought on his mind
we'd get it too was what we knew
   when night time would unwind
I 'cause each man knew just what was —
   for each Man wasent blind.

Skylark Sing
Your Lonely Song

The Lark and the Freedom Fighter

My grandfather once said that the imprisonment of the lark

is a crime of the greatest cruelty because the lark is one

of the greatest symbols of freedom and happiness.

He often spoke of the spirit of the lark relating to a story of

a man who incarcerated one of his loved friends in a small cage.

The lark, having suffered the loss of her liberty, no longer sang her little heart out, she no longer had anything to be happy about. The man who had committed the atrocity, as my grandfather called it, demanded that the lark should do as he wished: that was to sing her heart out, to comply to his wishes and change herself to suit his pleasure or benefit.

The lark refused, and the man became angry and violent. He began to pressurise the lark to sing, but inevitably he received no result. So he took more drastic steps. He covered the cage with a black cloth, depriving the bird of sunlight. He starved it and left it to rot in a dirty cage, but the bird still refused to yield. The man murdered it.

As my grandfather rightly stated, the lark had spirit—the spirit of freedom and resistance. It longed to be free, and died before it would conform to the tyrant who tried to change it with torture and imprisonment. I feel I have something in common with that bird and her torture, imprisonment and final murder. She had a spirit which is not commonly found, even among us so-called superior beings, humans.

Take an ordinary prisoner. His main aim is to make his period of imprisonment as easy and as comfortable as possible. The ordinary prisoner will in no way jeopardise a single day of his remission. Some will even grovel, crawl, and inform on other prisoners to safeguard themselves or to speed up their release. They will comply to the wishes of their captors, and unlike the lark, they will sing when told to and jump high when told to move.

Although the ordinary prisoner has lost his liberty he is not prepared to go to extremes to regain it, nor to protect his humanity. He settles for a short date of release. Eventually, if incarcerated long enough, he becomes institutionalised, becoming a type of machine, not thinking for himself, his captors dominating and controlling him. That was the intended fate of the lark in my grandfather's story; but the lark needed no changing, nor did it wish to change, and died making that point.

This brings me directly back to my own situation: I feel something in common with that poor bird. My position is in total contrast to that of an ordinary conforming prisoner: I am a political prisoner, a freedom fighter. Like the lark, I too have fought for my freedom, not only in captivity, where I now languish, but also while on the outside, where my country is held captive. I have been captured and imprisoned, but, like the lark, I too have seen the outside of the wire cage.

I am now in H Block, where I refuse to change to suit the people who oppress, torture and imprison me, and who wish to dehumanise me. Like the lark I need no changing. It is my political ideology and principles that my captors wish to change. They have suppressed my body and attacked my dignity. If I were an ordinary prisoner they would pay little, if any, attention to me, knowing that I would conform to their institutional whims.

I have lost over two years' remission. I care not. I have been stripped of my clothes and locked in a dirty, empty cell, where I have been starved, beaten, and tortured, and like the lark I fear I may eventually be murdered. But, dare I say it, similar to my little friend, I have the spirit of freedom that cannot be quenched by even the most horrendous treatment. Of course I can be murdered, but while I remain alive, I remain what I am, a political prisoner of war, and no one can change that.

Haven't we plenty of larks to prove that? Our history is heartbreakingly littered with them: the MacSwineys, the Gaughans, and the Staggs. Will there be more in H Block?

I dare not conclude without finishing my grandfather's story. I once asked him whatever happened to the wicked man who imprisoned, tortured and murdered the lark?

"Son," he said, "one day he caught himself on one of his own traps, and no one would assist him to get free. His own people scorned him, and turned their backs on him. He grew weaker and weaker, and finally toppled over to die upon the land which he had marred with such blood. The birds came and extracted their revenge by picking his eyes out, and the larks sang like they never sang before."

"Grandfather," I said, "could that man's name have been John Bull?"

Weeping Winds

Oh! cold March winds your cruel laments
    Are hard on prisoners' hearts,
For you bring my mother's pleading cries
    From whom I have to part.
I hear her weeping lonely sobs
    Her sorrows sweep me by,
And in the dark of prison cell
    A tear has warmed my eye.

Oh! whistling winds why do you weep
    When roaming free you are,
Oh! is it that your poor heart's broke
    And scattered off afar?
Or is it that you bear the cries
    Of people born unfree,
Who like your way have no control
    Or sovereign destiny?

Oh! lonely winds that walk the night
    To haunt the sinner's soul,
Pray pity me, a wretched lad
    Who never will grow old.
Pray pity those who lie in pain
    The bondsman and the slave,
And whisper sweet the breath of God
    Upon my humble grave.

Oh! cold March winds that pierce the dark
    You cry in aged tones
For souls of folk you've brought to God
    But still you bear the moans.
Oh! weeping wind this lonely night
    My mother's heart is sore,
Oh! Lord of all breathe freedom's breath
    That she may weep no more.

Modern Times

It is said we live in modern times,
    In the civilised year of 'seventy-nine,
But when I look around, all I see,
    Is modern torture, pain, and hypocrisy.

In modern times little children die,
    They starve to death, but who dares ask why?
And little girls without attire,
    Run screaming, napalmed, through the night afire.

And while fat dictators sit upon their thrones,
  Young children bury their parents' bones,
And secret police in the dead of night,
  Electrocute the naked woman out of sight.

In the gutter lies the black man, dead,
  And where the oil flows blackest, the street runs red,
And there was He who was born and came to be,
  But lived and died without liberty.

As the bureaucrats, speculators and presidents alike,
  Pin on their dirty, stinking, happy smiles tonight,
The lonely prisoner will cry out from within his tomb,
  And tomorrow's wretch will leave its mother's womb!

I Once Had a Life

The sun hung high above, seemingly like a gaping hole in the still blue sky, out of which the golden light came pouring down like honey to feed the land and ripen the barley, while sending shimmering hazes quivering above the melting tarmacadam surfaces. It was hot and humid. The beads of sweat lined my forehead like an ornate jewel.

I walked along the well-trodden path that lay on the perimeter of the forest and which rose steeply before me. I was in no hurry. I had plenty of time to take in and enjoy the beautiful surroundings. A gentle breeze sighed, sending ripples across an ocean of shining green and rustic brown ferns that lay ahead of me.

Clusters of timid yellow primroses lined both sides of my avenue. A young rabbit scurried across my path and vanished. Everything was alive and buzzing, but there was peace in the activity of nature. A passing crow cawed but the bees fed undisturbed upon the flowers, while the refreshing scent of pine carried upon the breeze.

I mastered the twisting rising climb and crossed a clearing of lush green grass, where a solitary young sycamore threw its shadow towards a family of bluebells that flourished by a little trickle of a stream. I sat down upon an earthen mound and gazed down the hillside at the sweeping landscape of deep green and every shade of brown, speckled with orange and yellow and splashed with a million white dots.

Where the life of the forest receded and fought to guard its flanks and outermost perimeter, a road in its infancy lay hollowed out in the black hardened clay, clustered with machinery. A row of houses appeared beyond, then another, leading to a massive concrete jungle where tiny figures moved to and fro.

There were deck chairs in the gardens where the sun-worshippers gloated in contentment. A group of young lads played with a garden hose, the cool white jet of water rising into the air before toppling down upon them in a thousand shining little silver drops.

To the right lay Belfast, belching out the sweat of the early morning risers, and the cranes of the shipyard towered towards the cloudless sky; in the distance stood another dogged giant, the Divis Tower, in the shadow of its like-named mountain; and, nearer by, "Napoleon's Nose" kept a watch on the city, perhaps in remembrance of Wolfe Tone who visited it all those years ago.

I retraced my gaze and found with ease our old house. Nobody I knew was there any more, just strangers, who trimmed the lawn around the ash tree that I grew up with. The fence needed a coat of paint and the front garden had been deflowered of its colour—my mother's and father's pride and joy. An old dog chased its tail on the street where we once played "kick the tin" and the old fellows made their way to the bookies for the first two across the card.

Farmer Thompson's old faithful dog brought his sheep in, a few fields away, and a wood pigeon fell to a distant shotgun, as I arose, not from my panoramic platform, but out of the inky blackness in the corner of my filthy, cold cell, where, wrapping a dirty, flimsy blanket around me to cover my naked body, I stepped towards the barred window and leaned my head against it.

The Fair People

In the blackened heavens silver sentries stood guard around an
    eloquent yellow Queen,
Off the Irish Sea came rain on gusty winds o'er hills and sunken
    valleys to wander through their dream.

The double latch of the half-door shot, bitter January bit both the
  fiery heart and the wretched soul,
When from humble home in black of morn came the fair people to
  dig that cursed coal.

Wild piercing eyes on heads tucked down watched their own feet
  cut through the muddy, watery slag,
Many of those feet were naked! the odd one shod: a few bound in
  disregarded rag,
But ever on went the pitter patter of the little naked feet and the
  weary trudging tramp of the very old,
When in the black of morn, half-frozen to death, went the fair people
  to dig that cursed coal.

Oh! cloaked by the chill of the biting winds, before the grey crow
  dared to caw on the wing,
Thousands were swallowed up by their motherland, an immoral
  sentencing,
Into the unstoked fires of hell they dropped where the years of like
  are stole,
Oh! when from the black morn to the black of hell, descended the
  fair people to dig that cursed coal.

While the robin sang by the greenwood thicket and the barges cut
  through ice on canal to town,
Your wee'ans cried and starved and died like your silver beads of
  gushing sweat that fell upon that blackened ground,
And as the den set upon your valley sides, the first light of dawn
  sought out every nook and knoll,
Oh! when but two hours on from the black of morn, the fair people
  had dug a thousand tons of that cursed coal.

Afore a hearthen fire of blazing log of pine sat the bossman with his
  steaming warming tea, brandy laced,
Upon fresh burning cakes of wheatenbread succulent golden streaming
  butter found a course to trace,
His fattened jollers quivering, his red rosy face blank like his thought
  toward that evil hole,

Where six hundred of the fairest, fair people stood knee deep in
    murky freezing water, digging that bastard's coal.

Aye, you Welsh charterists you were men, but will your likes e'er
    be seen again, your fair people to free?
Or will your tragic pitiful fair ghosts wander through your green
    valleys aimlessly?
Seven score of years have gone but still you hear the pitter patter
    upon your bones they stroll,
When in the black of morn, dearest God, ever still 'tis the fair people
    going out to dig that cursed coal!

A Thought in the Night

The wind howled mournfully and swept across the brilliance of a thousand
lights illuminating the surrounding sky, while from the outer darkness the
heavy rain came hurtling down in sheets of silver crashing upon the black
tarmac surface, sending a million fairy-like figures jigging and leaping in a
frenzy of movement.

A thousand miles of grey barbed wire wavered and shook in protest
as the wind weaved and attacked it relentlessly. An unlocked gate clanged,
and the panic-stricken barks of a distant guard dog hugged the wind and
were carried into the night. Then, as if the good Lord had snapped his fingers, a silence fell.

The wind was tamed and the fairies clung to the grey wire like a multitude of sparkling pearls. The ensuing calm and sudden hush were eerie
until disturbed by a moan from the unlocked gate and the sharp piercing
cries of the unseen night travellers, the snipe and the curlew. The pools of
silver rain glimmered as the passing night settled to recuperate from its raging ordeal and I gazed at a distant star to dream in the newly-born tranquillity, as the cold dampness of the December evening descended.

My thoughts were of my home and family, my wife and son. I tried to
visualise the fading faces of my mother and father whom I have not seen
for a long time, whom I fear I will not see again. Then came an old companion of mine: depression! It tore at my heart and engulfed me with its
unseen shroud of misery. The more I thought of home and family, the
deeper I plunged into its darkest depths.

The smile, the soft warm tender smile of my wife, kept coming up out of the darkness in front of me, and I heard her plaintive gentle voice: "I miss you, and I love you, come home." And my son lay sleeping like an angel, innocent and unaware of his mother's hardship and loneliness, with no father to tuck him into bed, to love or emulate as he grew; and he sighed as only an innocent sighs, and rolled over in his dreamy sleep.

Then came the faces of my family, my sisters and brother, growing up in my absence. And I knew just how much I loved them, and how I longed to share this short life with them and my poor mother. Lord, my poor tortured mother, grey and marked with a lifetime of worry and hardship that only she knows the entirety and toll of. And I said: "I'm sorry that you have suffered through my sufferings, mother." As ever, she replied: "Don't be humble. You're my son, and I'll always stand by you." My father, quiet as always in his own way, stood beside her. "Take heart, son," he said, " take heart."

The sky began to grey as the dawn threatened, and the birds awoke to proclaim the existence of life and nature. In the outer corridor of silence a key jingled and footsteps approached from afar. Depression slipped away unnoticed, as tension attacked my nerves and fear fell with the dawn.

Three hundred and fifty naked bodies stirred, a million thoughts and dreams fled, and a nightmare descended as the sun shone clear. Another day began. The footsteps grew louder and louder, and a voice said: "Get up, you bastards." I braced myself and thought: "Oh for the darkness of a stormy night."

McIlhattan

In Glenravels Glen there lived a man whom some would call a God
For he could cure the dead and kill the live for a price of thirty-bob.
Come winter, summer, frost all o'er or a jigin spring on the breeze
In the dead of night a man slips by—McIlhattan, if you'll please.

Chorus:
"McIlhattan, you blirt, where have you gone?" cry a million choking men.
Where are your sacks of barley? Or will your likes be seen again?
Here's a jig to the man and a reel to the drop and a swing to the girl
    he loved,
May your fiddle play and poteen cheer your company above.

There's a wisp of smoke to the south of Anne and the poteen's on the air.
The birds are up and the rabbits are out and there's drunkards everywhere.
At Skerries Rock the fox is out and be God it's chasing the hounds
And the only thing that's in a decent state are the dead below the ground.

Chorus:
In McIlhattan's house the fairies are out and dancing on the hobs.
The goats have collapsed, the dogs run away, there's salmon in the bogs.
He has a million gallons of wash they say and the peelers are on the glen,
But they'll never catch that heckler man 'cause he'll ne'er be back again!

"Come On, You Wee Reds"

The dim yellow lights from the rows of houses shone out, barely illuminating the shining bleak wet streets that lay before us. There were very few, if any, street lamps left in working order and the shadows crept up and along slogan-scarred walls, and silhouettes were upon me before I knew their origin or intentions and I wondered where "They" were.

"Keep your eyes open, Joe, only another twenty-five minutes to go, old son, and we'll have made it again. The rain's eased, thank God, but I'm wet and the very chill is biting through my saturated battle gear and creeping through my body. But they'll be making the soup for us now. Aye, I can almost smell it. Scalding, simmering country broth, thick and delicious."

"Top window ten o'clock, Joe!"

"Go home to yer ma's where yez belong and give's all peace."

"Jesus, Joe, you're not watching, the women are the worst. Always hostile, always ready to tear you to pieces. No sympathy from them and in a way I can understand them 'cause it's their sons and daughters who we've killed and gaoled, but I'm only doing a job, aren't I? Coming up to the chip shop now, Joe, just like the one at home, too, smell those fish 'n' chips. No chance of us buying any, they won't serve Brits. There's the usual crowd congregated outside listening to a transistor and the sound of Coronation Street comes drifting from the wee kitchen houses. I could be home, it could be Manchester if it were I standing eating those chips. Watch the crowd, Joe, and the girls with the long coats that hide the armalites, and that bastard of a sergeant has me perched up here like a coconut advertising myself to the whole of Belfast.

"Watch the crowd, those innocent faces hate you, Joe. If only I knew who was who or could see them, but you don't see them or even hear the sharp crack, and they know what they are doing. They're an army all right, a well-trained guerrilla army and they're determined to win their cause. Aren't they dying to prove it and rotting in gaols and in H Blocks and they told me it was a sectarian war and I would be a hero, saving the Irish from psychopathic killers. Some job, Joe. Some hero.

"Don't take your eyes off them, Joe old son. Going up Waterford Street now, not much light here either. Only shadows and the feeling that there is a gunman at every window and I wouldn't doubt it. Down Clonard Street and on to the Falls Road again. The crowd's still at the chippy but there are crowds watching you, Joe. They just watch and wait for the right moment. Some cars on the road and people going to the club and whatever pubs are left. The burnt-out shells of buildings tell the story of this war-torn town.

"Watch the doorways, Joe, where the courting couples stand. You're not in Germany now and there's no excitement and promise in this land, Joe. Jesus, it's cold but only six more minutes, old son, and you're home. Along Townsend Street and watch the Divis Flats, Joe. If they are there they'll be high. Track the windows with the sights, shoot first and ask later, Joe, these aren't your people anyway. You can't even understand them, the way they talk. Up the Grosvenor Road, Joe, going great! There's the Europa, no chance of me seeing too much of it in there, settle for a mug of soup, a few cans of beer and I'll write a letter to the missus and the wee one before I hit the sack.

"Leeson Street. Now watch the windows, Joe. Past the hospital gates and Dunville Park. I wonder how they're doing, she was three last month. Won't be long until I see them again tho', only a few more weeks, might not come back again.

"I'll fight for my country but not here, this isn't our problem, this isn't my people, no one can call me a coward. I don't even know why I'm here, what for? And where's it all going to end? At the junction of the Falls and Grosvenor Roads. One minute, Joe, watch the doorways old son, lights green, past Beacons pub and up the Springfield to the billet. They're opening the gate for us, smell that soup, Joe, hurry up! Big match on the telly tonight too, come on, you wee reds, watch the windows, Joe. I'll make sure I see the next one at Old Trafford, maybe even go to every home game.

"Watch the corners, Joe, take the missus to the club now and again and the wee lass to the zoo, hurry up! Maybe if I get a good job I could buy a car, moving in through the gates, or go to Spain for a holiday, watch the windows, Joe. I always wanted to go to Spain, almost there, Joe. Watch the doorway, Joe, come on the wee reds, scalding hot soup here I come."

Crack!

"You can't watch everywhere, Joe . . . '

The Harvest Britain Has Sown

A stretch of tarmac surrounded by barbed wire and steel is the only view from my cell window. I'm told it's an exercise yard. I wouldn't know. In my fourteen months in H Block, I haven't been allowed to walk in the fresh air. I am on "cellular confinement" today. That is the three days out of every fourteen when my only possessions, three blankets and a mattress, are removed, leaving a blanket and a chamber pot.

I'm left to pass the day like this, from 7.30 a.m. to 8.30 p.m. How I spend my day is determined by the weather. If it's reasonably warm, it's possible to sit on the floor, stare at the white walls, and pass a few hours day-dreaming. But otherwise I must spend my day continuously pacing the cell to prevent the cold chilling through to my bones. Even after my bedding is returned at 8.30 p.m. hours will pass before the circulation returns to my feet and legs.

Methods of passing the time are few and far between, so I am left with many hours of contemplation: good times, bad times, how I got here, but, most importantly, *why* I am here. During moments of weakness I try to convince myself that a prison uniform and conforming wouldn't be that bad. But the will to resist burns too strong within.

To accept the status of criminal would be to degrade myself and to admit that the cause that I believe in and cherish is wrong. When thinking of the men and women who sacrificed life itself, my suffering seems insignificant. There have been many attempts to break my will but each one has made me even more determined. I know my place is here with my comrades.

I think of the only break in the monotony, the forty minutes I spend at Mass each Sunday—"turn the other cheek," "love thy neighbour"—and I wonder, because over the months I know that bitterness has grown inside me. A hatred so intensive that it frightens me.

I see it also in the faces of my comrades at Mass: the hatred in their eyes. One day these young men will be fathers and these attitudes will inevitably be passed on to their children.

This is the harvest Britain has sown: her actions will eventually seal the fate of her rule in Ireland.

It is frightening to see men become aged at eighteen and nineteen. Young men, who were fit and strong in mind and body a year ago, now resemble shrunken shells of human beings. Every aspect of H Block life, from cold, empty cells and denial of every comfort, to refusal of medical treatment, is designed to grind down our resistance, but it will not succeed.

They may hold our bodies in the most inhuman conditions, but, while our minds remain free, our victory is assured!

The Refugees

A hurried worried people, a human stampede to God knows where,
Were spat out from the back streets, for God knows who to care.
Their little kitchen houses lit up the night around about
"For God and Ulster" was the reason that the refugees were driven out.

Oh little humble homes where the people hugged the open fire,
Oil-clothed floors and little ornamented cabinets that the neighbours
    would admire,
The little backyard havens where the youngsters would play
And in the hall the little font of holy water to bless you on your way!

They were little narrow streets where the door was never closed,
Where characters and folklore were born and not composed,
And where, by the street lamp by the corner, the children made a swing
In a concrete jungle where the hoker was the king.

Oh a kindly people, too clannish were they not,
A simple cup of tea or the milkman's price, were things that weren't
    forgot,
And when there was trouble sure didn't all of them muck in,
Wouldn't every man amongst them go out and get stuck in.

Ah sure some returned; others? God knows where they've gone,
Driven out in terror by that bigoted orange throng.
'Tis well I recall those hurried worried people, their little mansions
    burnt down,
As I watched them go in their thousands on the road to Gormanstown.

Fenian Vermin, Etc.

"Get those Fenian vermin out of that car," so ordered the Special Branch
man on the occasion of my arrest. I'd heard those words before and was to
hear them again a hundred times during my next six days of beatings and
torture in Castlereagh. In fact, the friendly "bobbies" used a whole variety of
descriptive addresses, like "tramp" and "gypsy," "vermin" and "scum,"
"filth" and so on, plus the usual vulgarities, threats and curses. These same
keepers of the law were quite good at describing what they had done on the
Fenian whores, as they called the Catholic girls they had interrogated.

Such descriptive vocabulary is quite fashionable in (for the want of a
better word) "authoritative" circles and I suppose that that included the
infamous Shankill butchers' team, seeing as the bulk of them were members of the UDR. I don't think anyone needs any reminders of the constant
use of such words during their bloody murderous orgies.

I now find that this "vermin" vocabulary is used probably more by
screws than anyone else. In the case of the bigoted screw it is not so much
aimed at degrading the prisoner (which it does, and the H Blocks are full of
that anyway) but, be it an RUC man or screw, the psychology remains the
same—to assert what they believe to be their superiority over the inferior
Fenians. It's the dictate of their sectarianism and loyalism to dominate,
degrade and terrify the second-class citizens and so on.

The extent of this practice in H Block would have to be heard and
seen to be believed. Sort of makes you think why they keep us locked up
and naked and filthy in disease-ridden, smelly concrete dungeon like cells,
unfit even for pigs. It is a mentality that makes it so easy for them to torture us, or butcher us when the opportunity arises. A mentality much the
same as those who maintained and organised the Nazi concentration camps
and the subsequent genocide of the Jews.

Tonight they'll go home to their wives and families and act like
civilised humans, just like the Shankill butchers must have done after their

bloody orgies. The Special Branch torture mongers and the other murder squads will do the same. But I'll just lie here and continue to resist them knowing that some day our day will come. For all their superiority they know that too; maybe that's why they sit with a gun constantly at hand listening for the alien sound and watching for a stranger. Tomorrow they return to their superior selves.

Me? I'll always remain the same—an Irishman fighting for the freedom of my oppressed people.

The Gaol Tunnel

He searched my clothing every part,
And fixed his evil eye,
Upon the store I'd braved to dare
And both met to defy.
He searched my hair and underwear,
Soles, ears and every thought,
All he found was pure disdain,
That time in gaol had wrought.

The handcuffs clinked and snapped with hate,
He sneered as if to say,
You'll bear a load of thirty years,
When you come back this way,
The tunnel door as once before,
Creaked open in my path,
And cheerful men who went there forth,
Came back without a laugh.

The tunnel wall was wet and grim,
The air was warm and thick,
We marched in almost funeral file,
In clickity, clickity, click.
This lonely tramp of condemned men,
Was an evil avenue,
The very devil hid in wait,
For souls that would go through.

Ghosts of men roamed this lonely way,
Their bodies lay in lime,
They bore the mark of hangman's noose,
Eroded ne'er by time.
They wore no face 'cept that of pain,
And clung they wall to wall,
And ne'er we see their ugly face,
We hear their eerie call.

They brushed against my biting chains,
I felt their creeping chill,
They courted pain and courted death,
In awful deathly drill.
The Screws ne'er dared to raise their eyes,
I heard the hangman's creek,
He laughed aloud and put a kiss,
Upon the devil's cheek.

We walked on by the courtroom door,
It thundered in our wake,
The very air was charged with care,
It made a body shake.
The pig in the wig sat in wait,
But ne'er I cared for him,
'Twas the awful thought, must I walk,
Back through that cave of sin.

A Place to Rest

As the day crawls out another night crawls in.
Time neither moves nor dies.
It's the time of day when the lark sings,
The black of night when the curlew cries.

There's rain on the wind, the tears of spirits,
The clink of key on iron is near,

A shuttling train passes by on rail,
There's more than God for man to fear.

Towards where the evening crow would fly, my thoughts lie,
And like ships in the night they blindly sail,
Blown by a thought—that breaks the heart—
Of forty women in Armagh jail.

Oh! and I wish I were with the gentle folk,
Around a heartened fire where the fairies dance unseen,
Away from the black devils of H Block hell,
Who torture my heart and haunt my dream.

I would gladly rest where the whin bush grows,
Beneath the rocks where the linnets sing.
In Carnmoney Graveyard 'neath its hill,
Fearing not what the day may bring!

The Rebel

There stood a beautiful lady frocked in a brilliance of white,
Her green body glistening in the silvery rain from the night.
The *slua sí* had been and danced and crept out of sight
To listen to the minstrel shake the hills with delight,

There he commanded the highest twig on that tree,
So the whole of Ireland might hear and might see.
Oh the *slua sí* cried that his heart still might yet be
As the mistle thrush sang of a land yet unfree.

But who heard this brave fellow's heart breaking, plead,
Save a *Rí na síogaí*, passing by on his swiftly brown steed.
And the creeping lord of the manor sat upon a black bloody deed,
Mortally wounded the minstrel, his land yet unfree.

Oh! how that woman's white frock turned so red where he fell
And the *slua sí* wept 'neath a limestone rock in the dell:

'Twas a little brown sparrow told me by the bars of my cell
How the *slua sí* buried a rebel next a lonely blue bell.

slua sí—fairies; *Rí na síogaí*—king of the fairies

Flowers, My Friends, Flowers

Flowers are gentle maidens. They radiate a breathtaking beauty and a fragrance that swoons the very birds. Symbols of love and peace are these little charmers of nature.

There is happiness to be found in every flower and the freshness and beauty of life for those whose own lives have grown stale and dull. They entice the bees and court the ladybirds, these little devils of colour. Flaunting to the breeze, dancing with the wind and shedding their dewy tears as they marvel at the glory of a new day.

Primroses are the joy of the poor man. The tiny, yet hardy, clusters of bright yellow that herald the death of winter, the birth of spring and the expectancy of summer. Jewels of the wild are the primroses, embedded on the sides of mossy banks and roving ways. 'Tis a stealing, poor place that has been denied the presence of the poor man's rose.

Bluebells are delicate, lanky souls. Somehow they remind me of oppressed, impoverished people, for they stand so humble, their heads drooped lest they offend the towering, ugly brambles and weeds—the parasites of nature. Yet these ladies of slender elegance, like the poor man, are the most precious and deserved of their kind.

Yellow and white are the colours of God and Easter. The Dutch yellow of the daffodil is a hauntingly beautiful shade. But yellow and white roses portray the purity of freedom and their scent has been drunk by the bondsman, arousing his heart. They have blossomed into murderous rebellions, these gentle roses. They've bled in pitiful agony before the callous winds of a foreign land. They are Pearse and Connolly, this terrible beauty.

Goddesses, queens, Angels of Glory! Such are the praises of flowers. The muses of the poet, the heart of the artist, and the sorrow of love once lost.

But there are none more courageous, nor sorrowful, than those oppressed flowers in Armagh Gaol. Irish women who, unlike the flowers of the wild, refuse to bow before the foreign winds of torture and inhumanity. The beauty of the nation is being scarred by pain and hate, it has been buried in dark dungeons; hidden from the light of day without which no flower can survive. It can be heard screaming in a tormenting agony that wrecks the heart. Yet these flowers refuse to be broken!

Heroines, the stars of a fettered nation, a flaming inspiration to all downtrodden and oppressed bondsmen, the spirit of ancient Ireland and the Republic to be—these are the praises of those flowers who epitomise the unconquerable spirit of Irish womanhood. Let no man dare to scorn these women and let your weeds of indifference and sleeping roses blush in everlasting shame.

We Won't Be Fooled

"Bloody dreaded boiled egg for tea tonight," says the effort.

"Ya'd think they'd take a reddener firing the like of that up to a man."

"Dead right," says I, listening to his knobbley knees creaking as he paces back and forth across the small space between the wall and the door.

"Long aul' day," says he, trying to catch a glimpse of sunlight at the blocked up window. "Must be near tea time," he added, goin' back to the dreaded egg theme.

"It's only half an hour since dinnertime," says I, looking at the two inedible dinners lying on top of the rubbish at the foot of the bed.

"Who-ssh," says the effort, his ears pricked.

"Is there a screw at the door?" I asked.

"Ah no," says he. "It's only them'ins in the housin' estate batterin' them big Lambeg Drums again. Ya'd think they'd take a reddener as well and give us a break. I hear they're up to their tricks again too," says the effort, pacing up and down still.

"What's that, comrade?" I asked.

"Sectarian murders," says he. "Hasn't there been three or four lately? All Catholics."

"You know who's behind that, don't you?" says I to the effort.

"Course I do," says he, "The Orangies! and if I'd my way I'd soon put a stop to that."

"Well, don't be too sure it's the Orangies," says I, to the effort.

"Well, wasn't there one of them caught and charged?" says he.

"You still can't be sure," says I. "For you see it's like this, the Brits are up to every trick and there's nothing that would suit them better at the minute than a bloody sectarian campaign flaring up, as you know yourself comrade, the Brits are in a very bad way at the minute, because the IRA are inflicting many kills and casualties upon them, demoralising them and winning the war against them. On top of this the people are fed up with the Brits, even this is beginning to show from the Loyalist side, their politicians are continually slabbering and issuing threats and for the Brit he can't even come up with a political initiative because of the war. The future holds no hope for a political forum in the North and by the looks of things the Brits haven't a dog's chance of ever retaining any sort of political stability. To make things really bad for them, their H Block Conveyor Belt, the tortures in Castlereagh and its likes, the mass torture in the gaols and H Block, in fact their whole bloody criminalisation/Ulsterisation policy has exploded in their faces. So *cara*, the best way for them to try and wriggle out is to distract people's minds away from all this that I just said and the Brits know that there's no better way to do this than through a good old sectarian murder campaign, hoping that the IRA will react to it and make it worse."

"But we're too sly for that," says the effort, suddenly catching on.

"*Sin ceart*," says I, "and don't forget it could be SAS men or any of the Brit murder squads doing the dirty work, Peelers, UDR, Orangies, even someone from our own districts, that's why the people must be alert to this type of thing, 'cause the Brit is out to confuse, to frustrate and anger the people into reacting without thinking, to sectarian murders, so as to distract and detract everyone from the war effort. The Brit will and does back the murder gangs no matter who they are, turn a blind eye to them as they've done in the past, to safeguard them and promote them—be they their own SAS murder squads, Orangies or someone they've bought, bribed, threatened or blackmailed into it."

"I see what you mean *cara*," said the effort, "and they could also try to trick the IRSP or Sticks into the same trap or go vice-versa, by doing it in Loyalist areas, murder them to spark the reaction."

"*Sin ceart*, comrade," says I, "and that's the little trick they've used for hundreds of years, divide and conquer so to speak, but more so diverting people away from the real cause of the people, they, the Brit, their presence in and occupation of Ireland."

"So we and our people must not allow ourselves to be fooled into being diverted and tricked by British sectarianism," says the effort. "*Sin ceart*, comrade," says I, watching him looking up at the blackened window.

"Who-sssh!" says I.

"Lambeg Drums?" says the effort.

"Dreaded eggs!" says I.

"The tea's up."

"Ah na," says he, "not the dreaded egg."

Comrades in the Dark

There came a splendid golden sun,
  Across the darkened skies,
It woke the bondsman from his dream,
  As it fell upon his eyes.
It lit the ways of freedom's path,
  Sent forth the singing lark,
And bore a weeping blossom 'pon,
  The flowers in the dark.

They bloomed by country lane and town,
  In freedom's fragrant scent,
Giving heart to a weary folk,
  When dark days came and went.
And grew they strong and beautiful,
  Midst fortune cold and stark,
The fairest flowers of their kind,
  These roses of the dark.

The winds of war came sweeping cruel,
  The blossom would not cry,
Oh how it broke the freeman's heart,
  To see the first rose die.
Some soldiers plucked the garden's joy,
  And left a burning mark,
Upon the silver petalled bloom,
  Now fettered in the dark.

These flowers weep in dank cold cells
   No sun to light the gloom,
They suffer torture's vilest scorn
   To wither in their bloom.
But ne'er they yield these lovely things,
   O hear they freedom's mark
They are the light to guide the poor
   These flowers in the dark.

I care not should we freemen die,
   To see the garden flower,
And humble bluebells lift their heads,
   To rise in all their power.
I hold a tear, torn sore in heart,
   'Twere e'r a Joan of Arc,
'Tis each one of these saintly flowers,
   Who be in dungeons dark.

Trilogy

1 The Crime of Castlereagh

I scratched my name and not for fame
Upon the whitened wall;
"Bobby Sands was here," I wrote with fear
In awful shaky scrawl.
I wrote it low where eyes don't go
'Twas but to testify,
That I was sane and not to blame
Should here I come to die.

I heard the creak of creeping sneak
The Watcher on his round.
'Twould be, I thought, but all for nought
If caught upon the ground.
My dancing eyes bore no disguise

They leapt like flames of fire,
When Christ I stared as at me glared
The death name of "Maguire."‡

I paled with fright was death all right
I stood like trembling bird,
And felt the look, the Watcher's duke
As he passed by unheard.
But one thought lay upon mind's bay
'Twas anchored deep, my friend,
'Twas that man's name and cruel pain
That seen him to his end.

The light burned bright was day now night
Who cared of such in hell,
For a man's mind spent all its time
On when he'd leave the cell.
For who knew when or there again
Just who knew if at all,
If the next creak or creeping sneak
Was death's breath come to call.

The floor was cold on stocking sole
And boots forbidden things,
For one might die if one might tie
A noose with lacing strings.
For tortured men seek death's quick end
And branch men know this too,
For stiffs won't talk so men must walk
The floor without a shoe.

I heard the moans and dreadful groans
They rose from some man's cell.
And knew I then that this poor friend
Had something big to tell.

---

‡ The RUC alleged that Brian Maguire hanged
himself in May 1978.

Bobby Sands

I'd heard him go some hours ago
His step was smooth and light,
But he'd come back like a crippled wreck
Or one who'd lost a fight.

All listened hard except the coward
Who squirmed upon his bed,
The pain of men just does not blend
With he whose silvers weighed.
It tore our ears and primed our fears
This man's tormenting groans
It made men reel for all could feel
The hurt on this man's bones.

I stewed like rat in Porter vat
Fermenting drunk with fear.
When would they come, who'd be the one?
The time was drawing near.
I worried sick and scurried quick
Like blindman in a storm,
I had no course but followed force
Of terror's blasting horn.

The light burned bright was day now night
Or was night turned to day.
Forty hours, I'd sweated showers
In panic-stricken fray.
This waiting game was greatest strain
And though I knew their ploy,
It did not ease nor did appease
But helped more to destroy.

My stomach turned, it churned and churned
Stirred fast by swirling dread.
'Twas times like this in wretchedness
A man fell down and prayed.
'Twas times like this in cowardliness
That men would break their code,

And spill the beans in cowardly screams
To shed this murderous load.

The groaning died, we tortured sighed
And silence fell again.
And so did that, that ties a knot
To choke the very brain.
Depression, friend, it did extend
In waves through every cell,
Crept up behind and bit the mind
Like shock from bursting shell.

I'd nought to do but see it through
I fought it tooth and nail.
It said to me in evil glee,
"Give up and go to jail.
The prison bars you'll see in hours
If you just sign your name.
Or just admit a little bit
Regardless who's to blame."

I heard the clink of metal link,
The Watcher was abroad.
He squeaked and creaked, tip-toed and sneaked
On shoes that were not shod.
Ne'er e'er he spoke and still unbroke
The silence hung in awe.
He watched you quake and watched you shake
And told them all he saw.

When he had gone I sat upon
The monstrous heavy bed.
What little air there was to spare
Was pumped out overhead.
It came through vent to no extent
To barely fill the lungs,
So ate we crust of dirty dust
And choked upon our tongues.

Bobby Sands

And who could sleep in sweltering heat
With rattle of the vent.
'Pon canvas sheets caked firm in pleats
With sweat that men had spent.
The bright white light gave no respite
And cut the eyes to shreds,
And left an ache to devastate
Already bursting heads.

White walls! White walls! Torturous sprawls,
With ne'er a window space.
And so confined a quaking mind
Goes mad in such a place.
The monotony so torturously
Cuts deep into the mind,
That men lose hope and just elope
With charge of any kind.

There's one to eight left to deflate
Will e'er they come to end.
I rose depressed for who can rest
With torture to contend.
From wall to wall my thoughts did trawl
Behind my dragging wake,
And shouted they in disarray
"How much dare you to take?"

"How much! How much! for pain will touch
Your very spirit, man.
And what you doubt may well slip out
And fry you in the pan.
She, you, or he need bare no sin
They'll give you one for free.
If break you will they sure as hell
Will give you two or three."

The moans and groans they froze our bones
I heard the next man pray.

'Twas him again, said I in shame
"That poor lad's on his way."
The very air screamed in despair
Contorted with pure fear,
For 'twas a tap on outside flap:
The torture men were here!

The tension snapped like grizzly trap
It gripped me by the throat.
And every sense lost all defence
Like gale-lashed drifting boat.
And undisguised, my thoughts capsized
And drowned they in my fear.
And washed they out with any doubt
Of what was drawing near.

A death hush fell for none could tell
Where fate was going to fall.
All held their breath as pale as death
For pain had come to call;
And stood we still in awful thrill
I, trembling unashamed.
An angry wound flashed the room
'Twas fear of fear inflamed.

Their cramped slow steps eased through the depths
Of clinging floating fear,
I dared a sigh as they passed by
Like hunters stalking deer.
Then came the word like call of bird
They'd found their trembling prey,
And none knew whom was bound for doom
As they led him away.

Some hours had passed when someone asked
To see a certain fiend.
That timid voice had made his choice
'Twas clearly to be seen.

Bobby Sands

With coward's reprieve he took his leave
Midst cursing, silent flak.
Said I, with sigh, as he passed by,
"That scoundrel won't be back."

A prisoner's mind may pass the time
In dreamy hopeful thought.
In Castlereagh from day to day
A thought's a battle fought.
And sinking men cling fast, my friend,
To hope within a thought.
A cherished smile or voice of child
Are life rafts to be caught.

From cell to cell they moved 'round hell
With food to feed the starved.
And keeping rules, gave plastic tools
So wrists could not be carved.
On paper plate in greasy state
They placed it in your hand.
But who could eat the devil's treat
Or who could give a damn?

They watched you too, while in the loo,
They stood while you sat down.
But men must do what men must do,
So turn your head around.
And ne'er they slink in all men's stink,
And ne'er they flush or pale.
What kind of men are these, my friend,
Who walk the devil's trail?

As twice before, he groaned once more,
The rattling noise began.
I quickened pace to such a race
That God I nearly ran.
That neighbour prayed and bright light slayed
The Watcher came to peek.

I felt the ill of weakening chill,
Like wind around my feet.

This Citadel, this house of hell,
is worshipped by the law.
It's built upon a rock of wrong
With hate and bloody straw.
Each dirty brick holds some black trick
Each door's a door to pain.
'Tis evil's pen, a devil's den,
And Citadel of shame.

The Men of Art have lost their heart,
They dream within their dreams.
Their magic sold for price of gold
Amidst a people's screams.
They sketch the moon and capture bloom
With genius, so they say.
But ne'er they sketch the quaking wretch
Who lies in Castlereagh.

The poet's word is sweet as bird,
Romantic tale and prose.
Of stars above and gentle love
And fragrant breeze that blows.
But write they not a single jot
Of beauty tortured sore.
Don't wonder why such men can lie,
For poets are no more.

And where are those whose holy prose
Has gave them halo'ed fame?
They kneel and pray, or so they say,
And play their little game.
For politics and love don't mix,
As well the vanquished know.
So genuflect, you tortured wreck
And bear your cross of woe.

I slowed the pace, this terror race
Was never to be won.
For creak of bed sparked awful dread
And nerves would jump the gun.
'Twas ten to nine, for that's the time
I heard the Watcher say.
But was it light or was it night
I ne'er knew either way.

And some are wrought by sickening thought
It tears their very heart.
It eats their mind like burning lime
And rips their soul apart.
It puzzles men and muzzles them
It leaves each one distraught.
It is that fiend that asks unseen,
"Just how did you get caught?"

I'd torn my jeans twice at the seams
And hidden matches there.
For men must use each little ruse
And take each passing dare.
If one had luck a lousy butt
Could calm the nerves no end.
For cultured taste takes second place
When you're in hell, my friend.

The Watcher came to check again,
I froze with sound of key.
Like ticking clock, I stopped in shock
As time ran out on me.
And God forbid, but flew it did,
Like screeching blackbird flew,
Across the floor, through opened door
As he barked, "INTERVIEW!"

The dreaded word, like trapped bird,
Went shrieking above my head.

It screamed and screamed and God it seemed
Like calling of the dead.
He looked at me unenviously.
Said he, "They want you, friend."
I looked at him, like man in sin,
Goin' out to meet his end.

The Watcher signed and underlined
My name into the book.
But ne'er he'd sign departure time,
The devious, dirty crook.
He flanked my side like devil's guide
On lonely gallows trek.
And curiously, he stared at me,
Like one not coming back.

I felt the bite of chilly night
And warning in the air.
A yellow moon like eye of doom
Gripped me in its glare.
Down twelve iron steps to darker depths
Where lurking figures were.
A hurried swop, like smuggling drop,
And I was in their care.

A silhouette of heavy set
Spoke out in whispered tones,
"Our friendly quack must do his check
Before we break your bones."
From fore and aft there rose a laugh
That scraped my very spine.
And said a voice, "You'll get no choice,
For, by God, you're goin' to sign."

I saw him come, he looked quite done,
His eyes were red and swollen
And knew I then, that this poor friend
Had had his secrets stolen.

Bobby Sands

I caught his eye, as he passed by,
His terror-stricken form
Search out the air for nothing there
Like blind man in a storm.

The doctor stood a gaping prude
'Tis hard to hide distaste.
"All right," said he, officiously,
"Strip off, down to the waist."
He'd stop and stare both here and there
When fancy was his whim,
And gape at me quite hatefully
As if I'd bitten him.

He glared at me begrudgingly,
He asked if I were ill.
I shook my head, for sickening dread,
Could not be cured by pill.
I quaked like swine on slaughter line
As he said, "You're quite fit.
So send him on, he's good and strong,
And roast him on the spit."

They walked me through an avenue
Where devils lay in wait.
The very air was charged with care
For there lay evil fate.
A man could feel the agony steal
Quietly o'er his skin,
They looked at me expectantly
And each bore his own grin.

We came to halt for some default
Caused two groups to collide.
They looked perplexed stopped in their tracks
For passage wasn't wide.
They shuffled back, then made attack
Then shuffled back in shame,

For no one knew quite what to do
So all just tried again.

They led her by, her head held high
Their faces hanging low.
It seemed to me quite obviously
That they had come to woe.
She looked at me determinedly
Across that gap of doom,
And smiled did she so pitifully
Like rose in winter bloom.

And in her wake she left an ache
That gripped my very heart.
If men but knew what she went through
They'd tear their souls apart.
"In here," he said by nod of head,
The door closed like a cave.
I stood like one in face of gun
With one foot in the grave.

They both stood there, an awkward pair,
From toe to head they swayed,
With casual stands, pocketed hands,
Expressions carefully weighed.
So unalike as day and night
This sneaky shrewd duet.
These shark-eyed hawks of chatty talks
And I like etiquette.

They have their means to make you scream
And cower to their whims.
Some quake and shake before they break
Just fearing for their limbs,
Then fall like leaves from autumn trees
Before the axe has swung.
For such is fear that men adhere
To having themselves hung.

Bobby Sands

They have their means and dirty schemes
To loosen up your tongue.
Some talk so sweet you'd think their feat
Was one of pleasant fun.
But soon you learn and soon you yearn
For safety of the cell,
For what was thought was penance taught
Was but the gates of hell.

From day to day in Castlereagh
The hours tick by like years,
While to and fro men come and go
To play upon your fears.
And some wear masks for their grim tasks
To hide their black disgrace.
But what black mask, I dare to ask,
Could hide the devil's face?

"The law is right," the judge will cite,
"The public must have care.
A crime is crime in any mind
Committed anywhere."
Hypocritical, parasitical bastards
Cry, "Hurray!"
But they would yell like souls in hell
If locked in Castlereagh.

They do not watch while minutes hatch
Into eternities,
Reciting prayer in awful tear
Upon their bended knees.
Nor is each sound a worry found
Each creak the devil's tread.
Each shattered thought a battle fought
Within an aching head.

Nor do they twitch with nervous itch
As clouds of dread creep in,

Nor gaze upon a wealth of wrong
That stares at them like sin.
Nor do they sleep nor do they weep
In little lonely tombs,
For sleep they 'pon a bed of wrong
On others' bleeding wounds.

With sweating toil and bubbling oil
Men once tortured men,
On ghastly rack they broke your back
Until you broke, my friend.
But modern day in Castlereagh
The police persuade with care.
They draw a line, then walk your spine
Until you sign—in err.

Now some will say in sweetest way
They do not wish you harm,
They try to coax, they try to hoax
They murder you with charm.
They give you smokes, they crack you jokes,
Allaying all your fears,
Then beg you sign that awful line
To get you thirty years.

They flatter you and shatter you
With pleasantry and smiles,
They'd set you free quite readily
If you would mark their files.
They crawl to you and drawl to you
As sweet as violin,
But underneath there hides a thief
Whose tune is that of sin.

Some bear the stain of cruel Cain,
These are the men of doom.
The torture-men who go no end
To fix you in that room.

To brutalise they utilise
Contrivances of hell,
For great duress can mean success
When tortured start to tell.

Like withered leaf or side of beef
They hang you by the heels,
Then kidneys crunch with heavy punch
To torture jiggling squeals.
Bones are bruised 'cause boots are used
To loosen up your tongue,
So men admit a little bit
When nothing have they done.

They chop your neck, then walk your back
Spread-eagle you like pelt.
For private parts their special arts
Are sickeningly felt.
They squeeze them tight with no respite
Till a man cries for the womb
That gave him birth to this cruel earth
And torture of that room.

Some play with threats to seek regrets
Others play with bribes,
In Castlereagh they'd dearly pay
For what a secret hides.
And some poor folk throw off their yoke
To whisper what they know,
For price of gold they sell their soul
For men can sink that low.

From day to day in Castlereagh
The hours tick by like years,
While to and fro men come and go
To play upon your fears.
And some wear masks for their grim tasks
To hide their black disgrace,

But what black mask, I dare to ask,
Could hide the devil's face?

They came and came, their job the same,
In relays ne'er they stopped.
"Just sign the line!" they shrieked each time
And beat me till I dropped.
They tortured me quite viciously
They threw me through the air.
It got so bad it seemed I had
Been beat beyond repair.

The days expired and no one tired,
Except of course the prey,
And knew they well that time would tell
If I had words to say.
Each dirty trick they laid on thick
For no one heard or saw,
Who dares to say in Castlereagh
The "police" would break the law!

They poured it on, this boiling wrong,
The body burned with pain,
Till hefty throws and heavy blows
Came hurtling down like rain.
Till clumps of hair lay everywhere
And blood lay red as wine,
One would have thought a prey was caught
And butchered up like swine.

All things must come to pass as one
So hope should never die.
There is no height or bloody might
That a freeman can't defy.
There is no source or foreign force
Can break one man who knows,
That his free will no thing can kill
And from that freedom grows.

Bobby Sands

In despairing gloom, out of that room
They led me quite depressed.
This dirty horde their heads now lowered
For I had not confessed.
Down that aisle in funeral file
We shuffled in retreat,
And well I knew that this black crew
Were chewing on defeat.

And every pace was act of grace
For crying in my wake
Were tortured screams and bloody scenes
And all I had to take.
And charge of kind no doubt they'd find
And prison bars I'd face,
But worse again would be the shame
Of deep and dark disgrace.

They walked me through that avenue
Still devils lay in wait.
The very air was charged with care
For there lay evil fate,
And I could feel the agony steal
Quietly o'er my skin,
And knew I well that this was hell
And I was still within.

From day to day in Castlereagh
The hours tick by like years,
While to and fro men come and go
To play upon our fears.
And some wear masks for their grim tasks
To hide their black disgrace,
But what black mask, I dare to ask,
Could hide the devil's face?

As dawn converged the world emerged
Into a brand new day.

I stepped out to a sky of blue
Where silver fleeces lay.
The chirp of bird I plainly heard
And as the breeze went by,
I drank the air in thirsty tear
With greed upon my eye.

I drank the day o'er Castlereagh
Like one back from the grave,
And feasted high upon that sky
Like one with awful crave.
Each soothing breeze was laced with ease
Each golden ray with life,
Each little bird that chirped a word
Echoed sweet as life.

The Watcher gazed with deep amaze
Or as if he'd seen a ghost.
His face was set like losing bet
Or a hollow-ended boast.
Up twelve iron steps to silent depths
He led me to my cell,
He could not gauge for hate and rage
How another wouldn't tell.

He turned away in pure dismay
With shrug and sigh of hurt.
It seemed no more he'd sneak the floor
This dirty, low-down blirt.
And ne'er a sound was heard around
As the hours crept on by.
And, God, it seemed if some one screamed
The very air would cry.

This Citadel, this house of hell,
Is worshipped by the law,
It's built upon a rock of wrong
With hate and bloody straw.

Each dirty brick holds some black trick,
Each door's a door to pain.
'Tis evil's pen, a devil's den
And Citadel of shame.

I heard the clink of metal link
The Watcher was abroad.
He squeaked and creaked, tip-toed and sneaked
On shoes that were not shod.
Ne'er e'er he spoke and still unbroke
The silence hung in awe.
He watched you quake and watched you shake
And told them all he saw.

'Twas in the night the burning light
Grew dim and barely lit,
And shadows fell within the cell
To almost smother it.
'Twas hard to sleep for vigil keep
The tortured and oppressed,
And day to day in Castlereagh
The tortured know no rest.

The shadows crept and figures leapt
Across the murky beams
That stole in by the judas spy
In perpetuating streams. . .
Then, dearest Christ!! as if enticed
They danced around the wall
And peered at me so hauntingly
With faces white and small.

They moved around and moved around
Just staring at the bed.
They marched in pairs with tortured stares
For they were marching dead.
Each looked a loss, each bore a cross
Upon his bended back,

And on it plain was that man's name
For he'd known torture's rack.

Each gruesome weird had rambling beard
And wore a blanket coarse.
His flashing eyes spit out despise
With mystifying force,
And bloody tears in blushing seers
Cascaded through the gloom,
To paint a rose in trembling pose
Of beauty tortured bloom.

They courted pain and flaunted strain
Contorting in their throes
What these poor men had met, my friend,
A man dare not suppose,
For round and round and up and down
Their faces crissed and crossed
Till in a sea of purgatory
Their painful shapes were lost.

I heard the clink of metal link
The Watcher was not there.
And no bloody eye peeped through the spy
But someone cast a stare.
I felt the chill of creeping ill
Someone was abroad,
And knew I not, just who or what
But prayed my prayers to God.

The quaking cell as if in spell
Began to whinge and weep.
Then awful shapes with sinners' gapes
Stole by in ghostly sweep.
Wizened apes with stumpy napes
Danced by in shrieking fear
And cavalcade of evil grade
Filed by with dirty leer.

Bobby Sands

The howls of ghouls and hoots of owls
Rang round that little room,
And devils' rooks and phantom spooks
Sailed by in deathly gloom,
And hideous, perfidious—serpents
Snaked and hissed,
While silhouettes made pirouettes
In terrifying twist.

A demon came his eyes aflame
And round him was the law.
They danced like in Hades and rats in plagues
And Christ I froze in awe.
They spun a cord this gruesome horde
On loom of doom and sin,
To make a noose that would induce
A tortured soul within.

Oh! Gorgons and Morons
And vipers danced a ball,
Ugly beasts and Satan's priests
Stood naked 'pon the wall.
Crude and lewd the spectres spewed
And goblins jigged in rage,
While snarling shrimps and imps and pimps
Threw sins onto the stage.

The witch and bitch and thieving rich
Threw up a scaffold black
A Demagogue blasphemed to God
In mocking disrespect.
The devil's sons and evil ones
Gathered round like fire,
And, Jesus Christ, their sacrifice!
Was murdered Brian Maguire.

Wizards, Lizards, Sins in Blizzards
Swirled round above their head,

Squealing bats and snapping gnats
Would suck the bloody thread.
And all spat hate to that man's fate
And all cried, "Satan come!"
All praised the law in evil awe
For evil is but one.

They danced in gloom, they danced to doom
They waltzed with mortal sin
Shuffling and scuttling
'Fore dark and evil wind.
They inched and winched and pinched and lynched,
And 'pon that scaffold swung.
'Twas evil fray in Castlereagh
Until that man was hung.

The devils fled for life was dead.
The law hid in its shame.
The butchered air gasped in prayer
And tears fell down like rain.
The very walls were appalled,
My eyes were red as fire,
For I had cried a tearful tide
In mourning of Maguire.

This Citadel, this house of hell,
Is worshipped by the law.
It's built upon a rock of wrong
With hate and bloody straw,
Each dirty brick holds some black trick
Each door's a door of pain
'Tis evil's pen, a devil's den,
And Citadel of shame.

The Men of Art have lost their heart
They dream within their dreams.
Their magic sold for price of gold
Amidst a people's screams

Bobby Sands

They sketch the moon and capture bloom
With genius, so they say
But ne'er they sketch the quaking wretch
Who lies in Castlereagh.

The poet's word is sweet as bird
Romantic tale and prose,
Of stars above and gentle love
And fragrant breeze that blows.
But write they not a single jot
Of beauty tortured sore.
Don't wonder why such pen can lie
For poets are no more.

I heard the clink of metal link
The Watcher was abroad.
He squeaked and creaked, tip-toed and sneaked
On shoes that were not shod.
Ne'er e'er he spoke and still unbroke
The silence hung in awe.
He watched you quake and watched you shake
And told them all he saw.

A man must live, a man must give
By law and justice, friend.
Let all men know that it be so
That justice knows no end.
For king and knave, freeman and slave
Must face the king of kings,
And each must pay in his own way
For great and little things.

And he with shame and he with blame
Must answer every sin,
And no black lie or reason why
Will cleanse his soul within.
So listen well, you pimps of hell
You beasts of Castlereagh!

Both law and man will meekly stand
'Fore God on judgement Day!

In Castlereagh from day to day
The tortured know no rest,
And men don't sleep and men must weep
Until they have confessed.
Confessed to "crime" for sentenced time
Though guilt they may not know
But that is law however raw,
So bear your cross of woe...

2 Diplock Court

They walked me through the door of doom
Like pig to slaughter pen.
But pigs are treated better
Than prisoners are, my friend.
And I in lowly fetters
Of captured Irishmen.

The chains they clinked and drew the eyes
Of all assembled there.
They looked me up and looked me down
And fixed me in their stare.
And I felt the scorn in their eyes
Say—"Who are you to dare?"

They stared me up and stared me down
Distasteful leers and sneers,
They threw their dirty hate-you looks
Like burning, searing spears.
And said they all, "We'll get you, friend,
For thirty good long years."

A waster class these well-groomed brats
From a very evil field,
They'd gathered for the sentencing

Of one who would not yield.
He would not yield. "So break him then,"
The victim's fate was sealed.

That dock a lonely island there
And I a castaway,
The sea around alive with sharks
And hatred's livid spray.
But no one saw the wrecks of you
Or knew not where they lay.

The warders stood in perpetual stare
In regulation stance.
They watched each twitch and little move
In blank officious trance,
For ne'er this brat would take his life
Or even get the chance.

Silvery dust on beams of light
Ran by the curtains red.
I smelt the scent of affluence
And felt the creeping dread.
But lingering there unscathed by time
Was that, that courts the dead.

Hostile shadows, great swords of light
Stood guard in ranks of gloom.
Should e'er a truth be e'er conceived
It would die within the womb,
For truth is blackly murdered
In Diplock's room of doom.

"All arise," said a sharp-eyed rook,
And all arose but one.
The guest oppressed dropped timid eyes
The wretched few fell dumb,
For none were left in any doubt
The pig-in-wig had come.

The fat pig glared and all were sat
He moved his beady eyes
To fix them upon my worried look
In glare of pure despise.
And all the pawns fell into line
Disdain has no disguise.

The grunting pig he sneered and leered
And scratched his lofty snout.
He mumbled something rather snide
That died as it crawled out,
But carved a look upon his face
That cast aside all doubt.

A prosecuting hawk stood up
I sat as sparrow prey,
His shrivelled beak unleashed a shriek
That pinned me in my stay.
And ne'er I dared to even speak
For this was judgement day.

This case was clear cut, cruel by fear
And carved by hand of law,
The hidden hand that choked a man
His signature to draw.
While torturous screams haunt poor men's dreams
From deeds that no one saw.

The hovering hawk he swooped abroad
Arms outstretched as wings
His damning finger cut the air
In hurtling swishing swings,
And spat he venom 'pon the truth
In deadly lying stings.

There was no jury, none at all,
The pig-in-wig was right,
And only fools sought fit to stand

And challenge him with fight.
For this court is a farce, my friends,
And justice knows no light.

One by one they came slithering forth
And one by one to lie,
Those writhing snakes and dirty fakes
Called "witnesses" and why?
Because they witness what they wish
From closed or opened eyes.

They swear upon a holy book
They do so before God,
Yet they look toward the policeman
For prompting, wink and nod,
And don't you think, my honest friends,
That this is somewhat odd?

I saw them trip upon their ties
But ne'er they seemed to fall
For pig and hawk put words in mouths
That falter, stop or stall,
And who dare say that justice reigns
In Diplock's dirty hall!

There is no such thing as hope, friend,
Don't kid yourself, I thought.
Percentages of chance are years
And yours are truly wrought.
But don't despair, no ne'er do that,
Someday they'll too be caught.

"Me lord, the Special Branch have codes,"
Said he so honestly.
"We treat each suspect fair and square
No matter who he be."
A truth, I thought, they do at that
And do it murderously.

"Me lord, I gave him pleasantries
I gave him cups of tea.
I even begged him to confess
Upon my bended knee.
And after some more pleasantries
Me lord, he did agree."

"Sergeant, there seems to be some claim
That you forced him to confess.
And that you walked upon his spine
And beat him up, no less?"
"No! No! Me lord, that was his own
Self-inflicted mess!"

The doctor rose and took the stand
Said he just true to trait:
"Me lord, those words the sergeant said,
I must corroborate,
For it could quite well have been himself
Who made that bloody state."

"I can't accept that things weren't right!
Nor such a windy claim
That you were hurt in custody
And policemen were to blame.
For policemen do adhere to law
And I shall do the same!"

They do adhere to law, I mused,
But that law is their own.
It is a law unto itself
Whose face is never shown.
But I have seen it, yes I have
And brunt of it I've known.

I sat within the little dock
And gazed toward a friend.
He gazed right back with worried eyes

Bobby Sands

That said, this is the end.
And I just shrugged for well I knew
That this was usual trend.

They swore 'fore God, they swore 'fore man
They swore their lives away.
They 'dorned their halos jewelled with lies
The holy truth to slay.
And slew it cruel they did at that
And bled it where it lay.

They slew it with their devil tongues
Spat right into his face.
And crushed it in their bloody hands
In deathly black embrace,
And called on God they did, my friend,
To witness this disgrace.

The beady eyes they peered at me
The time had come to be,
To walk the lonely road
Like that of Calvary.
And take up the cross of Irishmen
Who've carried liberty.

That blackly little judge of man
He made his ritual speech,
"God's justice knows no bias," he said,
"'Tis dealt out fair to each.
For man must live and die," he said,
"'By every word he preach. . ."

"I've heard the words of honest men,"
The pig did dare to grunt.
"I see I have been met by truth
For truth stands at the front,
And only liars refuse to speak
When truth they must confront."

The liars have all been to the front
I thought—For what's the use,
Oppressed men are all born to death
They wear a ready noose,
But I have seen the rich man's "truth"
And shaken slavery loose.

"Thirty years," said the grey-wigged pig
"You'll count it, by the clocks.
Thirty years in a prison cell
By soothing, clinking locks.
And you'll rot in hell rest assure
In dungeons of H Blocks."

The pig he fled the room of doom
Judgement day was o'er.
The pawns they wore their evil smile
They'd done their evil chore.
And I was left in silent awe
With thirty years before.

They walked me through the door of doom
Like pig to slaughter pen.
But pigs are treated better
Than prisoners are, my friend.
And I in lonely fetters
Of captured Irishmen.

And men asked why men rise to fight,
To violence do resort,
And why the days are filled with death
And struggles' black report.
But see they not, these blinded fools,
Lord Diplock's dirty court.

Let all men know and know it well
That rich men judge the poor.
Working man 'fore bossman's eyes

Is just a sweating whore.
And rich men ne'er will bow to words
Of that, my friend, be sure.

'Tis but working men strong and bold
United, tight as one,
Who may hope to break the tyrant's grip
And see that splendid sun.
The splendid sun of freedom born,
A freedom dearly won.

3 The Torture Mill—H Block

On others' wounds we do not sleep
For all men's blood is red,
Nor do we lick the poor man's sore
Nor drink the tear he shed,
For king and knave must have a grave
And poorest are the dead.

And poorest are the lonely dead
Who stare at earthen sky,
And rot alone in skin and bone
Upon the spot they lie.
But poorer still are stupid fools
Who think they'll never die.

They found him on his own door-step
In crimson pool he lay,
His deathly eyes in fool's surprise
Stared blankly at the day,
For plain it seemed he'd never dreamed
That death would come his way.

In draped pine box he made his way.
To that hole of no return,
The morbid band moaned death's lament

So his very soul would churn,
But this sly soul had tortured men
And surely had to burn.

His black splashed hat lay 'pon the box,
'Twas flanked by ten and two.
Twelve grim men of this dead friend
That vengeance came and slew,
That haunting ghost that catches most
Had caught this bugger too.

The grave is deep, the grave is cold
A murky red clay tomb,
While underneath the body rots,
Above, the primrose bloom.
So do not cringe and do not whinge
For each will be there soon.

From dust to dust, ash to ash,
The wizened parson said,
As sprinkling clay in loud dull thuds
Fell down above the dead,
And covered up forever more
That fiend that luck had fled.

For he had tortured men no less
And by God he done it good,
For treacherous are the cunning cowards
And devious are the shrewd.
But bastards are the hated Screws
Who torture men in nude.

And he had tortured men no less
For he was such a Screw.
Yet! whinging voices cried aloud
What did this poor man do?
He only done what madmen done
Upon the silent Jew.

Bobby Sands

So bury him and let him lie
And play your brass tattoo,
But write above his marble stone
"Here lies a stinking Screw,"
For if men knew what he had done
They'd turn their backs and spew.

We do not sleep on others' wounds
Or lick their bleeding scars,
By avenues of marble halls
Citadels or towers.
For prisoners lie in darkened depths
Behind the prison bars.

So sleep we 'pon each day of pain
That screams within its wake,
And screeches at each shattered mind
How much dare you to take?
How much, how much, for pain is such
That even heroes quake.

Pitiful is the lonely man
Who watches night go by,
To hear the screams from comrades' dreams
The gentle sob or sigh.
But wretched is that lonely man
Who knows that he must die.

And who are we but mortal men
Who burn in others' hate,
And slump beneath the murderous load
Of torture's gruelling weight.
But though we slump we do not fall
And endless is our fate.

And endless is the fate of we
Who fight within the gloom,
For we have been imprisoned,

Since conceived, within the womb,
But freedom's fruit will blossom too
In the darkness of the tomb.

He will lie within the grave,
The grave he dug with pain,
And pain of those who wear no clothes
And he dug it with disdain.
So there he lies 'neath earthen skies
In everlasting shame.

There was no star nor heaven's blaze
No trumpet blast nor horn,
No angel chorus sang in praise
To harken forth the morn.
For freemen lay in tears of grief
No saviour to them born.

Blessed is the man who stands
Before his God in pain.
And on his back a cross of woe
His wounds a gaping shame.
For this man is a son of God
And hallowed be his name.

The word came up the frozen pipes
That one was *off the air,*
And each man knew a dirty Screw
Had got his dues somewhere.
And each man knew we'd get it too
But who could give a care.

The whispered word the naked heard
Was passed from cell to cell,
And each soul smiled like naughty child
At what he had to tell.
For though we lay in slow decay
We heard his requiem bell.

Bobby Sands

He sat upon the filthy foam
His piercing eyes ablaze.
He stared as if he did not know
Like one within a daze.
But all men wear this crazy stare
Within the dirty Maze.

He stared upon nightmarish walls
As if they held the key.
To some dark secret of his soul
That would not set him free,
That hidden cleft through which but death
May find tranquillity.

He did not smile like naughty child
'Pon hearing what had passed,
Nor did he muse the morbid news
Nor question did he ask,
But unleashed a yell that frightened Hell
Like Gabriel's trumpet blast!

He laughed aloud behind a shroud
Of yellow skin and beard,
His blazing eyes burned with despise,
And madness of the weird.
And thought I then, to this poor friend,
A devil had appeared.

But knew I well in this dark hell
That torture does such things,
And leaves the brain like bare terrain
From which but madness springs.
And knew I well that in each cell
The sanest hung on strings.

We do not wear the guilty stare
Of those who bear a crime,
Nor do we don that badge of wrong

To tramp the penal line.
So men endure a pit of sewer
For freedom of the mind.

Nor do we bend to black-clad men
When torture scream is shrill,
They who slight God's given right
Of each to his free will,
So bend the back upon the rack
Of H Block torture mill.

Each cell does smell within that hell
Where the naked cough and spit.
Each wall is smeared with something weird,
So the governor must admit,
On jail cement is excrement,
But what he means is shit!

And so it is this pit of his
Is reeking high and low,
This dirty mess he made no less
By casting men to woe.
And now he squirms not from the germs
But what the world may know.

They tramped us down into the ground
And righteous men ne'er spoke.
And in our nude they fixed us good
For freemen must be broke.
What could be done but smear that scum
And Christ it is no joke!

They do not call you by your name
Nor nickname try to fix,
For love and hate are hard to mate
And right and wrong don't mix.
You have no name but number plain,
"Move on, ten sixty-six!"

Bobby Sands

They call us "cons" to right their wrongs
They do it with a pen.
They call us "crims" to suit the whims
Of politics, my friend.
But they can call us all they want
For the people call us Men.

From wall to door he walked the floor
Listening for a sound.
Each sudden creak or sneaky squeak
Sent him swishing round,
His bulging eyes so terrorised
Near fell upon the ground.

That eight foot space 'twas freedom's grace.
To exercise the bones,
With every step the body wept
In awful moans and groans,
And sounded like the gnawny grind
Of some one rubbing stones.

Beneath the sky men live and die
For man must die from birth.
And some ne'er see the flower or tree
Or know their lovely worth,
But in the gloom or prison tomb
Men crave for Mother earth.

There are no trees or cooling breeze,
To soothe our reddened eyes,
Like clinging briar the grey blade wire
Strangles cloudy skies,
And every cloud's a bleeding shroud,
And crowned with thorns it cries.

To dance and prance to love's romance
Is elegant and neat.
To wine and dine on red port wine

Is such a tasty treat.
To eat and sit where you've just shit!
Is not so bloody sweet!

Shocked you are, by far, by far
But shock you do now know.
Perhaps you say this poet's way
Is crude and very low?
But in the blocks men have had shocks
That filled the very po!

You do not quake each day you wake
To a hymn of dawn that roars,
When stern-faced rats in black splashed hats
Steal in for Satan's chores,
And with their batons high and hard
They batter down the doors.

You do not lie like pigs in sty
Upon a concrete bed.
Or watch them come before the sun
To count the living dead,
And ask of Christ this sacrifice
Maybe your penance paid.

You do not pray through each long day
Or pray into the night,
Take air in sips with prayer on lips,
To sleep may steal your fright.
And cross your head in silent dread
As darkness turns to light.

From wall to door he walked the floor
Like a man trapped in a mine,
And looked at me quite desperately
Behind a mask of grime.
For with each step he sank a depth
From which he had to climb.

And time is but an endless rut
And each man in his own,
And some climb out and some do not
And some lie dumb and prone,
While time goes by like cloudy sky
Its destiny unknown.

Now keeping time to squelch of slime
He marched a quickened pace,
Those blazed eyes like angry skies
Rolled round his ashened face,
And on he went like a regiment
That fled the battle place.

He ran that floor from wall to door
And glared at me quite dumb,
And I at him like mortal sin
For words just would not come.
For this was hell and in this cell
A soul was on the run.

Each wretched soul in that vile hole
Had one thought on his mind:
We'd get it too was what we knew
When night time would unwind,
'Cause each man knew just what was due
For each man wasn't blind.

For come the morn as day is born
And all is deadly still,
The dirty Screws on muffled shoes
Creep in to make a kill,
But first of all they shriek and bawl
Like madmen doing drill.

They'll let us know it's time to go
And gauntlet they will form,
From wing towing their blows will sting

Like hornets in a swarm,
And naked men must run its end
Like seabirds in a storm.

So each man knew just what was due
And each man paced the floor.
A creeping dread was greatly fed
As one would think once more,
And dread set in and ate like sin
Right to your very core.

Some rant and rave with awful crave
For nicotine and smoke,
To such degrees that 'pon their knees
The very dust they hoke,
Elusive ends in gasping bends
To kill their choking yoke.

And some inhale to such avail
The smouldering blanket shred,
For nerves are terse and options scarce
To tame the killing dread,
So pale as death with burning breath
They drag each reddened thread.

The crawling day just ran away
For time runs fast 'fore dread,
And near and near we came to fear
As minutes fell down dead.
And any hope we tried to grope
Jumped up and promptly fled.

The dying night was bleeding white
The dark was on the run
And dawning day drove it away
Before the blood-eyed sun,
And by the shadows on the walls
We knew that they had come.

Bobby Sands

There was no star nor heaven's blaze
No trumpet blast nor horn,
No angel chorus sang in praise
To harken forth the morn,
For freemen lay in tears of grief
No saviour to them born.

Blessed is the man who stands
Before his God in pain,
And on his back a cross of woe
His wounds a gaping shame,
For this man is a son of God
And hallowed be his name.

They beat the flaps with drumming wraps
And banged the pipes and doors.
So terrified we almost cried.
Before their vicious roars,
And though we froze for lack of clothes
The sweat oozed out our pores.

The dirty Screw wears black and blue
The devil knows him well,
And he and they from grey of day
Call into every cell,
And stoke the fires that search desires
Within the blocks of hell.

Still keeping time to squelch of slime
He marched a quickened pace,
Those blazened eyes like angry skies
Rolled round his ashened face,
And on he went like a regiment
That fled the battle place.

He ran that floor from wall to door
And glared at me quite dumb.
And I at him like mortal sin

For words just would not come.
For this was hell and in this cell
A soul was on the run.

Then came the reek of stomach weak
For some men retch with fear,
And worse again and ne'er the shame
The bowels of men appear.
For listen, friend, we don't pretend,
There are no heroes here.

The double-lock flew back in shock
Then came the first man's name.
'Twas times like this that cowardliness
Would leave a man in shame,
'Cause each man knew just what was due,
For all would get the same.

He ran wild-eyed like screaming child
Before a horde of rats,
They beat him down upon the ground
With thumps and thuds and slaps,
And then within a ring of sin
They kicked him to collapse.

They sneered and cheered, leered and jeered
At their dirty handiwork.
Each dirty Screw knew what to do,
Each wore a dirty smirk,
They flaunted hate, these men of state,
And each one went berserk.

They grab your legs like wooden pegs
And part them till they split.
They pry and spy and even try
To look in through the split.
Both north and south to find your mouth
To try look "out" of it.

To roll and droll on country stroll
Is quite a pleasant flip,
To chase and race through open space
Is such a thrilling skip,
To trot like swine through one's urine
Is not so nice a trip.

The dirty Screws they stand in two's
Along that tortured way.
Their batons drawn to beat upon
The frantic screaming prey,
"Tis but a job," they whinge and sob,
And take the devil's pay.

And scruples none, not even one,
Do hold this gruesome band.
How they debase their own cruel face
Is hard to understand.
But to remain untouched by shame
Is damning to their clan.

He ran that floor from wall to door
And glared at me quite dumb.
And I at him like mortal sin
For words just would not come.
For this was hell and in this cell
A soul was on the run.

And on and on they moved along
While we listened to the fray.
And somewhere near I chanced to hear
The first bird of the day,
Its dawning tune rang out like doom
And died in disarray.

They search your hair with greatest care
Shine lights inside your nose,
Your mouth and ears and very fears

They scrutinise like crows,
And may I ask, what is their task,
For we men wear no clothes?

They search your back and every crack
Gloomy-faced and stern,
And scrape and gape at every space
Like doctor seeking germ.
But lewd and crude they fix you good
To make the patient squirm.

There is no crime in deed or mind
No dirty evil lure,
That any Screw would rue to do
To each let this be sure.
They stoop so low they undergo
The morals of a whore.

To bask 'neath sun is lazy fun,
To sport a tan is swell,
Complexions fair and dusky hair
Are like a wispy spell.
But torture's mark is grim and stark
And does not suit so well.

They squat us o'er the blackened floor
Upon a mirror clear.
They shine a light for better sight
To see what may appear.
I sometimes think they have a kink
The way they jook and peer!

And blood is hot and blood can clot
For I saw it on the ground.
It seems to say that gone this way
Was pack of horse and hound,
But no smart cox or shrewdest fox
Could take this hunt to ground.

The medic's job though somewhat odd
Is to patch a body's hurt.
To nurse a man not curse a man
When body is inert.
Though in the Blocks these humane chaps
Just rub your face in dirt.

Like screaming child I ran wild-eyed
Before that horde of rats.
They beat me down upon the ground
With thumps and thuds and slaps.
And then within that ring of sin
They beat me to collapse.

Like drunken man who cannot stand
I swayed like wavering tree,
And felt worse than a sea-sick man
Upon a raging sea.
And worse again I bore a pain
That almost scuttled me.

The ace of spades is sign of Hades,
The Screw the sign of shame.
Whoever mates with these black apes
No doubt will bear the same;
And in their grave they'll rue and rave,
The marriage of that name.

In angry tear with grip of hair
They dragged me at a trot,
They strangled me, entangled me,
Like squeezing tight garrotte,
Then threw me in a cell of sin
My body in a knot.

He ran wild-eyed like screaming child
I heard their bawling cries.
And ran he did to painful bid

With terror in his eyes,
Until he fell into that cell
In lemming-like surprise.

"Hurry up!! and scurry up!!"
They screamed at tearing men.
We heard the cracks and baton whacks
For every step were ten,
And every man swore by their clan
To kill the cutty wren.

Then all went still they'd had their fill
And Christ they had it full.
To do such things take special things
Learnt in the devil's school,
For when it comes to gauntlet runs
The wicked are no fool.

'Tis joyful thing in early spring
The morning lark to hear,
The mistle thrush on far-off bush
Crooning sharp and clear.
But who may know if lark or crow
With bleeding, busted ear?

Or who may sniff the fragrant whiff
Of daffodils and rose,
The wild green hills in autumn trills
Awaiting winter snows,
When worse the course you have to nurse
A broken bloody nose.

We fought back tears and scorned our fears
And cast aside our pain
And to our doors we stood in scores
To conquer their black fame
For loud and high we sang our cry
"A Nation once again!"

Bobby Sands

There was no star no heaven's blaze
No trumpet blast nor horn,
No angel chorus sang in praise
To harken forth the morn,
For freemen lay in tears of grief
No saviour to them born.

And blessed is the man who stands
Before his God in pain,
And on his back a cross of woe
His wounds a gaping shame.
For this man is a son of God
And hallowed be his name.

They lounge in might and glory bright
This empire once so grand.
With bloody fleets and dirty feats,
They built it without span.
But tank or gun they have not one
To break a blanket man.

We do not wear the guilty stare
Of those who bear a crime,
Nor do we don the badge of wrong
To tramp the penal line.
So all endure this pit of sewer
For freedom of the mind.

Nor do we bend to black clad men
When torture scream is shrill
They who slight God's given right
Of each to his free will.
So bend the back upon the rack
Of H Block Torture Mill.

The Battle for Survival

The greatest part of each seemingly eternal day that I face is filled with thought. I have nothing else to help pass the time during the long, never-ending hours. Boredom and loneliness are terrible things, continual and unrelenting. I have but one weapon to overcome them: my own thoughts.

To pass the time and to keep warm I pace the floor. Sometimes I stand gazing out of the cell window at the grey barbed wire or simply just sit upon my dirty damp mattress on the floor in the corner of my dungeon-like tomb. But all the while I'm thinking of something, somebody, or some place. It may be deep, serious thought or daydreaming to escape the reality of my nightmarish situation.

Again, I might be, and often as not I am, worrying, thinking of what is going on around me, or what may lie before me. Each day my comrades and I face a psychological battle for survival. It is a very intense struggle and the enemy is unmerciful.

For someone who is contented, or unconcerned with any worry, living what is termed an everyday life, you may find my psychological circum-stances hard to comprehend. For two reasons: firstly, my inability to describe the psychological struggle of myself and of my three hundred and fifty comrades; secondly, it is terribly hard, if not inconceivable, to conjure up in one's imagination the pain and stress of psychological torture or to know its many forms or to understand its various effects.

Imagine how it would feel to be locked up naked in solitary confine-ment, twenty-four hours a day, and subjected to total deprivation of not only common, everyday things, but of basic human necessities, such as clothes, fresh air and exercise, the company of other human beings.

In short, imagine being entombed, naked and alone, for a whole day. What would it be like for twenty torturous months?

Now again, with this in mind, try and imagine just what it is like to be in this situation in surroundings that resemble a pigsty, and you are crouched naked upon the floor in a corner, freezing cold, amid the lingering stench of putrefying rubbish, with crawling, wriggling white maggots all around you, fat bloated flies pestering your naked body, the silence is nerve-racking, your mind in turmoil.

You are sitting waiting on the screws coming to your cell to drag you out to be forcibly bathed. You have heard and seen the horrible results of this from many of your comrades at Mass. You know only too well what it means: the skin scrubbed from your body with heavy brushes. The screws have told you that you are next. You wait all day, just thinking. Your mind is wrecked. Maybe they've forgotten, you kid yourself; but you know they never forget.

They don't come. The next day is the same, and the next, and the next. You become more and more depressed. For days your thoughts have been the same, a mass of fear, fearing what lies ahead.

Consider being in that frame of mind every day! Knowing in your mind that you're to be beaten nearly senseless, forcibly bathed, held down to have your back passage examined or probed. These things are common facts of everyday H Block life.

It is inconceivable to try to imagine what an eighteen-year-old naked lad goes through when a dozen or so screws slaughter him with batons, boots, and punches, while dragging him by the hair along a corridor, or when they squeeze his privates until he collapses, or throw scalding water around his naked body. It is also inconceivable for me to describe, let alone for you to imagine, our state of mind just sitting waiting for this to happen. I can say that this physical and psychological torture in the H Blocks has brought many men to the verge of insanity.

We are in a very, very bad state now. What will we be like at the end of the day, or in the years to come? My mind is scarred deep. It is as equally a worrying thought that we may end up unable to even think at all! With that in "your" mind, I will leave off. Think about it, but just don't leave it at that.

Bury Me in My Blanket

"Well, how are ye'z?"

Dear God not him again! I said to myself. It was yer man the screw round to pester us once again in his spare time. He sounded so happy I thought Deputy Governor Miles had been spotted in the car park.

"Well how are ye'z?" he said once again, receiving an overwhelming tumultuous reply of dead silence.

"I've some bad news for ye'z," he said.

"Ah Dear God!" I knew it. "Deputy Governor Miles was spotted in the car park," I speculated aloud.

"No, no! Far worse than that," he said.

"Brian Faulkner's alive and well," someone else ventured.

"Yez'll not laugh in a minute when ye'z hear what I have to say. Don't ye'z want to hear what I have to say?" he said once again receiving a tremendous encouraging piece of continual dead silence. Taking a reddener, which now came natural to him, he said, "Well ye'z are going to hear it anyway," in his naa, na, naa, na, childish voice which also came natural to him (spoilt brat).

"Mr Mason," he said, bowing his head at the very mention, "Mr Mason has stated that your families are encouraging you to stay on this blanket protest 'cause the IRA are paying them money!"

This vital unparalleled piece of useless information was received by what could only be described as an uncontrollable vulgar noise from out of a nearby cell, followed by the now almost customary burst of dead silence. Well, yer man, not to be outdone (which he always was), slipped the key into the lock in my door and slid the cell door open.

"How are ye doing?" he asked.

"A lot better than you have been this past five minutes," I answered in the faint hope of getting rid of him,

"What'd ye think of Mr Mason's comments?" he chirped, bowing his head again at the very mention and sounding as happy as Larry.

"Pretty exciting," I answered as sarcastically as I could in another attempt to get rid of him.

"Truth hurts," he said foolishly and edged himself in through the entrance of the door.

"Mind them poor wee maggots on the floor," I said, prompting a two foot withdrawal and the first tactical success to myself as he jumped back. "Well," I said, "it seems to me that Mr Mason . . . is there something the matter with your neck?" I interjected. He took a reddener and I carried on. "Well, it seems to me that your hero says the most foolish things of which only equally as foolish people care to pay heed to. I mean," I said watching his mouth drop, "thirty months we've been here, languishing naked, rotting away while being subjected to the most callous and brutal inhumanities and tortures, proclaiming our right as political prisoners of war, in pursuance of an ideal that cannot be bought or won with all the money in the world, and you and your little idiotic dictator are trying to tell us that what is keeping us going and what is fuelling our resistance is a god-damned few shillings that our families have never seen and who are pressurising us for a non-existent few bob! What is keeping us going is called the spirit of resistance, so tell that to Mr Mason. Are you bloody well sure that there's nothing wrong with your neck?"

He turned slamming the cell door behind him and stormed down the wing screaming, "Yez are all mad, Yez are all mad! Did ye hear me?" And once again this was greeted by a coordinated outstanding ovation of dead silence!

Five minutes later and no doubt having torn up all our priceless parcels of Kleenex tissues, he returned and worked his way back in to my cell.

"Spirit of resistance!" he sniggered. "Ideals," he mimicked. "We'll see bloody well all about that if you have to bloody well die here," he said.

"I've thought about that too," I said, "and it's hard to say to oneself that one is prepared to go to such an extreme, but then we are special prisoners and we are struggling for a special cause, so if I should die here, tell "Mr Mason" to bury me in my blanket and for God's sake keep your head at peace and you have yours examined like a good lad."

The Window of My Mind

When one spends each day naked and crouched in the corner of a cell resembling a pigsty, staring at such eyesores as piles of putrefying rubbish infested with maggots and flies, a disease-ridden chamber pot, or a black, disgustingly scarred wall, it is to the rescue of one's sanity to be able to rise and gaze out of a window at the world.

My cell window, fortified by thick concrete slabs which serve as bars, affords me with a view of nothingness, unless a barbed wire jungle and rows of blank, faceless tin timbers offer an artistic appreciation unknown to me. It's what passes by, lingers, or materialises in front of my humble little window that saves me, that can dampen depression, allow me to contemplate, serve as an enjoyable distraction from my surroundings, and provide me with a once unknown pleasure.

On a dreary, dull, wet, morale-attacking November afternoon, when one's stomach is empty, and when the monotony begins to depress and demoralise, it is soothing in many respects to spend a half an hour with one's head pressed against the concrete slabs, gazing in wonder, and taking in the antics of a dozen or so young starlings bickering over a few stale crusts of bread. Circling, swooping, sizing up and daring an extra nibble, continually on their guard, and all their tiny nerves on end, the young starlings feud among themselves, the greedy one continually trying to dominate and always wanting the whole haul to himself, fighting with his comrades whilst the sparrow sneaks in to nibble at the spoils.

But the ruler of the kingdom of my little twenty-yard arched view of the outside world is the seagull, who dominates, steals, pecks, and denies the smaller birds their share. The seagull takes it all. In fact, his appetite seems insatiable. He goes to any length to gorge himself. Thus I dislike the seagull, and I often wonder why the starlings do not direct their attention to the predator, rather than each other. Perhaps this applies to more than birds.

During the summer months, finches were abundant, and the music of the lark a constant symphony of sound and a reminder of life. The various crows, the odd magpie, and the little wagtails are still to be seen and heard from dawn to dusk.

In the late evening, when most of the prisoners of war are sleeping, when a hush descends, amplifying the gentle sound of a breeze, one can gaze upon the ocean of sky and the multitude of stars that seem embedded and ablaze in that black root of nothingness that not even the moon in all her beaming regalia can penetrate, and one can dream a thousand dreams of yesterday, of childhood and happiness, of love and joy, and escape through make-believe and fantasy. The evils that engulf each day are forgotten about, and tomorrow as far away as the unreachable stars.

On many a summer evening and cold winter night I stand with only my old shabby blanket wrapped tightly around me, my breath pouring out into the blackness, in ghostlike clouds, just dreaming. Many a day in the eternal hours, I stand watching the birds and listening to the lark, trying to discover its whereabouts in that stagnant blue ocean above me that represents the outside world, and I long for the liberty of the lark.

I suppose, to many, a few birds, the sound of a lark, a blue sky, or full moon, are there, but stay unnoticed most of the time. But, to me, they mean existence, peacefulness, comfort, entertainment and something to view, to help forget the tortures, brutalities, indignities and evils that surround and attack my everyday life.

Today, the screws began blocking up all the windows with sheets of steel. To me this represents and signifies the further torture of the tortured, blocking out the very essence of life: nature!

A few words I once read came echoing back to me today: "No one can take away from a person his or her ability to contemplate. Throw them into prison, give them hard labour, unimaginative work to do, but you can never take away from them the ability to find the poetry and music in life." And I also realised that, here, my torturers have long ago started, and still endeavour, to block up the window of my mind.

Wing Shift in H Block

The boys all knew two days before
It always was that way.
It gave a man two days respite
To worry sick and pray.
And some grew ill and some went dumb,
Some paled with awful fear.
I heard the very birds walk by
As crossing day drew near.

The minutes ticked from hour to hour,
The days stole blackly in,
He looked at me with scary eyes,
And I with same at him,
And ne'er we spoke but paced the floor,
And wished it was our day,
For greatest curse was listening
While comrades ran the fray.

They beat their batons on the pipes,
And roared in wild-mouthed glee,
'Twas times like this a man grew weak,
And buckled at the knee.
We knew their terror game all right,
And they our trembling fright,
He looked at me and I at him,
In matching deathly white.

The grillman called the dreaded words,
My God, the whole block shook,
"Lock 'em up," he cried and cried again,
"No witnesses may look."

We stewed like prunes in deathly hush,
And stomachs gave to fear,
For men do mess the corner floor,
When crossing time's so near.

We glided back and forth the cell,
Our blankets swishing time,
And each little creak echoed loud,
In startling eerie chime.
The quiet pressed in silent squeeze,
'Twas a petrifying thing,
I said to him in whispered dare,
"The devil's in that wing."

He passed me by like flitting ghost,
I met his eyes aglare.
They danced like hurtling raindrops do
Cascading everywhere.
And we heard the slam of heavy door,
'Twould not be long we knew,
We sighed the sigh of fettered men,
To brave the tempest through.

We heard the first one come afar,
Like thunder in the clouds,
He rolled across from "B" to "C,"
Sent on by yelling crowds.
We heard the stamp of heavy boot,
The slap and crash of hand,
That left us squirming nought to do,
Like fish upon dry land.

Dear God we sensed their evilness,
Each blow we felt at heart,
As comrades fell upon the ground,
It tore our souls apart.
"Move! Move!" they screamed, those cowardly Screws,
And move by God they did.

Bobby Sands

What naked man would dare defy,
The batons wacking bid.

They hung the boys like spit-eyed pigs,
O'er table top spread rude,
Where they would kick like new born child,
Embarrassed in their nude.
They pulled each limb so far apart,
You felt the body tear.
They crucified you in your fear,
And hung you in the air.

The mirrors shone by flashing lights,
Detectors bleeped for steel,
But all the dirty probing tools,
Could sense not what we feel.
He passed me by as white as chalk,
His eyes in hateful glow,
Says he in choking trembling words,
"There's twenty more to go."

"There's twenty more to go," said he,
As they ran in naked file,
And smashed 'gainst grills and wielding blows,
In reeling drunken style.
They beat their batons loud and hard,
As beaters of the hunt,
Like white gazelles the naked fell,
Brought down by torture's brunt.

The silence came in wake of pain,
For all had run that hell,
And lay they panting sore and glad,
Of reaching that dark cell.
And lay we now with beating heart,
For next to move were we,
Such are the trials of blanket men,
In the depths of H Block Three.

I Fought a Monster Today

I fought a monster today and once more I defeated the monster's army. Although I did not escape, I survived to fight another day. It was hard; harder today than ever before, and it gets worse every day. You see I am trapped and all I can do is resist. I know some day I will defeat this monster, but I weary at times. I think and feel that it may kill me first.

The monster is shrewd. It plays with me, it humiliates me, and tortures me. I'm like a mouse in comparison to this giant, but when I repel the torture it inflicts upon me I feel ten feet tall for I know I am right. I know that I am what I am, no matter what may be inflicted upon me, it will never change that fact.

When I resist, it doesn't understand. You see it doesn't even try to comprehend why I resist. "Why don't you give in to me?" it says. "Give in! Give in to us!" the monster's army jibes. My body wants to say: "Yes, yes, do what you will with me. I am beaten, you have beaten me." But my spirit prevails. My spirit says: "No, no, you cannot do what you want with me. I am not beaten. You cannot do what you want with me. I refuse to be beaten."

This angers the monster. It goes mad. It brutalises me to the point of death. But it does not kill me. I often wonder why not? But each time I face it, death materialises before me. The monster keeps me naked. It feeds me. But it didn't feed me today because it had tried so hard to defeat me and failed. This angered it once more, you see. I know why it won't kill me. It wants me to bow before it, to admit defeat.

If we don't beat it soon it will murder me. Of this I am certain. It keeps me locked up in a dark smelly tomb and it sends its devils to keep me on edge, to keep the torture going. Each time the door of my tomb opens, the black devils attack me! They nearly won yesterday. It was inhuman. They beat me into unconsciousness. I think, "Is this really happening to me?" and, "Can this happen in this day and age?"

Monsters do not exist. Nor do devils. There cannot be so many devils. I'm mad. Yes, that's it, I'm insane. But my pain, suffering, and grief are real. It must be all real. No, I'm right, I know I'm right. I must resist, I have nowhere to run. My tomb may be my grave. I'm surrounded by a barbed wire jungle. The monster roars at me: "You shall never get out of here. If you don't do as I say I shall never release you."

I refuse.

My body is broken and cold. I'm lonely and I need comfort. From somewhere afar I hear those familiar voices which keep me going: "We are with you, son. We are with you. Don't let them beat you." I need to hear those voices. They anger the monster. It retreats. The voices scare the devils. Sometimes I really long to hear those voices. I know if they shout louder they will scare the monster away and my suffering will be ended.

I remember, and I shall never forget, how this monster took the lives of Tom Ashe, Terence MacSwiney, Michael Gaughan, Frank Stagg, and Hugh Coney, and I wonder each night what the monster and his black devils will do to me tomorrow.

They always have something new. Will I overcome it? I must. Yes, I must. Tomorrow will be my seven hundred and fortieth day of torture—an eternity. Yes, tomorrow I'll rise in the H Blocks of Long Kesh. Yes, tomorrow I'll fight the monster and his devils again!

Alone and Condemned

The heavy steel door of the punishment cell slammed shut behind me. In a bewildered daze I vaguely heard the jingle of keys and the steady footsteps fading away in the wake of its thunderous echo. An ungodly silence fell, leaving only the sound of my sharp rasping breaths.

My eyes flashed at the bareness of my humble surroundings. A wooden board for a bed, a concrete block for a stool, a concrete slab as a table. A bright light burned high above me, reflecting off the chalk-white walls, and the severe cold bore through my body and numbed my bare feet. Naked, alone, and condemned, I began to pace the small, freezing cold cell; my thoughts in an entangled mess, riddled with panic, worry and fear. Condemned! "We'll be back in eight hours," that's what they said. Jesus, what time is it now? Eight hours, that's all I've left.

It will hurt. I know it will hurt. Everyone says it hurts. Oh God, it's not happening to me. It's not happening, I'm trapped. Entombed! No escape! Nowhere to hide. And nowhere to run. I'm condemned to face what awaits me in eight hours. I can't appeal, I can't plead. They won't even listen, they just laugh, they're glad, they revel in it. That's why they give me a warning of eight hours, to watch me sweat and worry. They have it well planned.

They're watching me now. They're watching me through that little slit in the cell door. They won't give me peace, but what peace can I find? I'm so scared, I can't even think right. I wish I was at home. I wonder what the family are doing now? Sitting around the fire in a nice warm room having tea. Jesus, it's getting colder. My feet are blue. I wonder what they are thinking? What would they think if they knew what is to happen to me? It would only make it worse, they would suffer, they would worry so much, but maybe they have secretly been expecting this, and never said so. Maybe it's better they don't know.

They won't break my spirit. I won't let them do that. They can do what they will with me, and I won't concede my spirit. Yes, that's it. Calm down, fight back, show them your spirit, settle down, and get ready for the ... There's a Bible in the corner—flick through it and stop thinking about it. Six hours! Take heart. . . . The prophet Sirach: "Blessed is he whose heart does not condemn him, and who does not give up his hope." Remember that. Remember those words. I'm all right. I won't give up hope. No, I won't give up hope.

They're watching again. Ignore them. Let on you don't see them. Jesus, it's freezing. It's so quiet, it's ghostly. Walk again, keep moving, get your body warm. How long left now? What time is it? I'm losing track. Have a guess. Five hours left, maybe less. I must be ready. I'm shaking again. Don't fail now. Get it right, they'll be back. I'm depressed! Jesus Christ! I'm cracking, I'm going insane. . . I wish I had someone to talk to, even for a few minutes.

Keys! The jingle of keys. Footsteps! They're coming back. Jesus it's not time yet. They've tricked me, they're coming for me now. Don't fail, remember your spirit. "Blessed is he who does not give up his hope." Jesus, Mary and Joseph, watch over me and protect me. Key in the door. It's open. Oh, dear God. . .

"Grub up! What are you gaping at, son? Take it." (You'll pay some day, you bastard, you'll pay.) "Don't stir. Take it in, you tramp." Got it. He's shutting the door. Slam! Keys jingling. They're going, they're leaving. Thank God. Thank God, they've gone. Don't give up hope, there's hope still.

Cold food, no knife, no fork, only a plastic spoon. I'm not hungry, my stomach's turning. Nerves again. I must calm down. Meet them with dignity. That's a word: "Dignity." They can't take that from me either. Naked as I am, treated worse than an animal, I am what I am. They can't and won't change that. A cigarette would be nice. It's so long since I've had a cigarette or warm clothing or slept in a dry bed. I forget what it's like to live. I must be shocked, I don't even feel the cold any more. I've lost the feeling in my poor tortured feet. It doesn't matter. It won't be long now. It's creeping closer.

Two hours. Time waits on no man. I'm exhausted. God, I'm tired. I wish I could lie down and go to sleep, and wake up out of this nightmare. They're watching me again. Keep walking. I'm sure they don't even feel guilty. Money consoles their conscience. That is their purpose in life, to gain as much of it as possible. They're mindless, merciless parasites. Torture mongers. Yes, that's what they are. Some day their turn will come. They'll have to answer for everything!

It's getting dark. Winter nights. I hate winter. It's so cold and dark and lonely. I wish I was free. . . . God, my head's splitting, migraine again. I feel really bad. It's the waiting, that's worse than anything. When it happens it will be over and that will be it, but it's the waiting.

I feel like the only person left in the world. I'm so isolated. Fear is a terrible thing, but I must keep my head up. My spirit will survive. They expect me to give up, to break down, but they're going to be disappointed. I shall resist. It's only natural that I should be afraid. Who wouldn't be? It must be nearly time. I can hear them moving about. There will be plenty of them, there always is. God, life is hard for the oppressed, but to fight back is a victory. To remain unbroken in spirit is a great victory.

Here they come, keys jingling and their heavy footsteps clattering. Get ready, face them. Jesus, this is it. This time, dear God, protect me. "Get on your feet, tramp, we're coming." I'm shaking again. Remember your spirit. They won't break that. Keys in the lock, the door is open. Jesus, there must be a dozen of them. "Right, you, let's go."

"I'm. . . I'm not going."(Laugh all you want you torture-mongers.)

"What did you say?"

"I said I'm not going." (Some day you will all laugh on the other side of your faces.)

"You're going all right, son. Get him out."

Jesus, they're on top of me, kicking and punching . . . I'm out of the cell, and in the corridor. Jesus, they're dragging me by the hair. My head's on fire, my eye is bleeding, they'll kill me!

"Right, get him into it. Get him into it!" Jesus, it's stinging the eyes out of me! "Get the brushes." They're scrubbing the skin from my back, my flesh is burning, they're murdering me. My face and body are covered in blood and marks.

"Give it to him right. Give it to him right, so the rest of these bastards will see what they're going to get too."

Jesus! They're killing me. They're killing me. My head's light.

Remember your spirit. "Blessed is he who does not give up his hope."
Don't give in, don't give in, they can't break your spirit, they can't. . . .

A Tribute to Screws

In the blackness I awoke like a corpse in the grave,
Engulfed by the fear of a ghostly wave.
There were devils and angels by the foot of my bed
And they fought for my soul to the night sky fled.

With trembling lips I prayed in the gloom
Questioning my birth to die in a tomb.
The silence was angry and it bit deep in the mind
And it screeched in my face, "You're here for all time."

Four bare walls make this prison cell
The eight by eight space the prisoners call hell,
A concrete burden that is borne on the back
And some call it "bird" and some call it "wack."

'Tis a terrible feeling to be naked and down
To be dirty and itchy and to sleep on the ground,
'Tis a terrible feeling to live and feel like a rat
But 'tis worse again still to be treated like that.

They're ungodly dungeons these blocks of stone
Where a man meets himself and finds he's alone,
And black devils walk their inner ways
Where weeks seem like years and minutes like days.

Each morning they come banging on the doors
And bid us good morning with obscenities, strings of curses and roars.
Those murderers of hope, those rogues of the mind,
Oh, those god-fearing Christians when it comes dying time.

They're the dregs of the earth and the prisoners' curse.
Some call them Screws, but more call them worse.
They watch while you weep, they watch while you kneel
They watch while you die, your death's secret to steal.

'Tis hard to believe and yet even harder to take
Why a man will stoop lower than the belly of a snake.
Some plead greed of money, some just out of trait,
But the blackest devil is out of bigoted hate.

I've been locked in old dungeons and I've been locked in a Cage
And I've watched these scoundrels play their lives on a stage.
These rough and tough cowards, these hypocritical fools,
Who beat men to pulp and forget their own rules.

Is there such a damning indictment to this class of scum
Than the million crimes they have already done?
Be it in an African dungeon or the old Bastille
Their cruelty's no different, nor the pain that we feel!

Has ever such slyness been born 'fore men's eyes
Than these conniving bastards, these lovers of lies,
Has ever such a profession been developed so pure
That in lowliness it stands higher than the back of a whore.

Have ever such talents been seasoned to prime
Has ever such evil been born in a mind,
They make Judas seem innocent, they degrade even sin,
They'll be ejected from Hades, should they ever get in!

I know them I tell you and I know their stare,
And the crunch of their batons that reddens the hair.
I know their bravado, when they stand six to one
And likewise their cringing cowardliness, when they stand one to one!

They've broke our women's hearts, these dastardly fiends,
They've built towers of worry and crushed our young dreams,
They have greyed our poor mothers and helped dig our graves,
Is there one among you unsickened by the deeds of these knaves?

Was it only but yesterday that I sat in the space
With thirty Screws encroaching my thirty minutes' grace,
In the space of a pen where the families trade tears
In hushed whispers we tremble, betraying our fears.

And they, these magpies of expression and thought,
They cling to every syllable that our secrets be caught
Those sneaks, those creeps, those evil foxes,
Degrading the meek in dirty little visiting boxes.

There is no place more lonely than the prison cell
But 'tis a hundred times worse in this living hell.
Oh I have eaten rubbish, I live with maggots and flies,
Yet it's the human parasites I've learned to despise.

Filthy ragged threads clothe our pale bodies no end
We political dungeon dwellers—we oppressed blanket men.
We stand in the face of all—we bow to none,
For in the depths of the dungeons, there is nowhere to run.

People of Ireland, dwell well on these lines
They hold no joke nor jest nor simply rhyme,
If you knew but the torture, that the prisoners know well
You'd storm these dungeons, you'd tear down this hell.

But it's more pity that I hold for these exploiters of pain
Than a deep-scarred revenge for to see them in flame,
For be it heaven or the Republic, or what may come to pass
'Twill be woe to the devils of this murderous class.

They will be saluted with hatred, they'll be acknowledged by scorn,
And our ghosts will haunt them, and theirs not yet born.
Prisoners and bondsmen, mark me well you shall see
These whores of justice perish—at your liberty.

Christmas Eve

Something woke me, an unidentifiable sound that came sneaking through
the darkness and fled before the last clouds of sleep left me. In the blackness of my little cavelike surroundings I lay motionless on my bed, a damp
mattress upon the ground, listening to the gentle mourning sighs of the
wind passing through the night. A depressing silence surrounded me, broken only by my gentle breathing and the sighing wind.

The cold crept under the old worn blankets that covered me, and tortured my naked body. All hope of further escape through sleep departed, leaving me to my thoughts in the still night.

I've been here quite a long while now, an eternity. Sometimes I think it's not really happening—that I'll wake up out of this nightmare some time and it will be over. But it never happens, the pain never eases and the fear and tensions refuse to release their torturous grip. I think of life going on in the outside world, in faraway countries and at home, of people going about their daily lives.

From the darkness of my lonely tomb I feel as if I am buried without an existence, that my only purpose is a body to be tortured. My mind conjures up colourful images of smiling girls and laughing children, sunny days and summer evenings and God I long to be free, with my family. I long to be far away from the evils that confront me each day. My body is dying before its time and my limbs have been dormant for so long that my body aches.

How I long for a walk through the countryside, to touch the lush green grass, where there are open spaces, to hear the birds sing and to breathe fresh clean air. To live again, that's it—to live again. I'm not living now, I'm being tortured to death in this vile tomb where they have held me naked for so long, in so much pain.

The night is passing, my naked comrades lie sleeping and dreaming. They are with their families and friends for another short while. But the nightmare will return with the dawn and all comfort will flee with the dying night. All the little children will be wishing this night away. Tomorrow will be a day of delight for them.

All the mums and dads will be sneaking back to bed now, happy and contented, for their children's wishes have been met. Their reward will be great when tomorrow comes; the happy, smiling faces will tell all. Screams of delight will warm their hearts, but I shall see no smiling faces or hear those screams of delight, of the happy excited children. Only the screams of terror from the naked, wretched souls around me. Who will it be tomorrow or the next day? They never leave us alone. They never cease in their callous tortures to destroy our spirit. Dear God the night is dying once again.

My bed upon the ground is damp. I can find warmth nowhere. A warm clean bed would be so nice, or to sit in front of a grand fire with a good book. It's been years since I saw a book or a newspaper. I often wonder is the outside world still the same. Dear God, I sometimes ask myself is there nothing left but torture and misery?

I'm hungry and cold, but the world goes on. There will be warmth and happiness elsewhere this day. Dear God, don't let this night die on us so soon. It is dawning but I cannot see the light for they have blocked up my little window. But I can hear the birds sing. It's just another day for them.

The tensions and fears are descending and the evil is flooding the air. There is no music in the birds' song, only sorrow. Gates are beginning to clang and footsteps are breaking the dying silence of the already dead night. The jingle of keys—those hated keys, are sounding, giving warning to the sleeping souls around me.

It is time for "the families" to depart, for another day has dawned and a million dreams are fleeing as hundreds of naked bodies awake cold and hungry to confront yet another nightmare. The air is heavy, like the calm before the storm, and the gentle humming of "Silent Night" echoes from a nearby tomb. But there is no one smiling, there is no one screaming with delight, there is no happiness, just heartbreak and pain. Dear God, it's Christmas Day.

> The Screws they came early this morning,
> Of what was to come I had no warning.
> From my bed they dragged me naked and cold,
> No reason or cause was I told.
> I was put in a bath of scalding water,
> With every punch and kick it seemed to get hotter.
> My skin did blister, I had to get out.
> I didn't notice my cries my friends told me about.
> The Screws they laughed and thought it great fun,
> When they scrubbed my skin till the blood did run.
> Then the freezing cold water, I lost my breath.
> I would surely catch pneumonia, or even my death.
> But it didn't finish there, they had more in store
> As they spread-eagled me face downwards on the floor.
> They shaved my head and my beard to follow,
> While the hair and the dirt they made me swallow.
> By the feet they dragged me back to my cell,
> With the dirt and pain I was back in hell.
> To stop this torture we all must strive,
> But I'll never forget it while I'm alive—A bath!

I hate this place with all my heart
My cell, this prison every part.
For me it is a living hell
With dirt and pain and a stinking smell.
The Screws they have orders to break us all.
They do their best for it is Mason's call.
So they beat and starve us every day
While they seek a rise in their daily pay.
They have blocked our windows, we cannot see,
Is it snowing or is there a drought?
For us the sun it never shines
There's just the darkness and the lonely times.
I hate this place with all my heart,
Could you blame me, from the start?
But I tell the Screws and Mason too —
To break a blanket man you cannot do!
—I HATE THIS PLACE

Wing Shifts

Wearing halos of hate like Pharisees they stood.
Cloaks of purple more apt to their silver and black.
Calvary or Dachau a more fitting place for their deeds,
Gathered like wolves the oncoming naked to attack.

The air was tinged with fragrant violet,
A camouflage that the lingering ungodly stench tore through,
Tension held its breath like a silver guillotine, then fell!
As a steel gate yawned open and a voice said, "Right you!"

A lamb to the slaughter, a lark to the hawk,
So naked among many, with so many eyes burning hate!
Inspectors with detectors, forceps and reflectors,
Hang one's body like a pig to be left to much the same fate.

Hands tore at rings—the bonds of lovers—or the legacies of ghosts
   gone by,

Stripping a man of his very pride and all that he adorns,
Seeking for the secreted? Perhaps the flame of a spirit,
But you will be free, you naked men! who wear this crown of thorns!

"The Renegade"

I have chosen to forsake my principles and my whole person for favours
and alms, though I am unsure as to why I have done so. As I am unable to
distinguish between the truths and the untruths that I tell myself to justify
the harassing guilt that in times of loneliness and depression often plagues
me. Perhaps I am a weakling? But I could have shed my physical burden
and left it at that, but I didn't! I chose to go further, my mind overriding
my person, involving me deeper and deeper, causing me to perpetuate callous and evil deeds, diminishing the character of he who was once me, and
throwing him into the abyss of shame and no return.

But I never fought or even attempted to suppress my actions. Dare I
confess that I often revelled in them, and at times excelled myself to please
those to whom I have debased myself. I realise now that I am dependent
upon them, at their mercy. But my actions are not necessarily their bidding,
as I must continue to strive at every opportunity to satisfy their insatiable
appetite for misery and brutality, a brutality that must be inflicted upon
those I once knew and who once knew me, who now lie naked and rotting
and hating me.

Their fate should be my fate. Now it partly rests in my hands. They
hate me more than they hate their captors.

"RENEGADE!" they rasp at me in bitterness, thoughts of bloody,
gruesome revenge screaming from their eyes as I hand them their mutilated, cold and meagre evening tea. I feel no remorse then, I'm even somewhat glad that I have deprived them of their proper amount of food. I can't
stand the look on their wretched, pale faces. I would have done it anyway.
Yes! even if the screws had not willed it, I would have done it to them. I
won't let them look at me like that!

The screws give me cigarettes.

I blow the smoke into their wretched faces. I taunt, them, jibe at
them and insult them. I have mastered the art of humiliation well: upon
them! I laugh at them as they crawl upon the dirty floor to eat their scant

offerings in the total darkness that I have made. But out from the corners of the blackness come the screaming, piercing eyes of hatred and revenge and I feel glad that I have given the screws a hand to beat them.

I watch the screws literally slaughter them! hosing them down, battering their dilapidated shells of bodies with powerful jets of water, and I clap my hands in encouragement and delight. And when they lash the sickening, crippling, fuming disinfectant into their tomblike cells, I urge them on and laugh at their snide remarks and insults.

When they dragged them out of their filthy tombs, naked, and by the hair, to beat them into a bath of cold disinfected water to scrub the skin off their broken bodies, I screamed, "Give them more, give them more!"

But that deadly look in their stonelike eyes never vanished. They won't submit and be like me. Their spirit won't yield, only their bodies have succumbed and behind the facade of my invented confusion and untruths, I wish I were one of them!

But it is only he screaming back at me from within the realms of the bottomless pit of shame, and I delude no one with the thought of what I shall do when my time comes; the thoughts of what I shall do when I am released are of faraway lands that seem so inviting and colourful. I am bound there, my home town to be forgotten along with its valleys and fields and all the familiar voices and faces, sights and sounds and laughter.

My childhood and past and the avenues of my life are gone, never to be walked again. Foreign sounds and sights and alien voices and faces await me and who will know me, or know what I have done, except he who continues to remind me. There is no green in the colour, and who can I turn to? I can never turn back, for those screaming piercing eyes will never forget me! Nor I them.

Chest Out, Chin Up

He comes in the morning, well fed and fresh,
With a red tint to his cheeks, an even bronze on his flesh.
His clickety shoes check the rhythm of his step—
Chest out, chin up (*the old army deportment*) at which he's adept.

Like a barrage of cannon, steel monsters gape open and close,
Rippling the night tide that came from the hose.

He counts out the corpses barely covered by thread,
With his chest out, chin up, he cares not if they're dead.

He checks that the hungry are kept hungry when fed,
That the weary stay weary upon their damp bed,
That the fires of this hell burn the naked with cold,
With his chest out, chin up, he does what he is told.

"1066" his body stiffens in a jerk,
"Put on prison clothes and march out to work."
But for his military manner and authoritative tone,
With his chest out, chin up! he leaves on his own.

But in his regimental style with a stiff upper lip,
He never says die, no indeed, he never says quit.
He'll be back in the morning, when reveille is blown
With his chest out, chin up! No mercy to be shown!

"I Am Sir, You Are 1066!"

I must have died last night, because when I awoke this morning I was in hell. I don't really know how I got here. I don't think I've done anything to deserve being here. But I am here, and I am suffering terribly. I think I am in some sort of tomb. I can not see, as everywhere is in total darkness. I have no clothes on, except some sort of rag around my waist.

The floor of my tomb is covered in a wet mushy substance, the source or nature of which I don't know. There is a revolting stench lingering in the darkness and the air is warm, heavy and humid. There is something soft and damp lying in the corner, which seems to be some sort of bedding to lie upon.

I can hear heavy booming noises echoing all around me like thunder. Somehow it reminds me of heavy doors closing. I check the four walls of my tomb; there appears to be some sort of a door in one of the walls.

I can't understand my being here. What, I wonder, will become of me? I know I am a human being, although I'm naked and bearded. I can think and breathe. Am I in hell or some sort of limbo?

I can hear heavy footsteps approaching. They stop quite near to me.

There is someone or something nearby. I can hear it moving and breathing. It is watching me. More noise directly outside my tomb, a rattle of metal against metal. A square form of light begins to materialise, revealing an entrance as a door swings open. A figure stands in the grey dim light of the doorway. It is a human figure, dressed in what appears to be some sort of black uniform. It stands scrutinising me in silence for several seconds before letting out a terrifying yell that sends shivers through my body.

"I am Sir!" The words echo around my tomb. "I am Sir!" it bellows again. "I am Sir, you are 1066!" The door slams shut with a loud explosive boom, killing the dim light where the entrance had been. Still afraid to move I stand in the total darkness.

What is 1066, I think? Obviously it is me, but I can think, speak, smell and touch. I have all my senses, therefore I am not a number, I am not 1066. I am human, I am not a number, I am not 1066! Who, or what, is a Sir? It frightened me. It was evil. I sensed its hatred of me, its eagerness to dominate me, and its potential violent nature. Oh, what will become of me? I remember I once had a family. Where are they now? Will I ever see or hear of them again?

It's watching me. Once more the door opens. The dim light gives off a little illumination, revealing the black uniformed figure at the doorway. "I am Sir," it says, "Here is your food, 1066." A bowl is thrust into my hands as the door slams. Before the light dies I catch a glimpse of the floor. It is covered in filth and rubbish. There are several maggots clinging to my legs. The walls are covered with a mass of fat bloated flies.

Once again I am terror-stricken. I pace the floor, aghast at my surroundings. The bowl in my hand is cold, it contains some sort of porridge or gruel. The smell from it revolts me. I set it down on the floor. Pacing the floor in total darkness, I become engulfed with depression and despair. I wish I was dead. "But I am dead," I say aloud: I can't even kill myself, I think.

A breeze: I feel a breeze coming from the wall behind me. Feeling about, I touch a piece of cloth. I tug it and it falls. A light of great intensity hits my eyes, temporarily blinding me. My tomb becomes illuminated with light, revealing a window divided with concrete bars, Stepping closer, thousands of lights of every size and colour appear in my view. These lights are perched upon mountains of barbed wire that glitter and sparkle on the ink-black horizon.

Another step forward, and still looking straight ahead, a small building looms up in front of me, displaying a dozen or so windows all of which are brightly lit up. Several naked figures appear at the windows. The building is thirty yards away. I can see that all the figures are bearded, they all seem to be fairly young, but all their faces are pale and haggard. They are young men but have old men's faces. Am I gazing at death? These figures keep staring out at nothing, or pacing to and fro.

Footsteps again! I turn, apprehension again gripping me, to await my door being opened again. My new-found curiosity having diminished, I fall deeper into the depths of depression and despair. The thought of what lies on the other side of that door tortures me.

The door swings open, and several black uniformed figures stand there, surrounding a very small, fat, evil-looking person who evidently is their leader. They all glare at me, and then begin to shout at me: "I am a Sir," "I am a Sir," "You will conform," "Conform," "Conform."

They all grab me and start to beat and kick me while screaming: "You will conform," "You will conform in H Block. . ."

I awake, shouting and rolling in a filthy mattress on the floor. "Where am I?"

"Are you all right?" asks my cellmate.

"Where am I?"

"You are in your cell, you must've been having a nightmare," he says.

Our cell door opens and a black uniformed figure stands there, "Food," he says.

"What was that, Mister?" I ask.

"You call me Sir. You're in the H Blocks now! You're in H Block . . . Don't forget it, 1066!"

A Break in the Monotony

A thin layer of virgin snow covered all but a few spaces on the raven-black surface of the small, barren tarmac yard which lay dormant outside my cell window. The first snow of an unwelcome winter had just fallen as the grey light of another dying day faded.

The sky was a swirling mass of white snow clouds which hung threateningly, biding their time, waiting to release their monster load of freezing wintry flakes to consume the land and to paint the countryside a brilliant white. It was bitter cold. I had been huddled up in the corner of my freezing cell. The thin foam mattress which serves as my bed upon the cold concrete floor was damp, worn and dirty. I was sitting upon it trying to find some warmth with the flimsy worn blankets that I had tightly wrapped around my body.

Suddenly I was drawn to the window by the burst of chatter and excitement that came from two or three of my naked comrades a short distance away, as they announced the nasty change in the weather from the windows of their cavelike cells. It was a break in the almost eternal boredom and an unexpected change in the eyesore scenery of the grey steel crisscrossed wire and corrugated timbers.

The thin covering of snow glistened and glittered, blocking out the greyness and painting a new picture. It was something new to view to help pass the neverending hours, and, with the imminent promise of more to fall, the attraction drove the rest of the lads to the windows and the chatter built up.

Old, almost forgotten memories of winters gone by were dug up from the backs of scarred minds and were shared one after the other out the windows. The latest news was passed across to the boys on the other side of the wing who, being unable to see out of their recently blocked-up fortified windows, were driven to their doors by curiosity to seek the answer to the abnormal commotion from their excited comrades.

Another thin fall of snow fluttered through the descending darkness and a thousand coloured lights of orange, white and red illuminated the surrounding area, sparkling and reflecting off the frosted timbers, flashing upon the miles of snow-covered barbed wire, varnishing the smooth carpet that lay upon the yard. The snowflakes appeared like magic from out of the blackness above, floating as if to the music of the sighing wind to their earthly destination.

Clouds from my warm breath departed out of the paneless window into the night. Flakes of snow and frost clung to my long shaggy beard, and my eyes watered as the cold cut at my face and attacked my naked body. Who would imagine such a beautiful night could be found in a place filled with so much misery and pain, I thought, as I rubbed my hands and stamped my bare feet in an attempt to bring some warmth back into them. The chatter was dying at the windows, only the hearty and lonely remained braving the cold. Another sleepless night, I thought.

The concrete floor was so cold that to pace the floor would be impossible in bare feet. Three small flimsy blankets and lying upon a damp mattress would not provide enough warmth for escape through sleep. This night will be another night, huddled up in the corner, fighting the intense cold amid despairing thoughts, when pain and depression become almost overwhelming.

The wind is rising and growing angry; it will carry the blankets of falling snow in through the paneless windows. I am very, very cold now. I can stand here and freeze at the window gazing upon this barbed-wire jungle of colour and whiteness, or I can retreat to my little den in the corner of my tomb and gaze at my nightmarish surroundings, upon the dark sinister shadows which the filthy walls conjure up, or on the piles of scattered, once putrefying, now stinking rubbish which scars the floor.

Cold, tasteless porridge for breakfast tomorrow morning, the promise of yet another beating and another eternity, and another cold, cold night.

The monster is shedding its coat of a million snowflakes, the other monster is sleeping somewhere, tomorrow is the last day of the year. No one else is at his window now.

Dear God, I wonder how things are in Siberia?

The Privileged Effort

"Well?" says I to the effort as he limped into the cell with a grimace of pain on his face and his boggin' teacloth-like-towel hanging precariously around his waist.

"Well," says he, his eyes blazing as the screws slammed the door behind him. "Look at that," he motioned, stroking the backs of his two bare legs that were scraped, cut, bruised everywhere. "I'm *scríosta*,"says he. "They near broke my two legs."

"I got the same myself," says I, walking up and down with only a teacloth around me, trying to get warm.

"*Tiocfaidh ár lá*," says the effort, mumbling and cursing away to himself and mentally killing all sorts of screws.

"Three times they booted me over the top of that mirror," says he, all flushed and raging. "And then they got me squatting over the top of it naked, and jumped on my legs until I fell on top of it and smashed it."

"I heard the crash," says I, thinking it's only a quarter to eight in the morning, and here we are naked and freezing, cut, bruised and beaten up, following another torturous wing shift.

"G. B. Shaw was right," says the effort, still inspecting the damage.

"A good judge of character," says I, thinking of what G. B. said about screws.

"Well, that's it to the next time," says the effort testing his footing.

"We'll probably not get the blankets till six o'clock tonight," says I, as the effort, driven by cold, began limping up and down the bare and empty cell.

"Right parcel of efforts up there this morning," says he, going back to the subject of the wing shift again.

"Well, you should know them all by now, aren't they all the same," says I, "and if you'd have noticed who was among that shower up there this morning, you'd have seen a few ex-peelers, B-Specials, UDR and Brits."

"I did notice," says the effort, and that's what makes it bloody worse, 'cause it's always them, and we're always on the receiving end."

"*Sin ceart*," says I. "Hasn't it always been the same, hasn't there always been two sides—the privileged (them) and the oppressed (us). It's one half jailing the other, oppressing the other, murdering the other or whatever."

"And we're always the other," says the effort. "Bloody brassnecks saying that they're only doing a job." "Well, they're only telling the truth," says I, "'cause the screw's job, just like the job of a peeler, Brit, UDR man, civil servant, MP or in fact the whole privileged side of the fence, is to oppress, to keep us down and make sure that their wee slice of the British cake is secure."

"I'm foundered," says the effort, looking whiter than usual.

"I'm starving," says I, noting the sound of the Dublin train passing by on the not-too-far-away railway.

"Dreaded boiled egg for the tea tonight; that should cheer us all up," said the effort laughing. "I wonder who's getting beaten up in Castlereagh now?" says he as an afterthought.

"Well, it's no one from the Antrim or Malone roads," says I.

"And with all their bloody money that these screws are getting, it won't be too long until they're all living there too," says the effort, starting on the screws again.

"*Sin ceart beor*," says I, "and the not-so-funny thing about it is that just like the peelers, civil servants, councillors, MPs or whoever, they'll never be out of a job, 'cause to maintain their privileged positions, their better and well paid jobs, their better housing and comfortable lives and all the rest, they keep us down, keep us bottled up in our ghettos, without work and in bad housing, in concrete jungles like Divis and Unity Flats, deprive us, rob us, oppress us, for they have a lot to lose; we have nothing to lose but our misery and chains."

"And they spent £8,000,000 on H Block to torture us, and look at the slums our people are living in," says the effort, quite rightly.

"And they'll grow fat, wealthy and happy with the likes of the Sticks and the SDLP falling over themselves to help them," says I.

"And when any of us attempt to change it we end up here in the H Block, and in Milltown Cemetery."

"And people wonder why we fight and what's it all about," says the effort.

"Well," says I, "if everyone were to just sit down and ask themselves, what have the Brits, or the Stormont crew or the SDLP ever given to us, 'cept oppression, everyone's answer would be the same: nothing!"

"Well," says the effort, "maybe they will sometime and maybe they'll do something to change it so as we can all get a good night's sleep, like the super-Brit."

"The Brits don't boot his door in," says I.

"Neither does he get the dreaded egg, or dragged naked over a mirror for an intimate search at half seven in the morning," says the effort.

"Ah well, on to the socialist Republic," says I.

"The onward march of a risen nation," says the effort, God help him, limping up and down the cell.

The Rhythm of Time

There's an inner thing in every man,
Do you know this thing my friend?
It has withstood the blows of a million years,
And will do so to the end.

It was born when time did not exist,
And it grew up out of life,
It cut down evil's strangling vines,
Like a slashing searing knife.

It lit fires when fires were not,
And burnt the mind of man,

Bobby Sands

Tempering leadened hearts to steel,
From the time that time began.

It wept by the waters of Babylon,
And when all men were a loss,
It screeched in writhing agony,
And it hung bleeding from the Cross.

It died in Rome by lion and sword,
And in defiant cruel array,
When the deathly word was "Spartacus,"
Along the Appian Way.

It marched with Wat the Tyler's poor,
And frightened lord and king,
And it was emblazoned in their deathly stare,
As e'er a living thing.

It smiled in holy innocence,
Before conquistadors of old,
So meek and tame and unaware,
Of the deathly power of gold.

It burst forth through pitiful Paris streets,
And stormed the old Bastille,
And marched upon the serpent's head,
And crushed it 'neath its heel.

It died in blood on buffalo plains,
And starved by moons of rain,
Its heart was buried at Wounded Knee,
But it will come to rise again.

It screamed aloud by Kerry lakes,
As it was knelt upon the ground,
And it died in great defiance,
As they coldly shot it down.

It is found in every light of hope,
It knows no bounds nor space,

It has risen in red and black and white,
It is there in every race.

It lies in the hearts of heroes dead,
It screams in tyrant's eyes,
It has reached the peak of mountains high,
It comes searing 'cross the skies.

It lights the dark of this prison cell,
It thunders forth its might,
It is "the undauntable thought," my friend,
That thought that says "I'm right!"

The Union Man

We were proud.
Aye, we were at that as we stood in long lines
Although weary, hungry and hurt.
Proud! Proud that we had left our fetters behind us
In the rubble and the blood-splattered dirt
And the drizzle fell lightly upon our blood-blistered hands
And wet our dirty, blackened faces.
Our ragged clothes smelt of battle, burnt and scorched
With the fight, a terrible fight
And smeared with all its bloody ugly traces
And the morning air was silent
But shaking the roar of the murderous cannon,
Dead at least for now.
And life stirred as we marched through Dublin streets
At the point of gun
Where peeping angry eyes from behind drawn curtain
Upon us glared
And voices spoke, hatred, whispering and scorning us,
Tho' we knew not what they said
And the foggy dew fell down behind us to shroud our Fenian dead.

'Twas a sorrowful time, but a great day.
A great day for the fighting, workin' man.

But the workin' man was blind, blind to the bloody rose
That had bloomed upon the land.
The workin' people, dear God, my own very brothers,
Dubliners too to a man
Turned and spat into my reddened eyes and I told myself
They ne'er understood and I pitied them, God, I pitied them
That they ne'er heard the dying Fenian cries.
And I think, where is Connolly who stood for the workin' man
And that man Pearse and the old fella Clarke who finally won his day?

Aye, and for a nation's sake did the sleeping West awake
And plunge into the fray.
I am hurt and tired and captive but
The Irish Citizen Army has trained me well
And I'll tell you—
For my nation and James Connolly I'd rise again,
Aye, I'd rise again and fight my way to Hell.

Teach Your Children

There are ladies dressed in silk and satin, arrayed in velvet gowns
Wearing plastic, painted, perfumed smiles and silly smirks like clowns.
They sip chilled wine and titter and toast the fat man and his joke
Whilst strings produce gaiety 'midst the chandeliers and smoke
And a sapling fair, a dying child, screams and scorns the human race
That dances to the sound of strings while the rat bites at its face
And the fat man claps his little hands and slobbers in
    greedy-eyed delight.
He's sold for gold the tools of genocide, the tools of power and might
And roaring migs and 5rs spit death upon unseen ants in foreign land.
While in the banquet hall one and all raise a toast to the common man
But the common man's burning, mutilated ridden body lies strewn
    upon the earth.
Where scavenging dogs lick the bloody flesh of those condemned
    to death from birth.
And there's worry and confusion and bustle and men rush to and fro
And figures climb and fall and climb and the dollars grow and grow

Percentages and investments depict the fate of the wretched soul
Poverty and blood and death are mixed to produce capital returns and
    wealth and gold.
And in labour concentration prison camps weary tortured men arise
    to face another day
This is the life of the common man, it has always been this way.
Teach your children all you oppressed and wretched men of
    passing time
Unveil the guise and cloak of those that trample upon the very soul
    of all mankind.
Arise rebel, and strike and fight and raise your battle cry to heaven.
Teach your children the only law and word that fat men fear
The power of an AK47.

Strolling

Reddened, dirty feet pace to and fro
Carrying souls with nowhere to go.
Back and forth in endless flight
Like ghosts into the night.

The weary bodies of weary men
That pace three steps and turn again.
Old brown blankets cover naked paling skin
Clinging to bodies, frail and thin.

Journeying endlessly in an endless time
To defeat the enemy that attacks the mind.
In tombs of misery 'midst the shrouding fear
Where the only warmth found is in the trickling tear.

Time comes and goes, unseen, unheard, on by
And the darkness cloaks the pain-filled face that never sees the sky.
And somewhere each minute reddened feet pace a lonely tomblike cell
The daily stroll in H Block, or an eternal walk through Hell!

And Forward Went the Fool

My pain is great, but great is the pain that wrecks my heart
And the shame that besets my soul.
There are no comforting hands to cradle my cheek
Only this dark lonely bloody foreign soil that I will die upon.
And the ungodly fray goes on
And screaming, mutilated men die like the day as the blue skies
Of freedom grow black and clouded by death, and mock me.
And I have played the fool while better men than I
Die in my wake for the freedom of a proud and aged woman.
They rest easy in her bosom
Heroes to a man they be—"Forward, keep moving forward I say"—
And, dear Jesus, why was I the fool?

There is no promise or excitement in this graveyard
Where potential corpses rush past me like the wind into eternity.
And who will wet my parched lips?
Death falls by my side to taunt me in my shame and dying minute,
"Forward, keep moving forward I say"—but the corpses laugh in silence
And the sound of cannon comes in whispers as my tears fall
Upon a land that knows not me nor I her.
And I wish I were not the fool but the hero of my proud and aged mother.

"Forward, keep moving forward, I say."

The Window to Your Mind

The daylight began to fade and die. As dusk fell I was just about able to
distinguish the changing light and no more through the new contraption
that encased my cell window. Perched somewhere in the jungle of grey
gruesome barbed wire a robin sang its heart out in the last dwindling shadows of daylight. A few of the lads were arguing the possibility of the
singing robin being a thrush. But no one could be positive as no one could
see out of their cell window to identify it.

This was the latest measure of torture and attempt to break our spirit
by depriving us of sunlight, the meagre amount of fresh air that we got and

the precious little view which we had of nature and the outside world. If the slits in the back wall ever resembled a window, they had certainly lost all appearance of it now. For where the window had been was now a fortified mass of steel and wood and plastic! The inside of the window was blocked by a heavy steel frame and grill; then came the four reinforced concrete pillars that served as bars on the outside. A box type housing shrouded the outside of the window. It was a wooden and corrugated plastic structure that prevented all view of the outside, but there at the top of the structure disgustingly and unashamedly was a little sheet of clear perspex glass to "generously" facilitate the unfortunate inside with a no doubt "privileged" view of a few square inches of barbed wire and sky which disappeared as quickly as the dirt clogged up the perspex. I could not see out and not so much as a passing sparrow could see in! The air was stuffy and hot and I thought it very appropriate timing that they, the prison administration, should, after letting us literally freeze to death during one of the coldest winters for years, with snow falling in through the open windows upon our naked bodies, suddenly decide to block up the entire window that would turn our tomblike cells into ovens, when the long scorching hot summer days came. But that's a minor point in comparison to putting things, in general, into their proper perspective. For instance, the reason behind completely entombing naked men, who are already being deprived of exercise, fresh air and further deprived of natural light, a view of the clouds, the stars and the moon and everything else for that matter. Couple that with a burning white light that is continually kept on in the cell. Surviving on restricted diets and sleeping upon an old damp, filthy foam mattress upon the floor and you have an extremely good reason. "A Special Control Unit" type cell where the naked blanketman, having had the only distraction he had taken away from him, is left to stare at the empty, filthy surroundings of his cell turned tomb.

It's all psychology and meant to create frustrations, depression, despair and what have you!

All geared to break your spirit, to wear your mind and resistance down, if you allow it to! One can gain a distraction and pass time by simply just looking out the window, by observing the birds or gazing at the clouds or occasional aeroplane that may pass overhead. A red sky or inky blackness lined and tinted by sparkling stars, things like that are pleasurable distractions and in distressing depression or severe boredom can be very welcome and alleviate one's mind. One only becomes more depressed staring at a "filthy po" or four dirty smelling walls all the time. So, depending on what side of the window you're on, there is a very good reason behind blocking up the cell windows where Republican POWs are held. It all adds up to the massive torture campaign being perpetrated upon hundreds of naked political prisoners. Today I heard the lads say, "I wonder what time it is?" "Is it raining?" "What sort of day is it?" Tomorrow no one will bother asking as no one will know. Perhaps after a while no one will care. We might even forget about what's out there. They say what good is a pair of eyes that can't see? But what good is a pair of eyes that can only see a constant living nightmare?

The Loneliness of a Long-Distance Cripple

I was shaking like a leaf. The air was tense and filled with the cold chill of winter that bites deep into the lungs and reddens the nose and cheeks. There was an excitement that was almost overwhelming, and a silence and seemingly eternal stillness disturbed only once by a curious unperturbed mistle thrush, and a lone roaming gust of wind came and passed on by, ruffling my hair and flapping the sides of my flimsy vest as it passed on its way to nowhere. As the sky grew grey and overcast and rain threatened, a voice barked a command and I stiffened. On both sides of me a hundred others did the same. Another gust of wind whipped at my bare legs, and the first drops of rain fell upon my marked arms unnoticed as I held my breath.

"Bang." The thrush fled and I sprang forward. The marshy ground churned and sucked and squelched as hundreds of foreign spiked feet mutilated and scarred its face. Across an open field we charged in a bunch. My mind was racing as I tried to weigh up the situation and opposition as the lay of the land was seen, then gone, in a matter of a few strides. Bellowing puffs of smoke appeared as panting warm breath met the freezing, frosty country air and we leapt ditch and jumped gaps, splashing through a swampy pond that had been sleeping. Black, murky, icy water lashed and flayed at my naked, plunging, trudging legs as I fought my way through it, and some fell and others gave up, and behind the once sleeping pond was now a swirling, bubbling torrent of waves and activity. Jaggy nettles stung at me, and brambles clawed and tore and scratched the skin.

My heart pounded like the tramp of an army but I could do it, I knew I could do it as I burst forth, passing those whose strength and hope were fading and failing them fast, and I leapt the ditch once more, forging and forcing my weary legs to carry me up the last heart-destroying, body-wrecking hill. I mastered it and with the refreshing wind and lashing rain in my face I sprinted for home, towards where the crowd stood, towards where the finishing line lay, and I never heard the cheering voices or saw the smiling congratulating faces as I broke the finishing tape, breathing like a racehorse in deep, vast gulps.

Victory was mine and I felt like an Olympic champion. I was fourteen years of age. It seems like only yesterday and not so many years have passed by since that day.

Today, I feel like a living corpse. The legs that once ran miles, leapt ditches and climbed hills, that once kicked football and loved swimming and sport are longing to relive and participate in such sport and games again, but are dying, maybe even dead well before their time, perhaps never to see the like of it again. Reduced to pacing the darkened inner confines of a filthy depressing tomb of misery and pain and the three steps forward and three back again become increasingly less, perhaps for a few minutes a few times each day. My legs are heavy and weak and sore and pained and I tire like an old man and my head feels light and exhaustion falls upon me like a shadow and I can't believe that I am unable even to walk the floor for five minutes. I who ran miles in gruelling cross-country races and swam miles and kicked football can now barely walk the length of myself, and as time goes on I become more weary, not just my legs but my whole body, and perhaps soon my mind will follow, and I think at least in the tiger cages of Saigon they could see the sky. And I feel like a cripple, maybe even a corpse, but a corpse doesn't feel torture and doesn't wake up in the dead of night terrified or feel the pain of humiliation, degradation, torture or inhumanity. I run another race in my mind and the wretchedness that engulfs and envelopes me laughs at me as I stare at my legs and naked body in disbelief—the rigours of total solitary confinement in H Block have taken hold.

The Rose of Rathfarnham

Shadows climbed the ancient walls and far away a bell tolled as if in warning.
Young and gentle like a silver petal upon a rose, she awoke in the damp cold of the morning.

The day came hesitantly, seemingly knowing that it carried the last few
living hours of a man.
And she arose with a thought to him and the others as the sun poured
forth like honey upon the land.

She thought of the small white-washed cottage out Rathfarnham way
Where flitting silent secret figures came and went from day to day,
Where silver birch was put to pike and shot for musket made
And the arms for the ill-fated rising in the dusty rafters laid.

In the hush that hung, footsteps broke upon the courtyard outside her
lonely cell,
'Twas the man from God knows where himself, a soft sigh bade him
a last farewell.
Oh, and where was Henry joy and Munroe and her own blood
O'Dwyer,
And where was he, the boldest of them all, that sparked the freedom
flame afire.
Only that, the day would reveal and it came and passed on by,
And they took her to find out his fate, when the rising sun was high.

To Dublin she was taken in a coach, that drew still aside a crowd
Where women wept and men squirmed as the death drums rolled aloud,
Upon a scaffold, bound in bonds, but proud and free in spirit
He stood like a hero to meet the bloody death that he'd inherit.
And the drums rolled and men found tears as he was hanged and drawn
and quartered,
And the rose of Rathfarnham screamed! 'Twas bold Robert Emmet
they slaughtered.

And time passed and the torturers sought her secrets to unfold
A nation and another generation had been sold to men, by men, for gold.
Tone had gone and Emmet after, Munroe and Henry Joy,
Thomas Russell hung in Downpatrick gaol.
And she sat watching shadows and her heart cried out, for the United
men, who died to free the Gael.

Ghosts in My Tomb

I joined them somewhere on the road from Clare
Their expressions familiar like living corpses
Their grey sunken eyes peered through tattered hair.
A dying hoard of ragged, wretched suffering,
Pained brows on frail bodies, ghosts in the night to Galway went shuffling
Curlews cried in still of night, Róisín Dubh was dying
Clinging to her mother's shroud a dying child sat crying.
In the wayside ditch the emancipated body of Mother, a mother of Mary
    had fell
Lost to the breeze that sighed through the night o'er the land of a living
    hell!

The frosted road bit hard at naked feet that passed
While in a glen of hazel wood beyond lay a manor of the upper class.
But in their wake nothing stirred or dared to move, 'cept a creeping rat
And the English Lord on the pheasant fed and dined and wined and grew
    fat.
Around Galway town we skirted as the dying night prepared to flee.
The first light broke upon the dew around the hawthorn tree
And an old dog howled in misery but his master was long dead and gone
And ne'er a bird rose to sing as the forlorn of another morn was born.

Upon the brow of a little hill the ragged band grew still
Their tattered hair laced in the wind and the February chill.
Their spirits bruised they trampled on, although their bodies broke
For there below in Galway Bay sat a saviour, *The Star of Hope*.
At a sea torn pier a starving folk dropped upon their knees
Clare's bedraggled children screamed and mothers wailed, before the
    saving sea.
"Lord, let the trade winds blow and guide us on our way
For Róisín Dubh we leave behind for far America."

The salted air came on the breeze, the seagulls shrieked in terror,
Boston bound on *The Star of Hope* or Hades?
Time would tell the error.

The Star of Hope, a merchantman rolled gently on the swell
The oaken lids of darkened holds opened up the path to hell.
Silver doweries died, the rings of generations ceased
For a place in McKnight's darkened hold his bloody hand was creased.

While down below six score or more sat meekly in their tomb
McKnight the English captain sent three score more down to their doom.
The hatches were all battened down upon the cries of grief unheard
On Galway Bay the rigging flayed, Atlantic-bound they fared
And upon a walnut table, the blood-money piled high
McKnight sat down to dine and watch the wretched die.
Ten days out of Galway with a full wind in her sails
The seasoned bow of *The Star of Hope* met the February gales.

The dying and the dead of Clare lay rotting in their slime
And in the inky gruesome darkness they screamed for her behind,
The smelling loathsome stench of rotting flesh hung in the air
A sea of putrefying human waste engulfed them everywhere.
The little helpless children cried no more in hungrying pain
'Neath Atlantic waves in watery graves ne'er they'd cry again.
For seven days a tempest raged and the coffin ship was tossed
And when a calm fell upon the earth the pride of Clare was lost.
Ne'er a man among the men or woman 'mongst her kind
Would e'er again see a grassy glen or the dream they hoped to find.
Roísín Dubh in a tear-soaked sleep cried out to her silent throng
But their pikes remained in rafters bare, like the Wild Geese they had gone.

But down the years her tortured heart was warmed by a risen spirit
A resistance sown by her sons of sons that we today inherit.
And at night I hear the rat go creeping and *The Star of Hope* sails by
The walnut table has turned to gold but the fat man will not hear my cry.
And the stinking filthy stench of rotting flesh and waste, screams out, a
    living Hell!
'Tis my body dying in my coffin ship in this lonely tomblike prison cell.

The Bold MacKillen

I cut and slashed the strangling bramble,
Of ditch and rolling glen
With steel long and sharp and tempered,
In the scarlet blood of Antrim men.
A claymore cold and shining
That took the Clann and Blood MacCoy
Aye! One less Scotch Dragoon
To torture Henry Joy.

Antrim is lost! But we rose and fought
As Antrim men or better,
There's a gleam upon the pike heads
And the aged rust has left the fetter.
The blood! and death! and battle hate
Antrim town is lost!
A hunted rebel now I am
MacKillen of Abbots Cross.

In ditch I lay by light of day
Two days from Ballyclare.
Three nights in fields by Ballyrobert
There were Redcoats everywhere.
I have ate the bones of swiftly hare
And sucked the same grass
And whitened by the tombstones
As ghost and Redcoat came to pass.

Their yellow lanterns flicker
Upon the gorse, where Tone took oath and swore
The southern sky has been ablaze
From where the cannon roar.
Jesus, kill those screeching cries!
Oh, our tortured butchered women
To Badgers Rock in Carnmoney Hill
Go I, the fleeing MacKillen.

Bobby Sands

'Tis Belfast town by Lagan stream
I see yonder in the night
Where they shape the haunting scaffold high
To hang McCracken come first light.
And County Down sleeps peacefully
Across the blackened, lifeless Lough
Yet Ballynahinch burns this very night
Where Munroe has rose and fought.

On the birth of morn from Troopers Lane
And Carrickfergus town they came
Those Scotch and English Redcoats
Their murderous hunt begun.
Oh with drunken eyes and hateful hearts
They'll earn their bloody shillin'
But some will take it to their grave
Afore they take the Bold MacKillen.

The dawn she breaks and stirs my heart
Like Áine in the night,
Yet Monkstown sleeps and Cloughfern too
And White Abbey out of sight.
To the hiding place of the holy monks
I go to seek the spring
To quench my thirst and cleanse my soul
In Belfast the death bells ring.

The lightning black and creamy white
Of the swallow cuts the sky
In the spring pool lies a shimmering face
Of a rebel. It is I.
Hush! The morn's been murdered
A shrieking blackbird leaves the moss
'Tis the time to fight or the time to die
For MacKillen of Abbots Cross.

Three wolves on feet and a horseman come
I shall come upon them on the path,

'Tis the blade of this Scotch claymore
That'll carry MacKillen's wrath
For Antrim and McCracken!
I shook Carnmoney's side
The searing claymore cut down three
As the brown mare pranced and shied.

A burning dagger found my skin
And bit my tired bones
Afore the horseman fell down screaming
To die in bloody groans.
The breeze she stirs the hazel tree
The watercress is red,
Oh, the lightning swift and silver swallow
Have stole the sky and fled.

To Michael Dwyer in Cill Mantáin
Or the Devil pay the cost
On this surging mare across the sky
Goes MacKillen of Abbots Cross.

A Burning Thread

The seagulls are crying
Swirling up the spray
Upon the ocean of my mind
Blown, by a breeze of yesterday.

Oh! the simple gentle thoughts
The loneliness of the prisoner
To see the golden mermaid of the rock
Yet, to be cut adrift from her.

The mind knows no doors
A burning candle in the night
To seek the green or grey of yesterday
Or the "if" the "wish" or "might."

In the tomb the darkest depths
The candle flickers dying
Death is slaying life unseen
While the seagulls are crying.

The Voyage

It was 1803 when we sailed out to sea
And away from the sweet town of Derry
For Australia bound and if we didn't drown
The mark of the fetter we'd carry.
Our ship was *The Gull*, fourteen days out of Hull
And on orders to carry the croppy
Like a ghost in the night she sailed out of sight
Leaving many a wee'an unhappy.
In our rusty iron chains well we sighed for our wee'ans
And our good wives we'd left in our sorrow
And the main sails unfurled our curses we hurled
At the English and the thought of tomorrow.

At the mouth of the Foyle we bade farewell to our soil
And the sea turned as blue as the heavens.
The breeze filled our sails of a yellowish pale
And the captain lay drunk in his cabin.
The Gull cut the sea carving our destiny
And the sea spray rose white and came flying.
O'Docherty screamed, awoken out of his dreams
By a vision of bold Robert dying.
The sun burnt us cruel as they dished out the gruel
And Dan O'Connor lay dying with fever.
Sixty rebels today, bound for Botany Bay,
God, how many would reach the receiver.

I cursed them to hell as our bows fought the swell
And we danced like a moth in the firelight.
White horses rode by as the devil passed by
Taking ten souls to Hades in the twilight.

Five weeks out to sea we were now forty-three
And the strongest wept bitter like children.
Jesus, we screeched and our God we beseeched
But all we got was a prayer from a pilgrim.
In our own smelling slime we were lost in a time
Hoping God in his mercy would claim us.
But our spirits shone high like stars in the sky
We were rebels and no man would tame us.

We were all about lost, two round score was our cost
When the man on the mast shouted, "Land hoe!"
The crew gave a cheer as we cradled our fear
And the fathoms gave up and we swam low.
Van Diemen's land a hell for a man
Who would live out his whole life in slavery,
Where the climate was raw and the gun made the law
And neither wind or the rain cared for bravery.
Twenty long years have gone and I've ended my bond
And my comrades' ghosts walk behind me.
A rebel I came and I died just the same
It's on the cold wind at night that you'll find me.

The Lonesome Boatman

In the middle of the sleeping lake
The lonesome boatman dwells.
Around him rise the bracken hills
The dreamy glens and dells.
The skies are red and rolling
Tinted in the twilight's velvet hue
The ragged scarecrow peers in relief
To where the crackling crows have flown.

The lonesome boatman doesn't move
His clothes are old and worn.
Oh, lonesome boatman reveal to me why,
Why you look forlorn.

Is it life's sorrows
Or a forgotten memory that you have found
Or do you listen to the wind
For the boatmen you've seen drown?

Oh, lonesome boatman, there's a gleaming star
High above your head.
The waters glisten in the dusk
Are they the tears that you have shed?
Oh, lonesome boatman, the birds are here,
The morning shadows fall.
Oh, friends, why must you be
But a dying shadow on my lonely cell wall.

And So Life in the Living Hell Goes On

My body is broken, my heart sore, more sore than the pain that wrecks my body. The sound of screaming men tears at my heart and attacks my mind and I wish to God it were I again, for the pitiful cries of my comrades being tortured are harder to bear than the physical hurt that besets my brutalised body!

The ground is cold and black, yet warm and wet where the hot blood lies in thick red splashes. But yet I feel calm and unafraid. I know I am shocked and that when the tranquillising shock flees I will be the terrified, shaking, naked soul of wretchedness once again, and the tension will fall like a black sinister shadow upon me, but I think I just don't care any more. I have fought, we all have fought in our nakedness and we have fallen like the lamb before the wolf, and so we lie in our own spilt blood and I listen while the wolves savage the naked bodies of young men and not-so-young men who all resemble old men and older men and perhaps, I think, "dead men." And the wolves leave lifeless men upon the blackened, slimy, filthy, stinking floor of ready-made tombs to drift in their unconsciousness and those who are lost among the clouded tranquillity of senselessness, thank God.

And I have but the one thought—bloody unmerciful revenge—as I hear the screams of those who have never known life, only oppression and more oppression and the inhumanity of a monster who denies us our freedom. We have fought for freedom and we still fight for freedom with all we have left, our only weapon our spirit, but in our nakedness the spirit cannot repel the wolf or shield the blow of the baton or deflect the pulverizing, raining punches—it cannot repel torture!

But this spirit of ours is the spirit that says to me don't give up, don't give in, arise and face what they have, and another pitiful terror-filled scream pierces the air midst the melée of thuds and crashes and the sound of flying heavy spit and polished boots. And I think of those long lines of naked, ragged Jews in the midst of a jungle of grey gruesome barbed wire and I can hear their feet, the almost silent, shuffling, naked feet of wretchedness and inhumanity and the whispering, whimpering, weeping, shrieking, screaming sounds of torture and death and I hear them all right. They're screeching at me from all sides and the wolves of Dachau are no different from the wolves of this hell and, dearest Jesus, is this not hell? And I know I will die if I have to, we all will if need be to quench the flames of this hell, and my body aches and my mind is not my own, for the pain is tearing at my tortured body and the hovering tension and fear have fallen upon me and have clutched my very soul, and the screams, the heart-destroying screams continue. My spirit cries out, arise, but my body pleads for no more, for mercy, and it wants to lie upon the cold, black blood-splattered ground and die, to sleep, for it is weary and broken and perhaps dying each minute, each eternal minute. And my spirit says, get up, and I get up as the pain causes more pain, it is the pain of terror and fear, the fear of fear and the wolves laugh and I wonder do people really know and understand, for there is no relief or ease. And I keep seeing those lines of Jews and no one is listening to them 'cept I, for I understand. And I am shaking as the door of my tomb flies open and the mass of black uniformed, howling wolves attack me, and I know this is the price of resistance, the price of freedom, and the Jews scream in my mind and are drawn by the screams and suffering of the naked political prisoners that surround me and their screams are dying to whispers. And I just don't care any more as I think they can do no more to us except murder us. Over a hundred men in H Block have fallen and in their nakedness lie brutalised and savaged and beaten to pulp but I feel calm and unafraid as my blood bleeds and my heart breaks. But my spirit cries out, arise and, dear God, is there no end? And I arise, for the risen people can never be put down and so life in this living hell goes on.

Sad Song for Susan

I'm sitting at the window, I'm looking down the street
I am watching for your face, I'm listening for your feet.
Outside the wind is blowing and it's just begun to rain,
And it's being here without you that's causing me such pain.
My mind's wandering back again, to when you were here
And I wish I had you now, I wish that you were near.
I remember the winter nights when you warmed me from the cold
And in the spring when we walked through green fields and skies of gold.

You're gone, you're gone, but you'll live on in my memory.

In summer we played with the kids and you brought us young Jane,
But now—now it's lonely and cold and it's winter once again.
It's dark now, I see, the stars are out way up in the sky,
And oh! how they remind me of the sparkle in your eye.

I'm lonely, yes, I'm lonelier than the cold wind that blows,
Are you happy, are you all right? I suppose God only knows.
And darling all the people are going to bed and the kids are crying for you
—How can I tell them you're dead?

You're gone, you're gone but you'll live on in my memory,
You're gone, you're gone but you'll live on in my memory.

The Twilight Ballet

The last flitting sparrow passes by the dusty perspex pane.
The little squabbling citizens have all gone home.
The sky is silver and violet and the darker things are
Already beginning to creep above the ugly grey barbed wire, the day is on
    the run.
As if chased by the barking guard dogs who scent the first bold rats
    standing on the pipes,
The prisoner clutches the steel wire grill,

Fingers already beginning to flush he gapes out at the world
Hugging his shabby grey blanket he fights for balance.

His sickly yellow face is almost hidden behind his great rambling beard,
Matted, dirty, tangled clumps of hair hang like vines.
His eyes are hard fierce and ablaze with the piercing took of the
    insensitive and the insane,
Or perhaps it is a mixture of the rigorous torture and the sheer delight
    of a peep at a dying day.
He peers from his tomb like a re-incarnated caveman
But there is no breathtaking panorama, just the dying day
And the twilight ballet of the eloquent little wagtails
And the sky is now bleeding, the day has been wounded,
Mortally so, revealing a cloudy crimson hurt and darkness has captured
    the heaven.

The ballet is so beautiful.
In three pairs the dancing birds move with the grace of a veil in the breeze.
The prisoner grips the biting steel grill enthralled by the spectacle.
They run and leap into a high flutter, pirouetting on the wing,
Descending on the breeze, tails bobbing, rising and falling to their twitter.
It is not a song but a classical accompaniment.
The day had but one breath of deep purple left.
But even the night is repulsed by all.

A single ballerina flutters in the magnificence of a twilight star,
The moon has come to watch, the dogs howl
And the first rat scurries through the drainage here.
Night is now plunging down, the dancers disappear with the day
And the prisoner, the poor eye groping,
The prisoner can clutch the cold steel no longer,
He falls into the bowels of his dank dark tomb, a pathetic
    bundle of rags.
The twilight ballet is over but all the audience will not go home,
Perhaps he never will go home.

Stars of Freedom

The stars of freedom light the skies,
Uncrowned queens of yesteryear,
They were born 'mid shades of royal hue,
From mystic wombs they did appear.

Silver gems that pierce the dark,
Heavenly virgins in disguise,
That stir the heart with love and flame,
And light great flames in all men's eyes.

Oh! star of beauty in nightly hue,
You have inspired bondsmen to kings,
And lit the ways of despairing folk,
From dreams to living things.

In the seas of time you float serene,
Oh! silver stars of nations born,
And you draw a tear to free men's eyes,
Through dungeon bars forlorn.

Oh! star of Erin, queen of tears,
Black clouds have beset thy birth,
And your people die like morning stars,
That your light may grace the earth.

But this Celtic star will be born,
And ne'er by mystic means,
But by a nation sired in freedom's light,
And not in ancient dreams.

Dreamers

Through silver mist the war notes ran
The ancient Cú cried on the wind
Where an angel bore a shining blade,
Against all of them that sinned.

And I saw them ride from a thousand glens,
And I heard their battle song.
The Gael moving o'er the sweeping plain,
And they marched ten million strong.

And at their fore was Aodh Ó Neill
And by his side Aodh Rua,
O Ruairc, O Brian, Aodh Maguidhir,
And the Kings of a thousand tuath.

And I watch them march to the Bearna Bhael
And once again they fell to woe,
For they knew not just what they sought,
And they knew not how to go.

By the Rocks of Dún an Óir—1580

I saw her sails filled with the breeze,
And her long boats come ashore,
A Spanish lady on the seas,
By the rocks of Dún an Óir.

They bore silver swords and standards high,
In flashing ranks these men of war,
And their trumpet blasts reached o'er the sky,
By the rocks of Dún an Óir.

But 'twas not friend who heard their call,
For friend was dead in gore,
But lurking knaves of English gall,
By the rocks of Dún an Óir.

The Scoraveen bit their darkened skins,
And they ne'er saw death afore,
As they loudly sang their battle hymns,
By the rocks of Dún an Óir.

Bobby Sands

The warning cries of the sea birds rose,
As western monsters roared ashore,
But ne'er they heard the English close,
By the rocks of Dún an Óir.

And the King of Spain sips brandy wine,
Elegant courtiers grace the floor,
But Spanish troops lick salty grime,
By the rocks of Dún an Óir.

"Surrender!" came the English cry,
"Too late!" the Spaniards did abhor,
For there were Redcoats there 'fore every eye,
By the rocks of Dún an Óir.

Eight hundred Spanish musketeers
Trapped on Erin's shore,
Where they dropped their arms and clutched their fears
By the rocks of Dún an Óir.

But English chivalry came to play,
And they broke the oath they swore,
As those Spanish heroes knelt to pray,
By the rocks of Dún an Óir.

"For Queen!" they cried in bloody lust,
Slaughtering all before.
And they murdered all in bloody thrust,
By the rocks of Dún an Óir.

Now the Scoraveen ruffles Spanish graves,
A bloody mess of men no more,
Where I cursed the day, and Kings and Knaves,
By the rocks of Dún an Óir.

Unseen Sorrow

Her tears fall in the darkness as the rain falls in the night,
Silvery tears like silvery rain, hidden out of sight.
The stars fall from her eyes like floating petals from the sky,
Is there no one in all this world who hears this woman cry?

A simple little flitting dreamy thought has stirred this woman's heart.
The golden sleepy dream of yesterdays before they were apart.
What comfort can there be found for a petal so fair and slim
Alone in a forest dark of sorrow she weeps again for him?

Warm silver rolling tears blemish a once complexion fair,
That once shone in the fairest radiance 'midst a cloak of golden hair.
And the children whimper and cry for a father's care and love they've
    never known.
Who sees their little tears of innocent years as the winds of time are
    blown?

What sorrow will you know this night when all the world's asleep,
When through the darkness comes the sword that cuts the heart
    so deep.
For there is no one there to dry your tears or your children's tears
    who cling around your frock,
When there has been another bloody slaughter in the dungeons
    of H Block.

Silver Star of Freedom

The scarlet blazing hue climbed high to meet the night,
A Queen awoke to rattling chains in a bursting cascading radiance of light.
To the north a silver star of freedom shone out above her head
Then two horsemen came with dripping swords our crimson Celtic blood
    to shed.

Behind the aged walls of entries dark came the whispers of a few,
Aside a piece of faded yellow chintz, peered out eyes unsure of what to do.

Then came the Orange hordes and 'Specials, black like devils in the night,
And those whispers turned to battle cries, "Arise!" as the few went out to
fight.

An August shower fell down upon the blood where it lay so thick and cold,
To seep into her heart and fall upon the bones of Fenian men of old.
Our children clutched their mothers' skirts as their mothers screamed
aloud,
A Fenian tear from a faceless face rolled down upon a withered hero's
shroud.

Oh! and yet they came like their forefathers in their screeching thou-
sands—"No Surrender!"
A revolver barked in a shaking hand, 'twas resistance come to tender.
Oh! the star lit up the heavens high, men came forth like wisemen long
ago,
To seek the way of freedom that once was ours to know.

In Newry town and Crossmaglen and in the Antrim Glens asleep
From the gap of the North, through old Tyrone to the burnt out Belfast
street,
Upon Creggan hill, in Fermanagh far and where the great lough slept
serene,
Awoke the Northern Gael, a risen people now, to free their Celtic queen.

And we have fought and died, and upon our graves our children have
sworn your reign,
The Northern Gael shall enthrone you in all your glory, an emerald queen
again.
And the night is long now, have not we walked so very, very far,
But we glance to where the night is bright 'tis your freedom in that
shining, silver star.

Things Remain the Same—Torturous

"Things remain the same—Torturous."

Those are the seemingly perpetual words that inevitably filter out
each day from the H Blocks of Long Kesh on miserable scraps of stamped

government property toilet roll to our comrades on the outside world. Our smuggled messages today told of the vicious and callous beatings meted out by dozens of sadistic and sectarian-natured screws upon naked and very vulnerable Republican prisoners of war; of how last night we fought at our cell doors with blankets to try and stop the freezing jet of the high powered hose from saturating our pale skeletal bodies and our filthy, already damp, mutilated mattresses that lie upon the dirty, cold, concrete floor. And how we gave up, drenched, to retire to the furtherest corner, up to our ankles in water, to fight back with all we really have, "Our Spirit of Resistance."

We tell of how our food is restricted, cold, spoiled and meagre. We live in a continual state of hunger. It is a terrible thing, but to us here in H Block it has become petty and of little consequence in the face of the battered, bloody bodies of naked men.

But have things not always been the same for Irish Republican prisoners of war incarcerated in British hellholes? There is no future in Ireland under oppression, only the same tragic history repeating itself in every decade. Every decade has brought forth the same horrendous story of the brutality and inhumanity inflicted upon Irish prisoners of war, men and women alike and, least we forget, the subsequent murders. We need no reminder of the savage and barbaric treatment endured by Anne Devlin, incarcerated and tortured by English and quisling alike, over 175 years ago; or the unflinching determination and unconquerable spirit shown by Countess Markievicz in her steadfast resistance both in and out of gaol. For that same determination and spirit is being shown to us at this very time by the principled stand taken by Irish women incarcerated in Armagh Gaol, who like our Republican heroines of decades and centuries gone by have refused to be broken or to allow themselves to be treated or portrayed as common criminals. Indeed their spirit and determination is undoubtedly, unflinching and unconquerable, never to be broken.

Similarly we Republican blanketmen in H Block remember only too well our countless James Connollys, Robert Emmets, Frank Staggs, Terence MacSwineys, and never do we forget that be it the English devil or the lackey devil, the result is always the same—oppression and torture.

The Fianna Fáil regime of today and the treatment of Irish Republican prisoners of war held in Portlaoise gaol is remarkably the same and there is little or no difference from that of the treatment dished out to captured Republicans in '21 and '22, when Free Staters machine-gunned the very wings of the gaol and the exercise yard became execution yards. . . .

Likewise is the case of those Republican prisoners of war tortured during the '30s, '40s and '50s in Crumlin Road Gaol . . . The repetition continues as the present generation of Irish men and women likewise rot and die and are relentlessly tortured, and the next generation, and the following generations may prepare to meet the same fate unless the perennial oppressor—Britain—is removed, for she will unashamedly and mercilessly continue to maintain her occupation and economic exploitation of Ireland to judgment day, if she is not halted and ejected.

There is but one way to halt her and remove the aged enemy and oppressor. Once and for all, the only way! By physical force in the form of armed struggle. We Republican POWs in H Block, Armagh, Portlaoise and Crumlin Road Gaols, the cages of Long Kesh, along with our comrades incarcerated in English hellholes, have taken that stand and we continue to refuse to be subdued or broken even after capture and torture. We know that we, along with our comrades of Oglaigh na hÉireann on the outside and you the risen people, can and will achieve the victory that will envelope the future generations with peace and justice, happiness and prosperity and not oppression.

Indeed we must ensure that we see our present fight right through to the very end and the successful conclusion of the establishment of an Irish Socialist Republic, or indeed "things" most definitely will always remain the same.

"Always the same! if we allow it."

Thoughts from the Shadows

Darkness again. A man left the protest today. "I'm leaving," he said to a priest. No one tried to halt him, no one ever does, the protest is voluntary. His shaggy Bible lay in his tortured wake upon the filthy floor, pathetically worn down and tattered by excessive use. A tattered Bible, *The Book of Truth*? Read by those of us who have them in the unholy atmosphere and silence of our tomblike cells in the living hell of H Block. There is little or no change from the Victorian prison era of Tom Clarke, O'Donovan Rossa or the poet Oscar Wilde.

A book to save sanity or destroy a man's mind when it becomes an obsession, through sheer loneliness and depression. It becomes misused. There is nothing else to read. We balance precariously on the thin divide between sanity and insanity, every aspect of our existence is cloaked in torture.

Some weeks ago a man put on the prison garb, he left the protest, no one tried to dissuade him. Many were happy to see him go, yet sad. The man's mouth was so swollen he couldn't eat. He was literally starving to death. He was continuously pacing the precious few feet between wall and wall in almost a trance. The cause? Serious unrelenting toothaches—dentist treatment being continually refused to him. The man was being held to ransom, that he breaks his protest to receive attention—conform for mercy. The man in torturous agony left, leaving his torturous moans and groans ringing in our minds and echoing in the silent corridors at night, raising the now aged question, "When will it all end? What will it take? How big the sacrifice?" The little humble graves and heroes, plots scattered throughout the length and breadth of our occupied and still unfree country, may hold the answer.

Yet it is terrible to think that the blood of countless patriots has not been enough, that a new and blind generation demands fresh blood to open their eyes to the monster that has them by the throat tearing their heart out.

It's lonely in the shadows, and thoughts and memories can be frightening, but I shall stand beside James Connolly and Stagg. My thoughts ring tragically— a man left the protest today, they took him out in a coffin!!!

Darkness again. There is talk about families receiving letters from the N.I.O. and Prison Authorities, apologetic, concerned interest and the real truth, as they say.

Our people, we know, returned them, sickened by the audacity. What an H Block mother sees on her precious monthly visit is neither comforting nor reassuring—a thin, pale, bearded figure who somehow always manages to brave a smile between his sunken cheeks. No God's amount of well conceived lies and apologetic excuses will ever erase the scar so deeply embedded in my mother's heart, having seen what they have done to me and continue to do. Of course, there are toilet facilities available to every blanketman, there are also washing facilities, medical facilities and a wide variety of various other facilities—but at what price are they got? It is always at their terms, terms dictated by a bunch of sectarian bigots, the backbone of the sectarian state—"Empty your chamber pots if you wish," they say, "but only in the fashion that we can degrade you"—"Wash yourself, but only in a fashion that we decide!"—"Go naked—or wear prison underwear."

We all know the attitude. It is the same attitude of the same oppressive authorities outside: "Take a concrete tomblike flat in Divis Flats or live on the street," they say. "Work for little or don't work at all and starve," or, "You may vote every four years. If you don't like it, too bad," and that's that as "they" say!!

To a grievance in H Block, warders say, "Put your name down to see the Governor." Outside it is basically the same, in that it's "Go and see an MP." The results from both are always the same, as the housing and standard of living, the qualities of life, in Belfast and elsewhere and inside of H Block, so clearly display. If you step out of line you are thrown into H Block, if you rebel in H Block and refuse to be criminalised, you are tortured in a further attempt to make you bow, accept, submit.

Our mothers and you the oppressed people are not to be found so gullible as to be told, and seriously expected to believe, that torture does not exist in H Block. The same torture that is a stark reality of the pitiful existence of the oppressed Nationalist working class! We all know the reason that we are being tortured—because we are political dissidents, POWs, and we won't bow the knee or conform. The reason that we are here is as equally clear—because of the mess that Britain has created in our war-torn and economically deprived and exploited country. Letters to our families, like those sent by the torturers of naked men and defenceless girls, are but sick jokes, very sick indeed.

Darkness again, the devil's friend and the shadows paint old faces. My thoughts unwind in a tortured mind of memories and beloved places. "Are you there son?" (the heart is stirred), but 'tis only Rosy calling— "Bless yourself now, watch the road, and mind you don't be fallin'."

God bless her soul, I've seen her age; how often have I seen her crying, and now I can't bear to watch as the thing she loves is pitifully dying. And as they drag me from the cell, naked, beaten, always falling, I hear a voice say, "God bless you son" and I know it's Rosy callin'.

Poetic Justice

It was the strangest dream, sure enough,
Of all I've ever had,
I dreamt I had left this life,

And to be honest I felt glad.
And so I felt my soul ascending
I looked down to whence I came,
And all I saw was nakedness, suffering and pain.

Soon I reached a golden gate
Where other souls stood in line,
To meet the Lord I joined the queue,
My fate to be defined,
And gradually as we moved along,
Ever closer to the gate,
I saw some go in and some go down,
Testifying to their fate.

Then there came a familiar voice
That didn't take much tracin',
From the blackest soul in all the line,
It was that of Roy Mason!‡
To the other souls I heard him say
"I'm all right, I only did my job."
I shouted up the line to him
"That's another lie, just wait 'till I tell God."

Well, we reached the golden gate,
Where the Lord sat on his throne
And Peter called upon me
To come to them alone.
"Bob," said the Lord, "you done all right down there,
Of torture, pain and suffering,
Don't I know you had your share?"
"Let him in, Peter," said the Lord,
"And go in peace, my son,
For the Lord your God forgives you
For everything you've done."

---

‡ Roy Mason was Secretary of State in the North from 1976 until
1979 and personally supervised the criminalisation programme.

Well, was I a happy soul
For the good Lord had forgiven all,
I was just about to collect my wings
When I heard Roy get his call.
"Mason—Lord," said Peter,
"I think you know him well,
And by the colour of that soul of his
He's plenty there to tell."
"Peace be with you, Roy," said the Lord,
"Have you anything to confess?"
"Lord," said Roy, "You must believe me,
It was Cromwell made that mess,
And Merlyn Rees and Whitelaw,
They led me far astray,
Lord, what else could I do down there,
I could find no other way."

"And what about those H Blocks, Roy,
And all those naked men you kept?
Don't you know," said the Lord, "I watched them,
And every night they wept?
Roy, you tortured them
And you held them all those years,
Naked and suffering,
They wept a million tears."

"What is to be done?" said Peter,
"My Lord you must contrive."
"Poetic justice, Peter," said the Lord,
"Send him down to H Block Five!"

The Woman Cried

From humble home in dead of night,
A flitting shadow fled,
The yellow moon caught sharpened pike,
Where the night shades danced and played.

A bramble clawed at trembling hand,
And a night owl watched unseen,
Through bog and glen a United man,
Marched out to win a dream.

Cold black water lashed and splashed
And played around a tattered reed,
By dying embers, to God a woman prayed,
That the Gael might but succeed.

The silver nails of a rugged boot,
Scarred a lonely lifeless stone,
'Cross rambling hill he marched afoot,
To fight along with Tone.

Six days he fought,
Midst dying piles of gory mutilated heroes,
And the English cannon roared,
Upon the ghosts of Celtic bones,
A nation's blood was poured.

Thousands fell in screaming bloody terror,
Whilst the informer hid cowering close by,
But there were none left amongst that bloody fray,
To hear the woman cry.

Rodai MacCorlai

I am Rodai of Duncaney—MacCorlai—Antrim born!
This day in Toome I meet my doom for an oath that I have sworn.
On yonder oak on Roughery Hill a jackdaw I have heard,
It waits to steal my very soul, 'tis surely the devil's bird.

My greying mother Tara the pity, cut my silent father free,
Where he danced like a ship on an angry wave from yonder hanging tree.
And he felt no touch nor heard no scream his deathly gaze a loss,
As he slumped into her cradled arms, like the Christ did from the cross!

And 'twas when the wind blew down the Sperrins and 'cross the haggard
   land,
That she left, a broken woman, to roam like the tinker man.
There was no one to pay the landlord's sum, for we were the poorest
   of our kind.
Oh! how she walks the mist to screech and wail and haunt the Largy line.

And I am Rodai of Duneaney and I have watched a primrose cry.
And her dewy tear fell upon a land that watched its mother die.
So at Donegore I swore an oath and 'tis upon that oath I stand,
To Erin my life, by blood, my love, and damn to King and gombeen man.

'Twas a hurried time when we slipped the pike from 'neath the purple
   heathered hill,
With staved rods of silver birch, gleaming pikeheads men to kill.
Like the blackest marble the sky held death, the wolves were gathering
   round,
The Red Earl laughed, the jackdaw shrieked above the gallows in
   Carrick Town.

But yet they came the decent folk, from humble homes by moss and
   greenly glen.
They came with trembling heart to die, those bold Unitedmen.
And 'twas at Crosskeys the pikes gleamed white 'neath a telling
   yellow moon,
As the common folk (and there, there the poacher's son) went out to meet
   their doom.

The Northern Gael has risen, Abu! Abu! Our hearts burned sore with
   pride,
And Leinster's on the march, me boys, the noble French are on the tide.
At Antrim town the cannon roared, the ancient cú howled at the sight,
The primrose wept, the jackdaw danced, and black death ran through the
   night.

In the morning mist that came in silent dread the great laugh whimpered
   sore,
For a thousand souls had trod her breast and the lark would sing no more.
Along the aged Bann the children cried and Ulster screamed in vain,
The heart of Leinster had bled to death, the primrose blushed in pain.

Oh! I am Rodai of Duneaney and those of no property bear my name.
Those kingly freemen who sweat and toil and yet who never reign nor
    gain.
I love these wretched gentle souls, they! condemned to death from birth,
I stand by Tone and I stand by truth and the wretched of this earth!

And the wind may steal the powder smoke, the snow may wash the blood
    away,
But the spirit of freedom knows no end, nor ever shall decay.
Oh! the spring was born by lough and land when I chanced by Springwell
    Brae,
In the hope of a roof and a bite to eat and ship to Americay.

In Ballyscullion I spent some nights, in Bellaghy three or four,
Then I crossed the Bann with a fisherman to my native Antrim shore,
By the winding bog I came upon McErlain, and he with a grudge for me,
But he bade me day and asked me stay and share his hospitality.

The jackdaw fluttered and danced with joy and me the blinded fool,
For I slipped into Hell, and by the devil's fire I rested on my stool,
"You'll have some broth," said a greying soul, "and let me take your
    shoes,"
And she stirred the pot and stirred the pot, and I slept before her ruse.

McErlain the Curse had sent a man on the road from Moneyglass
    to Toome,
And Duffin the devil ran to The Rock for cruel Sam to fix my doom,
And the woman McErlain she stirred the pot and stirred and never
    would it warm,
'Till came the Fencibles in their coats of red and ne'er a one did warn.

And I am Rodai of Duneaney—MacCorlai—Antrim born,
This day in Toome I meet my doom for an oath that I have sworn.
On yonder oak on Roughery Hill a jackdaw I have heard,
He waits to steal my very soul, 'tis surely the devil's bird.

Be staunch my friends and never lose faith though freedom's struggle's
    long,
For the common men have a common cause against England's ancient
    wrong.

The drum beats loud, it scares a man, and the irons bite grim and cold,
But the gallows stand in ghostly hate and with terror a hundredfold.

Farewell, Duneaney! Farewell, my friends! And the sweet Bann 'neath
   my feet,
Oh farewell, ye Bold Unitedmen, will we chance again to meet?
Oh the rope is coarse, the air is still, and the river whispers why?
But she does not see the humble folk who come with tear in eye.

And the sun set red on Slievegallion Brae, the jackdaw hid in shame,
The primrose wept for Rodai boy, for MacCorlai óg was slain.
And along the Largy line a woman wails and tonight she'll roam the glen,
Oh Rodai of Duneaney!—MacCorlai—Antrim born—will e'er we meet
   again?

Dear Mum

Dear Mum, I know you're always there
To help and guide me with all your care,
You nursed and fed me and made me strong
To face the world and all its wrong.

What can I write to you this day
For- a line or two would never pay
For care and time you gave to me
Through long hard years unceasingly.

How you found strength I do not know
How you managed I'll never know,
Struggling and striving without a break,
Always there and never late.

You prayed for me and loved me more,
How could I ask for any more,
And reared me up to be like you,
But I haven't a heart as kind as you.

A guide to me in times of plight,
A princess like a star so bright,

For life would never have been the same
If I hadn't learned of what small things came.

So forgive me, Mum, just a little more
For not loving you so much before,
For life and love you gave to me
I give my thanks for eternity.

Danny Lennon‡

Gone are those weeping throngs of right,
Who marched upon your blood,
And upon the blood of little innocents,
To tramp freedom down into the mud.
Poor, poor fools, led by others' greed,
Where are those others now?
They've gone, comrade, with their bloody silver,
'Fore their masters' feet to bow.
Danny, we suffer in the long cold nights,
For they fear the freeman's will.
But they ne'er understand that the thing that makes that will,
Is a thing they tried to kill,
But you live, Danny! You all live!
And they quake, comrades, they quake in all their might!
For 'tis not sleeping graves these English knaves have made,
But unquenchable stars of freedom's light.
You are toppling H Block comrade,
And because of you and the many others
We oppressed men and women of no property shall realise
The Irish Socialist Republic.

*Go dtreoraí cuimhne d'íobartha agus íobairtí denár dtírghráthóirí,
náisiún beo bocht chun bua.*

---

‡ In August 1976 IRA Volunteers Danny Lennon and John Chillingworth were transporting an Armalite rifle in a car through Andersonstown in Belfast. The Armalite was not in working order and was being shifted to a dump for repair. British soldiers pursued the car and at

Tom Barry‡

For Barry's soul we prayed in hell,
Pathetic creatures adorned in pain
And we never heard his requiem bell,
But our own—in torture's livid strain.

In the southern realms of Munster world,
The humble whin bush sway,
Shedding yellow tears like child
For a legend passed away.

And they blow down lanes of time gone by,
O'er Crossbarry and Kilmichael grave,
And resurrect a battle cry,
"With Barry, boys be brave!"

In dusty light, by mist, o'er hills they tread,
A column on the run,
The ghosts of fighters long since dead,
Yet ne'er at rest, their guns still slung.

Now Barry leads them in the night,
Hardy souls of Cork Brigade,
To tramp the glens to morning light,
When their ghostly forms shall fade.

And we prayed tonight for Barry's rest,
Would Barry e'er be free,
As he tramps across old Munster's breast,
To blind eternity.

Finaghy Road North they opened fire on the two IRA Volunteers, instantly killing Danny Lennon who was driving the car and seriously wounding his comrade.
The soldiers continued shooting and the car, now out of control, mounted the footpath and crashed into Mrs Maguire who was going to the shops with her children. Mrs Maguire was seriously injured and her children, Joanna, John and Andrew, died of their injuries.

‡ Tom Barry, an IRA commander in the Black and Tan War, died in July 1980.

And in the darkened shadows, 'neath prison bars,
The hags of torture wave,
But we hear a voice that is of ours,
"With Barry, boys be brave!"

The Sleeping Rose

Barry's dead and Cork's asleep,
MacSwiney's cause been sold.
And the blood still lies on Kerry's roads,
Unwashed by winds of old.
The hares cross lonely, barren ways,
Where once columns tramped the night,
And but a few still whisper Tracey's name,
By hearthened fires in dancing light.

The Rose of Munster's dead boys,
She choked upon her blood,
And Barry's men died in her screams,
Trampled down into her mud.
Who cares for Kerry's lonely graves,
The King of Cashel's gone to Clare,
And those impoverished downtrodden fold,
As ever—laid naked, poor and bare.

Barry's dead, does no one hear?
Kilmichael's road,—what worth?
While Irishmen wear rusty chains,
That beset them by their birth.
Oh! Barry's gone let Munster weep,
His pleading ghost cries in the night,
But the Munster rose will only bloom again,
When Munster men join freedom's fight.

Training Camp

When a British cabinet minister contends that to grant political status to protesting Republican prisoners would be to create a training camp for the IRA, one can easily and deliberately be misled by such a statement. These words and supporting descriptions of prisoners carrying out various military lectures and drill are but a pathetic attempt to hide the real reason.

Any British army officer would be forced to admit that the worth of such theoretical training is in the main minimal, and that practical battle experience is what makes soldiers. Many of the same officers have admitted and as many have found out to their cost that the IRA Volunteer is a well-trained and competent soldier, a versatile and deadly guerrilla fighter—that the majority of captured IRA Volunteers are already obviously fully-seasoned freedom fighters. What Mr Rees and the other British warlords really mean and really fear is the future politicisation of these guerrilla fighters. An inevitability that fosters itself through a simple political awareness (that is, the realisation of the root cause of Ireland's perennial suffering—Britain) which grows to political maturity among captured POWs who hold the same ideals and principles and who, because of a deeply rooted desire for freedom, vigorously seek what is the very essence of political awareness—the truth.

Where such exists, so too exist "Freemen." People who can think for themselves and can form their own political opinions and judgment. People who will not be so easily fooled but, most significantly, people who, prompted by the discovery of right and truth, will use this awareness to combat and change the wrong by directing resistance against the very heart of the cancer—Britain. Therefore, it is by no means a group of posing militarists whom Mr Rees and Co. fear but a politically educated, armed guerrilla fighter who will not only use his political mind to guide his weapon, but to guide and teach his politically undernourished countrymen to steer their own destiny—the sure revolutionary recipe to British defeat.

It was with this black cloud hanging above the British government and the freedom of the oppressed ancient nation looming up on the horizon, that the British government, embarking upon a policy of Ulsterisation—re-Stormontisation—attempted to depoliticise the war of liberation in Ireland to portray the freedom struggle as purely sectarian strife, gangsterism or whatever would suitably belittle its real nature. Therefore, the attempted criminalisation of the Republican POWs up in H Block and Armagh Gaol is but one blatant facet of this policy.

H Block was blackly engineered to crush the political identity of the captured Republican prisoner, to crush his resistance and transform him into a systemised answering machine with a large criminal tag stamped by oppression upon his back, to be duly released back onto the street, politically cured—politically barren—and permanently broken in spirit.

With eight hundred years of experience of failure in oppressing the Irish nation, a British government has yet to recognise and admit that the spirit of resistance of the Irish Nation can not and never will be broken— the first British government to do so will be the last! Yet it has been for four long years and continues to be in this typically arrogant English "Croppy Lie Down" type attitude that the British government perpetrate countless inhumanities upon hundreds of naked men. But the Croppies in H Block have not and don't ever intend to lie down. We have resisted with the same undauntable Republican spirit of resistance that died in bloody mass at the gateway to New Ross, that met the might of the British Empire during Easter Week of 1916, and, like that, that died in great defiance in Michael Gaughan within a lonely prison cell. But yet tempered with the sacrificial blood of Irish patriots, it is vividly alive in H Block and the Northern War Zone! The British government may have succeeded in destroying us in body and driving some among us insane and others to the brink of insanity, but the thoughts of Connolly and Pearse are today the thoughts of the wretched of H Block.

Today in the dungeons of H Block the language of the blanketmen is the rightful language of the nation—*Gaeilge*—it is spoken with love and vigour. It is roughly scratched upon the filthy walls in poetry and sung with pride. The silver speech that our fathers knew has been revived in prison dungeon—the future of the liberation struggle and the road to the Socialist Republic is eagerly thrashed out in political discussion and debate. Every aspect of the life of the nation and the affairs and interests of the people are discussed so that we may not only know how to get to the Socialist Republic but what to do when we arrive there. We in H Block are actively tying our political resistance into the armed struggle. No amount of torture has stopped this. We have not been depoliticised, we have not been criminalised, if anything the incessant torture has stiffened our revolutionary resolve and determination, driving us to achievements and heights that we could never have hoped to gain. We have not been deterred from freedom's fight but rather rallied to the forefront. They have even sought to torture our women comrades but their unprecedented heroic resistance leaves us burning with pride and the torturers in utter dejection!

The face of British barbarity has once again been nakedly exposed in front of the world.

It has ensured that not only will the scars of the inhumanity which is H Block remain imprinted in the minds of us tortured prisoners but will burn deeply and for generations in the hearts of our sons.

H Block is the rock that the British monster shall perish upon, for we in H Block stand upon the unconquerable rock of the Irish Socialist Republic!

March 1981‡

Sunday 1st

I am standing on the threshold of another trembling world. May God have mercy on my soul.

My heart is very sore because I know that I have broken my poor mother's heart, and my home is struck with unbearable anxiety. But I have considered all the arguments and tried every means to avoid what has become the unavoidable: it has been forced upon me and my comrades by four-and-a-half years of stark inhumanity.

I am a political prisoner. I am a political prisoner because I am a casualty of a perennial war that is being fought between the oppressed Irish people and an alien, oppressive, unwanted regime that refuses to withdraw from our land.

I believe and stand by the God-given right of the Irish nation to sovereign independence, and the right of any Irishman or woman to assert this right in armed revolution. That is why I am incarcerated, naked and tortured.

Foremost in my tortured mind is the thought that there can never be peace in Ireland until the foreign, oppressive British presence is removed, leaving all the Irish people as a unit to control their own affairs and determine their own destinies as a sovereign people, free in mind and body, separate and distinct physically, culturally and economically.

I believe I am but another of those wretched Irishmen born of a risen generation with a deeply rooted and unquenchable desire for freedom. I am dying not just to attempt to end the barbarity of H Block, or to gain the rightful recognition of a political prisoner, but primarily because what is lost in here is lost for the Republic and those wretched oppressed whom I am deeply proud to know as the "risen people".

There is no sensation today, no novelty that October 27th brought [The starting date of the original seven man hunger strike]. The usual screws were not working. The slobbers and would-be despots no doubt will be back again tomorrow, bright and early.

I wrote some more notes to the girls in Armagh today. There is so much I would like to say about them, about their courage, determination

---

‡ For the first seventeen days of his hunger strike Bobby Sands kept a secret diary in which he wrote his thoughts and views.

and unquenchable spirit of resistance. They are to be what Countess Markievicz, Anne Devlin, Mary Ann McCracken, Marie MacSwiney, Betsy Gray, and those other Irish heroines are to us all. And, of course, I think of Ann Parker, Laura Crawford, Rosemary Bleakeley, and I'm ashamed to say I cannot remember all their sacred names.

Mass was solemn, the lads as ever brilliant. I ate the statutory weekly bit of fruit last night. As fate had it, it was an orange and, the final irony, it was bitter. The food is being left at the door. My portions, as expected, are quite larger than usual, or those which my cellmate Malachy is getting.

Monday 2nd

Much to the distaste of the screws we ended the no-wash protest this morning. We moved to B Wing, which was allegedly clean.

We have shown considerable tolerance today. Men are being searched coming back from the toilet. At one point men were waiting three hours to get out to the toilet, and only four or five got washed, which typifies the eagerness [*sic*] of the screws to have us off the no-wash. There is a lot of petty vindictiveness from them.

I saw the doctor and I'm 64 kgs [140.8 pounds]. I've no problems.

The priest, Fr John Murphy, was in tonight. We had a short talk. I heard that my mother spoke at a parade in Belfast yesterday and that Marcella cried. It gave me heart. I'm not worried about the numbers of the crowds.

I was very annoyed last night when I heard Bishop Daly's statement [issued on Sunday, condemning the hunger strike]. Again he is applying his double set of moral standards. He seems to forget that the people who murdered those innocent Irishmen on Derry's Bloody Sunday are still as ever among us; and he knows perhaps better than anyone what has and is taking place in H Block.

He understands why men are being tortured here—the reason for criminalisation. What makes it so disgusting, I believe, is that he agrees with that underlying reason. Only once has he spoken out, of the beatings and inhumanity that are commonplace in H Block.

I once read an editorial, in late '78, following the then Archbishop O Fiaich's "sewer pipes of Calcutta" statement. It said it was to the everlasting shame of the Irish people that the archbishop had to, and I paraphrase, stir the moral conscience of the people on the H Block issue. A lot of time has passed since then, a lot of torture, in fact the following year was the worst we experienced.

Now I wonder who will stir the Cardinal's moral conscience . . .

Bear witness to both right and wrong, stand up and speak out. But don't we know that what has to be said is "political," and it's not that these people don't want to become involved in politics, it's simply that their politics are different, that is, British.

My dear friend Tomboy's father died today. I was terribly annoyed, and it has upset me.

I received several notes from my family and friends. I have only read the one from my mother—it was what I needed. She has regained her fighting spirit—I am happy now.

My old friend Seanna [Walsh, a fellow blanketman] has also written.

I have an idea for a poem, perhaps tomorrow I will try to put it together.

Every time I feel down I think of Armagh, and James Connolly. They can never take those thoughts away from me.

Tuesday 3rd

I'm feeling exceptionally well today. (It's only the third day, I know, but all the same I'm feeling great.) I had a visit this morning with two reporters, David Beresford of the *Guardian* and Brendan Ó Cathaoir of the *Irish Times*. Couldn't quite get my flow of thoughts together. I could have said more in a better fashion.

63 kgs [138.6 pounds] today, so what?

A priest was in. Feel he's weighing me up psychologically for a later date. If I'm wrong I'm sorry—but I think he is. So I tried to defuse any notion of that tonight. I think he may have taken the point. But whether he accepts it will be seen. He could not defend my onslaught on Bishop Daly—or at least he did not try.

I wrote some notes to my mother and to Mary Doyle in Armagh; and will write more tomorrow. The boys are now all washed. But I didn't get washed today. They were still trying to get men their first wash.

I smoked some "bog-rolled blows" today, the luxury of the Block!

They put a table in my cell and are now placing my food on it in front of my eyes. I honestly couldn't give a damn if they placed it on my knee. They still keep asking me silly questions like, "Are you still not eating?"

I never got started on my poem today, but I'll maybe do it tomorrow. The trouble is I now have more ideas.

Got papers and a book today. The book was Kipling's *Short Stories* with an introduction of some length by W. Somerset Maugham. I took an instant dislike to the latter on reading his comment on the Irish people during Kipling's prime as a writer: "It is true that the Irish were making a nuisance of themselves." Damned too bad, I thought, and bigger the pity it wasn't a bigger nuisance! Kipling I know of, and his Ulster connection. I'll read his stories tomorrow.

Ag rá an phaidrín faoi dhó achan lá atá na buachaillí anois. Níl aon rud eile agam anocht. Sin sin.

[*Translated this reads as follows*: The boys are now saying the rosary twice every day. I have nothing else tonight. That's all.]

Wednesday 4th

Fr Murphy was in tonight. I have not felt too bad today, although I notice the energy beginning to drain. But it is quite early yet. I got showered today and had my hair cut, which made me feel quite good. Ten years younger, the boys joke, but I feel twenty years older, the inevitable consequence of eight years of torture and imprisonment.

I am abreast with the news and view with utter disgust and anger the Reagan/Thatcher plot. It seems quite clear that they intend to counteract Russian expansionism with imperialist expansionism, to protect their vital interests they say.

What they mean is they covet other nations' resources. They want to steal what they haven't got and to do so (as the future may unfortunately prove) they will murder oppressed people and deny them their sovereignty as nations. No doubt Mr Haughey will toe the line in Ireland when Thatcher so demands.

Noticed a rarity today: jam with the tea, and by the way the screws are glaring at the food, they seem more in need of it than my good self.

Thursday 5th

The Welfare sent for me today to inform me of my father being taken ill to hospital. Tried to get me to crawl for a special visit with my family. I was distressed about my father's illness but relieved that he has been released from hospital. No matter what, I must continue.

I had a threatening toothache today which worried me, but it is gone now.

I've read Atkins' statement in the Commons, *mar dhea!* [Atkins pledged that the British government would not budge an inch on its intransigent position.] It does not annoy me because my mind was prepared for such things and I know I can expect more of such, right to the bitter end.

I came across some verse in Kipling's short stories; the extracts of verses before the stories are quite good. The one that I thought very good went like this:

> The earth gave up her dead that tide,
> Into our camp he came,
> And said his say, and went his way,
> And left our hearts aflame.
>
> Keep tally on the gun butt score,
> The vengeance we must take,
> When God shall bring full reckoning,
> For our dead comrade's sake.

"I hope not," said I to myself. But that hope was not even a hope, but a mere figure of speech. I have hope, indeed. All men must have hope and never lose heart. But my hope lies in the ultimate victory for my poor people. Is there any hope greater than that?

I'm saying prayers—crawler! (and a last minute one, some would say). But I believe in God, and I'll be presumptuous and say he and I are getting on well this weather.

I can ignore the presence of food staring me straight in the face all the time. But I have this desire for brown wholemeal bread, butter, Dutch cheese and honey. Ha!! It is not damaging me, because, I think, "Well, human food can never keep a man alive for ever," and I console myself with the fact that I'll get a great feed up above (if I'm worthy).

But then I'm struck by this awful thought that they don't eat food up there. But if there's something better than brown wholemeal bread, cheese and honey, etcetera, then it can't be bad.

The March winds are getting angry tonight, which reminds me that I'm twenty-seven on Monday. I must go, the road is just beginning, and tomorrow is another day. I am now 62 kgs [136.4 pounds] and, in general, mentally and physically, I feel very good.

Friday 6th

There was no priest in last night or tonight. They stopped me from seeing my solicitor tonight, as another part of the isolation process, which, as time goes by, they will ruthlessly implement. I expect they may move me sooner than expected to an empty wing. I will be sorry to leave the boys, but I know the road is a hard one and everything must be conquered.

I have felt the loss of energy twice today, and I am feeling slightly weak.

They (the screws) are unembarrassed by the enormous amount of food they are putting into the cell and I know they have every bean and chip counted or weighed. The damned fools don't realise that the doctor does tests for traces of any food eaten. Regardless, I have no intention of sampling their tempting morsels.

I am sleeping well at night so far, as I avoid sleeping during the day. I am even having pleasant dreams and so far no headaches. Is that a tribute to my psychological frame of mind or will I pay for that tomorrow or later! I wonder how long I will be able to keep these scribbles going?

My friend Jennifer got twenty years. I am greatly distressed. [Twenty-one-year-old Jennifer McCann, from Belfast's Twinbrook estate, was sentenced to twenty years' imprisonment for shooting at an RUC man.]

I have no doubts or regrets about what I am doing for I know what I have faced for eight years, and in particular for the last four-and-a-half years, others will face, young lads and girls still at school, or young Gerard or Kevin [Bobby's son and nephew, respectively] and thousands of others.

They will not criminalise us, rob us of our true identity, steal our individualism, depoliticise us, churn us out as systemised, institutionalised, decent law-abiding robots. Never will they label our liberation struggle as criminal.

I am (even after all the torture) amazed at British logic. Never in eight centuries have they succeeded in breaking the spirit of one man who refused to be broken. They have not dispirited, conquered, or demoralised my people, nor will they ever.

I may be a sinner, but I stand—and if it so be, will die—happy knowing that I do not have to answer for what these people have done to our ancient nation.

Thomas Clarke is in my thoughts, and MacSwiney, Stagg, Gaughan, Thomas Ashe, McCaughey.

Dear God, we have so many that another one to those knaves means nothing, or so they say, for some day they'll pay.

When I am thinking of Clarke, I thought of the time I spent in B Wing in Crumlin Road jail in September and October '77. I realised just what was facing me then. I've no need to record it all, some of my comrades experienced it too, so they know I have been thinking that some people (maybe many people) blame me for this hunger strike, but I have tried everything possible to avert it short of surrender.

I pity those who say that, because they do not know the British, and I feel more the pity for them because they don't even know their poor selves. But didn't we have people like that who sought to accuse Tone, Emmet, Pearse, Connolly, Mellowes: that unfortunate attitude is perennial also. . .

I can hear the curlew passing overhead. Such a lonely cell, such a lonely struggle. But, my friend, this road is well trod and he, whoever he was who first passed this way, deserves the salute of the nation. I am but a mere follower and I must say *Oíche Mhaith* [good night].

Saturday 7th

I received a most welcome note tonight from Bernie, my sister. Good old Bernie. I love her and think she's the greatest.

I am now convinced that the authorities intend to implement strict isolation soon, as I am having trouble in seeing my solicitor. I hope I'm wrong about the isolation, but we'll see.

It's only that I'd like to remain with the boys for as long as possible for many reasons. If I'm isolated, I will simply conquer it.

A priest was in today, somewhat pleasant, and told me about Brendan O Cathaoir's article in the *Irish Times* during the week, which I saw. We had a bit of discussion on certain points, which, of course, were to him contentious. He was cordial in his own practised way, purely tactical, of course, and at the same time he was most likely boiling over inside, thinking of the reference to this week's *AP/RN* [February 28th issue] calling him a collaborating middle-class nationalist, or appropriate words to that effect.

He is too, says I, and I sympathise with those unfortunate sons of God who find themselves battling against the poverty, disease, corruption, death and inhumanities of the missions. . .

I am 61 kgs [134.2 pounds] today, going down. I'm not troubled by hunger pangs, nor paranoiac about anything pertaining to food, but, by God, the food has improved here. I thought I noticed that during the last hunger strike. Well, there is a lot at stake here.

I got the *Irish News* today, but there's nothing in it, that's why I got it.

I'm looking forward to seeing the comrades at Mass tomorrow, all the younger looking faces, minus the beards, moustaches, long rambling untamed hair matted in thick clumps.

One thing is sure, that awful stage, of the piercing or glazed eyes, the telltale sign of the rigours of torture, won't be gone—if it is ever removed. I wonder is it even conceivable that it could be erased from the mind?

We got a new comrade during the week. Isn't it inspiring, the comrades who keep joining us?

I read what Jennifer said in court. [On being sentenced, Jennifer McCann said: "I am a Republican prisoner-of-war and at the moment my comrade Bobby Sands is on hunger strike to defend my rights as a political prisoner."] I was touched and proud, she is my comrade.

I've been thinking of Mary Doyle and Ellen McGuigan and all the rest of the girls in Armagh. How can I forget them?

The screws are staring at me perplexed. Many of them hope (if their eyes tell the truth) that I will die. If need be, I'll oblige them, but my God they are fools. Oscar Wilde did not do justice to them for I believe they are lower than even he thought.

And I may add there is only one thing lower than a screw and that is a Governor. And in my experience the higher one goes up that disgusting ladder they call rank, or position, the lower one gets. . .

It's raining. I'm not cold, my spirits are well, and I'm still getting some smokes—decadence, well sort of, but who's perfect. Bad for your health. *Mar dheas anois, Oíche Mhaith.*

Sunday 8th

In a few hours time I shall be twenty-seven grand years of age. Paradoxically it will be a happy enough birthday; perhaps that's because I am free in spirit. I can offer no other reason.

I was at Mass today, and saw all the lads minus their beards, etc. An American priest said Mass and I went to Communion. One of the lads collapsed before Mass, but he's all right now. Another was taken out to Musgrave military hospital. These are regular occurrences.

I am 60.8 kgs [133.75 pounds] today, and have no medical complaints.

I received another note from my sister Bernie and her boyfriend. It does my heart good to hear from her. I got the *Irish News* today, which carried some adverts in support of the hunger strike.

There is a standby doctor who examined me at the weekend, a young man whose name I did not know up until now. Little friendly Dr Ross has been the doctor. He was also the doctor during the last hunger strike.

Dr Emerson is, they say, down with the flu . . . Dr Ross, although friendly, is in my opinion also an examiner of people's minds. Which reminds me, they haven't asked me to see a psychiatrist yet. No doubt they will yet, but I won't see him for I am mentally stable, probably more so than he.

I read some wildlife articles in various papers, which indeed brought back memories of the once-upon-a-time budding ornithologist! It was a bright pleasant afternoon today and it is a calm evening. It is surprising what even the confined eyes and ears can discover.

I am awaiting the lark, for spring is all but upon us. How I listened to that lark when I was in H-5, and watched a pair of chaffinches which arrived in February. Now lying on what indeed is my deathbed, I still listen even to the black crows.

Monday 9th

I have left this rather late tonight and it is cold. The priest Fr Murphy was in. I had a discussion with him on the situation. He said he enjoyed our talk, and was somewhat enlightened, when he was leaving.

On the subject of priests, I received a small note from a Fr S. C. from Tralee, Kerry, and some holy pictures of Our Lady. The thought touched me. If it is the same man, I recall him giving a lecture to us in Cage 11 some years ago on the right to lift arms in defence of the freedom of one's occupied and oppressed nation. Preaching to the converted he was, but it all helps.

It is my birthday and the boys are having a sing-song for me, bless their hearts. I braved it to the door, at their request, to make a bit of a speech, for what it was worth. I wrote to several friends today including Bernie and my mother. I feel all right and my weight is 60 kgs [132 pounds].

I always keep thinking of James Connolly, and the great calm and dignity that he showed right to his very end, his courage and resolve. Perhaps I am biased, because there have been thousands like him, but Connolly has always been the man that I looked up to.

I always have tremendous feeling for Liam Mellowes as well; and for the present leadership of the Republican Movement, and a confidence in them that they will always remain undaunted and unchanged. And again, dare I forget the Irish people of today, and the risen people of the past, they too hold a special place in my heart.

Well, I have gotten by twenty-seven years, so that is something. I may die, but the Republic of 1916 will never die. Onward to the Republic and liberation of our people.

Tuesday 10th

It has been a fairly normal day in my present circumstances. My weight is 59.3 kgs [130.5 pounds] and I have no medical problems. I have seen some birthday greetings from relatives and friends in yesterday's paper which I got today. Also I received a bag of toiletries today.

There is no priest in tonight, but the chief medical officer dropped in, took my pulse, and left. I suppose that makes him feel pretty important.

From what I have read in the newspapers I am becoming increasingly worried and wary of the fact that there could quite well be an attempt at a later date to pull the carpet from under our feet and undermine us—if not defeat this hunger strike—with the concession bid in the form of "our own clothes as a right."

This, of course, would solve nothing, but if allowed birth could, with the voice of the Catholic hierarchy, seriously damage our position. It is my opinion that under no circumstances do they wish to see the prisoners gain political status, or facilities that resemble, or afford us with the contents of, political status.

The reasons for this are many and varied, primarily motivated by the wish to see the revolutionary struggle of the people brought to an end. The criminalisation of Republican prisoners would help to furnish this end.

It is the declared wish of these people to see humane and better conditions in these Blocks. But the issue at stake is not humanitarian, nor about better or improved living conditions. It is purely political and only a political solution will solve it. This in no way makes us prisoners elite nor do we (nor have we at any time) purport to be elite.

We wish to be treated "not as ordinary prisoners" for we are not criminals. We admit no crime unless, that is, the love of one's people and country is a crime.

Would Englishmen allow Germans to occupy their nation or Frenchmen allow Dutchmen to do likewise? We Republican prisoners understand better than anyone the plight of all prisoners who are deprived of their liberty. We do not deny ordinary prisoners the benefit of anything that we gain that may improve and make easier their plight. Indeed, in the past, all prisoners have gained from the resistance of Republican jail struggles.

I recall the Fenians and Tom Clarke, who indeed were most instrumental in highlighting by their unflinching resistance the "terrible silent system" in the Victorian period in English prisons. In every decade there has been ample evidence of such gains to all prisoners due to Republican prisoners' resistance.

Unfortunately, the years, the decades, and centuries have not seen an end to Republican resistance in English hellholes, because the struggle in the prisons goes hand-in-hand with the continuous freedom struggle in Ireland. Many Irishmen have given their lives in pursuit of this freedom and I know that more will, myself included, until such times as that freedom is achieved.

I am still awaiting some sort of move from my cell to an empty wing and total isolation. The last strikers were ten days in the wings with the boys, before they were moved. But then they were on the no-wash protest and in filthy cells. My cell is far from clean but tolerable. The water is always cold. I can't risk the chance of cold or flu. It is six days since I've had a bath, perhaps longer. No matter.

Tomorrow is the eleventh day and there is a long way to go. Someone should write a poem of the tribulations of a hunger striker. I would like to, but how could I finish it.

Caithfidh mé a dul mar tá tuirseacb ag eírí ormsa. [*Translated, this reads as follows*: Must go as I'm getting tired.]

Wednesday 11th

I received a large amount of birthday cards today. Some from people I do not know. In particular a Mass bouquet with fifty Masses on it from Mrs Burns from Sevastopol Street. We all know of her, she never forgets us and we shan't forget her, bless her dear heart.

I also received a card from reporter Brendan Ó Cathaoir, which indeed was thoughtful. I received a letter from a friend, and from a student in America whom I don't know, but again it's good to know that people are thinking of you. There were some smuggled letters as well from my friends and comrades.

I am the same weight today and have no complaints medically. Now and again I am struck by the natural desire to eat but the desire to see an end to my comrades' plight and the liberation of my people is overwhelmingly greater.

The doctor will be taking a blood test tomorrow. It seems that Dr Ross has disappeared and Dr Emerson is back. . . .

Again, there has been nothing outstanding today except that I took a bath this morning. I have also been thinking of my family and hoping that they are not suffering too much.

I was trying to piece together a quote from James Connolly today which I'm ashamed that I did not succeed in doing but I'll paraphrase the meagre few lines I can remember.

They go something like this: a man who is bubbling over with enthusiasm (or patriotism) for his country, who walks through the streets among his people, their degradation, poverty, and suffering, and who (for want of the right words) does nothing, is, in my mind, a fraud; for Ireland distinct from its people is but a mass of chemical elements.

Perhaps the stark poverty of Dublin in 1913 does not exist today, but then again, in modern day comparison to living standards in other places through the world, it could indeed be said to be the same if not worse both North and South. Indeed, one thing has not changed, that is the economic, cultural and physical oppression of the same Irish people. . . .

Even should there not be 100,000 unemployed in the North, their pittance of a wage would look shame in the company of those whose wage and profit is enormous, the privileged and capitalist class who sleep upon the people's wounds, and sweat, and toils.

Total equality and fraternity cannot and never will be gained whilst these parasites dominate and rule the lives of a nation. There is no equality in a society that stands upon the economic and political bog if only the strongest make it good or survive. Compare the lives, comforts, habits, wealth of all those political con men (who allegedly are concerned for us, the people) with that of the wretchedly deprived and oppressed.

Compare it in any decade in history, compare it tomorrow, in the future, and it will mock you. Yet our perennial blindness continues. There are no luxuries in the H Blocks. But there is true concern for the Irish people.

Thursday 12th

Fr Toner was in tonight, and brought me in some religious magazines.

My weight is 58.75 kgs [129.25 pounds]. They did not take a blood sample because they want to incorporate other tests with it. So the doctor says they'll do it next week.

Physically I have felt very tired today, between dinnertime and later afternoon. I know I'm getting physically weaker. It is only to be expected. But I'm okay. I'm still getting the papers all right, but there's nothing heartening in them. But again I expect that also and therefore I must depend entirely upon my own heart and resolve, which I will do.

I received three notes from the comrades in Armagh, God bless them again.

I heard of today's announcement that Frank Hughes will be joining me on hunger strike on Sunday. I have the greatest respect, admiration and confidence in Frank and I know that I am not alone. How could I ever be with comrades like those around me, in Armagh and outside.

I've been thinking of the comrades in Portlaoise, the visiting facilities there are inhuman. No doubt that hellhole will also eventually explode in due time. I hope not, but Haughey's compassion for the prisoners down there is no different from that of the Brits towards prisoners in the North and in English gaols.

I have come to understand, and with each passing day I understand increasingly more and in the most sad way, that awful fate and torture endured to the very bitter end by Frank Stagg and Michael Gaughan. Perhaps,—indeed yes!—I am more fortunate because those poor comrades were without comrades or a friendly face. They had not even the final consolation of dying in their own land, Irishmen alone and at the unmerciful ugly hands of a vindictive heartless enemy. Dear God, but I am so lucky in comparison.

I have poems in my mind, mediocre no doubt, poems of hunger strike and MacSwiney, and everything that this hunger strike has stirred up in my heart and in my mind, but the weariness is slowly creeping in, and my heart is willing but my body wants to be lazy, so I have decided to mass all my energy and thoughts into consolidating my resistance.

That is most important. Nothing else seems to matter except that lingering constant reminding thought, "Never give up." No matter how bad, how black, how painful, how heart-breaking, "Never give up," "Never despair," "Never lose hope." Let the bastards laugh at you all they want, let them grin and jibe, allow them to persist in their humiliation, brutality, deprivations, vindictiveness, petty harassments, let them laugh now, because all of that is no longer important or worth a response.

I am making my last response to the whole vicious inhuman atrocity they call H Block. But, unlike their laughs and jibes, our laughter will be the joy of victory and the joy of the people, our revenge will be the liberation of all and the final defeat of the oppressors of our aged nation.

Friday 13th

I'm not superstitious, and it was an uneventful day today. I feel all right, and my weight is 58.5 kgs [128.7 pounds].

I was not so tired today, but my back gets sore now and again sitting in the bed. I didn't get the *Irish News*, which makes me think there is probably something in it that they don't wish me to see, but who cares. Fr Murphy was in tonight for a few minutes.

The screws had a quick look around my cell today when I was out getting water. They are always snooping. I heard reports of men beaten up during a wing shift. . . .

Nothing changes here.

Sean McKenna [the former hunger striker] is back in H-4, apparently still a bit shaky but alive and still recovering, and hopefully he will do so to the full.

Mhúscail mé leis an gealbháin ar maidin agus an t-aon smaointe amháin i mo cheann—seo chugat lá eile a Roibeard. Cuireann é sin amhrán a scríobh mé bhfad ó shin i ndúil domsa.

Seo é cibé ar bith:

D'éirigh mé ar maidin mar a tháinig an coimheádóir,
Bhuail sé mo dhoras go trom's gan labhairt.
Dhearc mé ar na ballaí, 's shíl mé nach raibh mé beo,
Tchítear nach n-imeoidh an t-iffrean seo go deo.
D'oscail an doras 's níor druideadh é go ciúin,
Ach ba chuma ar bith mar nach raibheamar inár suan.
Chuala mé éan 's ní fhaca mé geal an lae,
Is mian mór liom go raibh mé go doimhin faoi,
Cá bhfuil mo smaointí ar laethe a chuaigh romhainn,
S cá bhfuil an tsaol a smaoin mé abhí sa domhain,
Ní chluintear mo bhéic, 's ní fheictear mar a rith mo dheor,
Nuair a thigeann ar lá aithíocfaidh mé iad go mór.

Canaim é sin leis an phort Siún Ní Dhuibir.

[*Translated this reads as follows*:
I awoke with the sparrows this morning and the only thought in my head was: here comes another day, Bobby—reminding me of a song I once wrote a long time ago.
This is it anyway:

> I arose this morning as the Screw came,
> He thumped my door heavily without speaking,
> I stared at the walls, and thought I was dead,
> It seems that this hell will never depart.
> The door opened and it wasn't closed gently,
> But it didn't really matter, we weren't asleep.
> I heard a bird and yet didn't see the dawn of day,
> Would that I were deep in the earth.
> Where are my thoughts of days gone by,
> And where is the life I once thought was in the world.
> My cry is unheard and my tears flowing unseen,
> When our day comes I shall repay them dearly.

I sing this to the tune *Siún Ní Dhuibhir*.]

Bhí na héiníní ag ceiliúracht inniu. Chaith ceann de na buachaillí arán amach as an fhuinneog, ar a leghad bhí duine éigin ag ithe.

Uaigneach abhí mé ar feadh tamaill ar tráthnóna beag inniu ag éisteacht leis na preácháin ag screadáil agus ag teacht abhaile daobhtha. Da gclúinfinn an fhuiseog álainn, brisfeadh sí mo chroí.

Anois mar a scríobhaim tá an corrcrothar ag caoineadh mar a théann siad tharam. Is maith liom na héiníní.

Bhuel caithfidh mé a dul mar má scríobhain níos mó ar na héiníní seo beidh mo dheora ag rith 's rachaidh mo smaointí ar ais chuig an t-am nuair abhí mé ógánach, b'iad na laennta agus iad imithe go deo anois, ach thaitin siad liom agus ar a laghad níl dearmad deánta agam orthu, ta siad i mo chroí—oíche mhaith anois.

[Translated, this reads as follows:

The birds were singing today. One of the boys threw bread out of the window. At least somebody's eating!

I was lonely for a while this evening, listening to the crows caw as they returned home. Should I hear the beautiful lark, she would rent my heart. Now, as I write, the odd curlew mournfully calls as they fly over. I like the birds.

Well, I must leave off, for if I write more about the birds my tears will fall and my thoughts return to the days of my youth.

They were the days, and gone forever now. But I enjoyed them. They are in my heart—good night, now.]

Saturday 14th

Again, another uneventful somewhat boring day. My weight is 58.25 kgs [128.15 pounds], and no medical complaints. I read the papers, which are full of trash.

Tonight's tea was pie and beans, and although hunger may fuel my imagination (it looked a powerful-sized meal), I don't exaggerate: the beans were nearly falling off the plate. If I said this all the time to the lads, they would worry about me, but I'm all right.

It was inviting (I'm human too) and I was glad to see it leave the cell. Never would I have touched it, but it was a starving nuisance. Ha! My God, if it had attacked, I'd have fled.

I was going to write about a few things I had in my head but they'll wait. I am looking forward to the brief company of all the lads at Mass tomorrow. You never know when it could be the last time that you may ever see them again.

I smoked some cigarettes today. We still defeat them in this sphere. If the screws only knew the half of it; the ingenuity of the POW is something amazing. The worse the situation the greater the ingenuity. Someday it may all be revealed.

On a personal note, Liam Óg [the pseudonym for Bobby Sands' Republican Movement contact on the outside], I just thought I'd take this opportunity tonight of saying to your good hard-working self that I admire you all out there and the unselfish work that you all do and have done in the past, not just for the H Blocks and Armagh, but for the struggle in general.

I have always taken a lesson from something that was told me by a sound man, that is, that everyone, Republican or otherwise, has his own particular part to play. No part is too great or too small, no one is too old or too young to do something.

There is that much to be done that no select or small portion of people can do, only the greater mass of the Irish nation will ensure the achievement of the Socialist Republic, and that can only be done by hard work and sacrifice.

So, *mo chara*, for what it's worth, I would like to thank you all for what you have done and I hope many others follow your example, and I'm deeply proud to have known you all and prouder still to call you comrades and friends.

On a closing note, I've noticed the screws have been really slamming the cell doors today, in particular my own. Perhaps a good indication of the mentality of these people, always vindictive, always full of hate. I'm glad to say that I am not like that.

Well, I must go to rest up as I found it tiring trying to comb my hair today after a bath.

So venceremos, beidh bua againn eigin lá eigin. Sealadaigh abú.

[*Translated, this reads as follows:* So *venceremos*, we will be victorious someday. Up the Provos.]

Sunday 15th

Frank has now joined me on the hunger strike. I saw the boys at Mass today which I enjoyed. Fr Toner said Mass.

Again it was a pretty boring day. I had a bit of trouble to get slopped out tonight and to get water.

I have a visit tomorrow and it will be good to see my family. I am also looking forward to the walk in the fresh air, it will tire me out, but I hope the weather is good. I must go.

Monday 16th

I had a wonderful visit today with my mother, father and Marcella. Wonderful, considering the circumstances and the strain which indeed they are surely under.

As I expected, I received a lot of verbal flak from screws going and coming from the actual visit. Their warped sense of humour was evident in their childish taunts, etcetera.

I wrapped myself up well to keep me from the cold. My weight is 58.25 kgs [128.15 pounds] today, but I burnt up more energy today with the visit. I've no complaints of any nature.

I've noticed the orderlies are substituting slices of bread for bits of cake, etcetera—stealing the sweet things (which are rare anyway) for themselves. I don't know whether it's a case of "How low can you get?" or "Well, could you blame them?" But they take their choice and fill of the food always, so it's the former.

They left my supper in tonight when the priest, Fr Murphy, was in. There were two bites out of the small doughy bun. I ask you!

I got the *Sunday World* newspaper; papers have been scarce for the past few days.

There is a certain screw here who has taken it upon himself to harass me to the very end and in a very vindictive childish manner. It does not worry me, the harassment, but his attitude aggravates me occasionally. It is one thing to torture, but quite a different thing to exact enjoyment from it, that's his type.

There was no mirror search going out to visits today—a pleasant change. Apparently, with the ending of the no-wash protest, the mercenary screws have lost all their mercenary bonuses, etcetera, notwithstanding that they are also losing overtime and so on. So, not to be outdone, they aren't going to carry out the mirror search any more, and its accompanying brutality, degradation, humiliation, etcetera.

Why? Because they aren't being paid for it!

I'm continually wrapped up in blankets, but find it hard to keep my feet warm. It doesn't help my body temperature, drinking pints of cold water. I'm still able to take the salt and five or six pints of water per day without too much discomfort.

The books that are available to me are trash. I'm going to ask for a dictionary tomorrow. I'd just sit and flick through that and learn, much more preferable to reading rubbish.

The English rag newspapers I barely read, perhaps flick through them and hope that no one opens the door. A copy of last week's *AP/RN* was smuggled in and was read out last night (ingenuity of POWs again). I enjoyed listening to its contents (faultless—get off them!—good lad Danny [*Morrison*]).

I truly hope that the people read, take in and understand at least some of the truths that are to be regularly found in it. I see Paddy Devlin is at his usual tricks, and won't come out and support the prisoners. . .

Well, that's it for tonight. I must go. *Oíche Mhaith.*

Tuesday 17th

Lá Pádraig inniu 's mar is gnách níor thárla aon rud suntasach, bhí mé ar aifreann agus mo chuid gruaige gearrtha agam níos gaire, agus é i bhfad níos fearr freisin. Sagart nach raibh ar mo aithne abhí ag rá ran aifreann.

Bhí na giollaí ag tabhairt an bhia amach do chách abhí ag teacht ar ais ón aifreann. Rinneadh iarracht chun tabhairt pláta bidh domhsa. Cuireadh ós cómhair m'aghaidh ach shiúl mé ar mo shlí mar is nach raibh aon duine ann.

Fuair mé cúpla nuachtán inniu agus mar shaghas malairt bhí an Nuacht na hEireann ann. Táim ag fáil pé an scéal atá le fáil óna buachaillí cibé ar bith.

Chonaic mé ceann dona dochtúiri ar maidun agus é gan béasaí. Cuireann sé tuirse ormsa. Bhí mo chuid meáchain 57.50 kgs [126.5 pounds]. Ní raibh aon ghearán agam.

Bhí oifigeach isteach liom agus thug sé beagán íde béil domhsa. Arsa sé, "tchim go bhfuil tú ag léigheadh leabhar gairid. Rud maith nach leabhar fada é mar ní chríochnóidh tú é."

Sin an saghas daoine atá iontu. Ploid orthu. Is cuma liom. Lá fadálach ab ea é. Bhí mé ag smaoineamh inniu ar an chéalacán seo. Deireann daoine a lán faoin chorp ach ní chuireann muinín sa chorp ar bith. Measaim ceart go leor go bhfuil saghas troda.

Ar dtús ní ghlacann leis an chorp an easpaidh bidh, is fulaingíonn sé ón chathú bith, is greithe áirithe eile a bhíonn ag síorchlipeadh an choirp. Troideann an corp ar ais ceart go leor, ach deireadh an lae, téann achan rud ar ais chuig an phríomhrud, is é sin an mheabhair.

Is é an mheabhair an rud is tábhachtaí. Mura bhfuil meabhair láidir agat chun cur in aghaidh le achan rud, ní mhairfidh. Ní bheadh aon sprid troda agat. Is ansin cén áit as a dtigeann an mheabhair cheart seo. B'fhéidir as an fhonn saoirse.

Ni hé cinnte gurb é an áit as a dtigeann sé. Mura bhfuil siad in inmhe an fonn saoirse a scriosadh, ní bheadh siad in inmhe tú féin a bhriseadh. Ní bhrisfidh siad mé mar tá an fonn saoirse, agus saoirse mhuintir na hEireann i mo chroí.

Tiocfaidh lá eigin nuair a bheidh an fonn saoirse seo le taispeáint ag daoine go léir na hEireann ansin tchífidh muid éirí na gealaí.

[*Translated, this reads as follows*:
St Patrick's Day today and, as usual, nothing noticeable. I was at Mass, my hair cut shorter and much better also. I didn't know the priest who said Mass.

The orderlies were giving out food to all who were returning from Mass. They tried to give me a plate of food. It was put in front of my face but I continued on my way as though nobody was there.

I got a couple of papers today, and as a kind of change the *Irish News* was there. I'm getting any news from the boys anyway.

I saw one of the doctors this morning, an ill-mannered sort. It tries me. My weight was 57.70 kgs [126.5 pounds]. I had no complaints.

An official was in with me and gave me some lip. He said, "I see you're reading a short book. It's a good thing it isn't a long one for you won't finish it."

That's the sort of people they are. Curse them! I don't care. It's been a long day.

I was thinking today about the hunger strike. People say a lot about the body, but don't trust it.

I consider that there is a kind of fight indeed. Firstly the body doesn't accept the lack of food, and it suffers from the temptation of food, and from other aspects which gnaw at it perpetually.

The body fights back sure enough, but at the end of the day everything returns to the primary consideration, that is, the mind. The mind is the most important.

But then where does this proper mentality stem from? Perhaps from one's desire for freedom. It isn't certain that that's where it comes from.

If they aren't able to destroy the desire for freedom, they won't break you. They won't break me because the desire for freedom, and the freedom of the Irish people, is in my heart. The day will dawn when all the people of Ireland will have the desire for freedom to show.

It is then we'll see the rising of the moon.

Bobby Sands Trust

The Bobby Sands Trust was formed after the 1981 hunger strike when ten republican prisoners died to assert the political status denied them by the British government and its repressive prison regime.

On 1 March 1981, twenty-seven-year old Bobby Sands, after enduring years of solitary confinement and beatings, led that hunger strike, during which he was elected as MP for the constituency of Fermanagh and South Tyrone. He died after sixty-six days on 5 May 1981.

During his four-and-a-half year imprisonment in the H Blocks of Long Kesh concentration camp outside Belfast, Bobby wrote poetry, short stories, a poignant account of what the prisoners suffered (*One Day in My Life*), and kept a diary for the first seventeen days of his hunger strike.

He wrote on sheets of toilet paper with biro refills in a small, filthy cell covered with excrement. It was not all written at the one time, which explains a certain unevenness in the style and content. The written sheets were smuggled out over a period of time. The text and handwriting have been authenticated by the Sands family and the contents corroborated by other prisoners.

Certain sections of the original manuscript have been omitted from this book on legal advice. Otherwise only minor textual changes for the sake of consistency and clarity have been made.

It should be pointed out that the British and Northern Ireland authorities have denied that there were any beatings or torture in Long Kesh. But they have taken no effective steps to refute the masses of published material in books and journals alleging the existence of such torture, particularly in a book published in 1979 called *The H Blocks* by two responsible clergymen, Rev. Fathers Faul and Murray, in which scores of signed and witnessed statements from prisoners concerning their ill-treatment were published.

Royalties accruing from the sale of this book are paid to the Bobby Sands Trust Fund set up for the benefit of the wives, families and dependents of prisoners.

The Trust holds the copyright to all of Bobby's poetry and prose. It was established to publish, promote and keep in print the extraordinary writings of this young Irish man who, from prison isolation, became an international figure in 1981, and who, to this day, continues to inspire Irish republicanism in its pursuit of freedom from British rule.

The Trust is made up of comrades of Bobby and the Sands' family. The civil rights lawyer Pat Finucane, an advisor to the Trust, was assassinated by loyalist paramilitaries in collusion with British intelligence in 1989. His legal firm continues to act for the Trust.

In 1996, on the fifteenth anniversary of the hunger strike, the Trust recommitted itself to promulgating the works and writings of Bobby Sands in Ireland and abroad.

For further information contact: The Bobby Sands Trust, c/o Oifig na Sé Chontae, First Floor, Conway Mill, 5-7 Conway Street, Belfast BT13 2DE.